America's DIZZY DEAN

America's Dizzy Dean

by
Curt Smith

The Bethany Press

St. Louis, Missouri

Portions of Chapter One have appeared in slightly different form in an Associated Press feature article.

Grateful acknowledgment is made for permission to reprint excerpts from the following:

The Broadcasters, by Red Barber, reprinted by permission of the Paul Reynolds Agency, Published by the Dial Press, 1970.

The Summer Game, by Roger Angell, reprinted by permission of Simon & Schuster, Inc., 1973.

The Way It Was, edited by George Vecsey, reprinted by permission of Mobil Oil Co., 1974.

The Detroit Tigers, by Joe Falls, reprinted by permission of Macmillan Publishing Company, 1975.

Included are photos used by permission of the baseball Hall of Fame, Cooperstown, New York.

Layout and cover design by Roger Siebe

Library of Congress Cataloging in Publication Data

Smith, Curt.
America's Dizzy Dean.

1. Dean, Dizzy, 1911-   2. Baseball players—United States—Biography.   I. Title.
GV865.D4S59   796.357′092′4 [B]   77-29060
ISBN 0-8272-0014-5

Distributed in Canada by The G. R. Welch, Company, Ltd., Toronto, Ontario, Canada.
Printed in The United States of America.

For Mom and Dad—
who both admired Dizzy Dean.
Had Diz known them, no doubt, he
would surely have returned the favor.

His image was, and he loved this, the guy that just dropped off the back of the truck, barefooted, wandered into town and said, "Fellas, what's it all about?"

—Broadcaster Bud Blattner

Contents

An Acknowledgment

This book could not have been written without help from men and women of uncommon cloth. I want to thank all those who assisted with their memories and tales. Bud Blattner and Pee Wee Reese, announcers of superbly varied skills. Writers such as Ken Smith, John Kieran and Harold Rosenthal of New York, reporters the caliber of Ray Gillespie and Sam Muchnick, each of whom calls St. Louis home. Bill MacPhail and Billy Rogell, Paul and Patricia Dean. Residents of Bond, Mississippi, and Lucas, Arkansas, towns which speak movingly of a tranquil and more ordered land. Mel Allen, who rivaled Ol' Diz for the childhood cheers his rousing voice evoked. And Joe McCarthy, the greatest manager who ever lived.

Thanks, too, to Bob Broeg, one of America's finest sports journalists, who was kind enough to review my manuscript, make suggestions and write the introduction. My wife, Linda, provided more encouragement (and more typing hours) than I could possibly say. My dog, Checkers, now nearing three, provided comic relief. John K. Hutchens, former book review editor for the New York Times, was perhaps the first person to impress upon me Ol' Diz's national appeal. He urged the book along, offered counsel and support, and lent grace to his beseechings—as has always been his wont. Jack Redding, Librarian at the Hall of Fame, made available that museum's voluminous research files. Finally, Bob Broeg guided me to Stuart Johnston, Executive Vice President of The Bethany Press, who nursed the manuscript toward completion and uplifted its course. All were generous with their time and care—and I cannot help but be generous in my gratitude toward them.

Curt Smith
Clinton, New York

Introduction

No wonder young Curt Smith was completely captivated by Dizzy Dean, sufficiently moved to write a book that captured this colorful bit of Americana in baseball flannels, just as Ol' Diz himself first captured the country's fancy in the Depression Thirties.

Truth is, I fell for Dizzy myself when I saw him pitch his first big league ball game at a time I was twelve years old and he was just twenty, a lean, lanky, loose-jointed guy with high cheekbones and a flowing, fluid delivery that popped a fast ball into catcher Gus Mancuso's glove as if it were a high explosive. Come to think of it, it was—his high, hard one.

As No. 17 warmed up in 1930, I mustered up courage to go down to a box seat where St. Louis Mayor Victor Miller sat, leaning forward earnestly, talking to manager Charles E. (Gabby) Street, who leaned forward from the field, arms folded on his chin.

His Honor was congratulating Gabby and his Cardinals for having clinched the 1930 pennant the day before, a result of thirty-nine victories in their last forty-nine games. I was an inadvertent eavesdropper, waiting to get an autograph. Heck, no, not the mayor's, the manager's.

Suddenly, turning toward Dean, who had won twenty-five games and lost only ten at St. Joseph, Mo., and Houston, Tex., combined, in his first professional season, Mayor Miller said: "Say, Sarge, I've been hearing about this Dizzy. Is he as good as they say he is?"

Gabby Street, who had caught a foul ball dropped by Walter Johnson from the top of the Washington Monument when they were batterymates, was never sharper in his life than when he put the prophecy this way.

"Mr. Mayor," he drawled, smiling, "I think he's going to be a GREAT pitcher, but I'm afraid we'll never know from one minute to the next what he's going to say or do."

From the time that late September afternoon forty-seven years ago that Dizzy Dean broke in with a three-hit, 3-1 victory over the Pittsburgh Pirates, belting a base hit off the left field bleachers himself to beat lefty Larry French, he was a GREAT pitcher.

But from the time he had rented three rooms at three addresses at St. Joe, then asked hitters what they wanted thrown to them and then "fogged" the ball past them, no one EVER did know what Ol' Diz was going to do. Not even when he died of a heart relapse because, as always, he'd conned and sweet-talked his way out of a hospital.

The man was sheer delight. I don't think he ever met a stranger. So it's no wonder, as author Smith relates in a detailed summary of the situation, that a depressed nation took that big, gangling kid to its heart back there in 1934 when, as the spirit of the Gas House Gang, Dizzy promised that "Me 'n Paul," meaning his shy, rookie brother, would win forty-five games between them.

They won forty-nine, not counting two each in the World Series, and, for once Jay Hanna Jerome Herman Dean had to apologize for insufficient confidence.

But Ol' Diz, which he called himself when he was barely out of the cotton-chopping coveralls he'd worn as an Oklahoma itinerant scratching the soil for three squares a day, really wasn't timid.

Down the stretch in September of '34 when the Gang caught and over-hauled the New York Giants for the pennant, with Dizzy working six of the last nine games, the elder Dean brother pitched a three-hit shutout in the first game of a doubleheader at Brooklyn. Brother Paul topped it with a no-hitter in the second game.

"Dawgonnit," Dizzy protested, "if I'd-a known Paul was gonna no-hit 'em, I'd-a done it, too."

How could ANYONE ever really dislike a guy like that, a living legend even before, with foolish bravado, he tried to come back with a broken toe still in a splint and, favoring his arm, hurt the arm and lost his fast ball and his future, in 1937.

Gosh, he was only twenty-six years old—imagine!—and not even at an average player's peak, much less a super-star's, and he'd had behind him big league seasons of 18-15, 20-18, 30-7, 28-12 and 24-13. My, if Dizzy Dean, who threw so smoothly and effortlessly, hadn't hurt that resilient right arm, I'll bet he'd have pitched in the bigs into the early fifties and against the black stars he'd met on barnstorming tours—and respected.

But Jay—I always called him what wife Pat did—never lost a base-ball future, but merely re-directed it to first the radio booth and then cheek by jowl to a television monitor. His reputation didn't diminish, but, rather, was enhanced—with or without a lusty version of the "Wabash Cannonball" delivered in the nasal twang of his native Southeast.

Yes, Dizzy Dean's reputation in "retirement" grew as fast as he did, which was something, all right, because that skinny, underfed, slim-jim of pitching perfection ballooned into a fat man of the circus, yet still slick enough to spot a sucker just enough strokes on the golf course to persuade the other fella to come back another day to leave once more laughing when his pocket hurt.

General Dwight D. Eisenhower wondered aloud when they were in a celebrity foursome for charity how Dean could play golf so well so heavy or, rather, why such a great athlete would permit himself to become so overweight?

"Mr. President," Ol' Diz replied, brightly and lightly, "I was on a diet for twenty-five years. Now that I'm makin' some money, I'm makin' sure I eat enough to make up for the lean years."

The gregarious, good-natured big guy with the blue eyes, wide grin and western white hat could be spiteful at times, just as his wife Pat could be watchful and protective in a tender way. From the time she saved $1200 out of the $3000 he earned in 1931 at Houston, the year they were married, Patricia Nash Dean made certain that the big guy's easy-come, easy-go, boundless generosity knew bounds of limitation.

And when overweight and six years in drydock, deriding the humpty-dumpties of the old St. Louis Browns, Dizzy was persuaded to desert the radio booth for the pitcher's mound the final day of the 1947 season, Pat writhed uncomfortably in a box next to the Browns' dugout.

For four innings, Ol' Diz cunningly slow-curved the Chicago White Sox scorelessly with an exaggerated motion and corner-cutting control. Then he lashed a drive to left field, "slud" into second base with a double, as Dean would have described it himself, and got up limping. Pat Dean had had enough.

Leaning over the box-seat rail toward the Browns' dugout, Mrs. Dean persuaded manager Herold (Muddy) Ruel to get Diz off the field "before he kills himself."

Jay Hanna Jerome Herman (Dizzy) Dean was one of a kind, but, oh, it was so nice to have him and so pleasant to find a young man such as Curt Smith willing to do the research, travel the miles for interviews, and to do the detail with devotion and dedication to make Dizzy Dean live again.

Ol' Diz, the one and only, used to sit on the bench at Arizona State University when Dan Devine, later the football coach at Missouri, Green Bay and Notre Dame, coached the Sun Devils. Asked before a critical game to say a few words to the squad, Dean roared:

"Hit 'em hard and let 'em lay. I wasn't the greatest pitcher, but I was amongst 'em. You ain't the greatest football team, podnuhs, but you're amongst 'em.''

Sure, Arizona State hit 'em hard and let 'em lay that day. Dizzy Dean always was amongst winners, on and off the field, in the minds of the rich and the poor, the strong and the weak, the old and the young. He was as much an American legend as any ball player who ever lived.

BOB BROEG
Sports Editor, St. Louis Post-Dispatch
Veterans' Committee
Baseball Hall of Fame

Chapter One

From Bond to Wiggins

I

Ol' Diz was more than just an ol' hillbilly.

Why, to millions of Americans he was an authentic folk-hero, oft-remembered and revered, especially among the country folk who spoke his rural twang, and mirrored his homespun humor, and sensed the small-town values which stirred him.

Few who heard him, or remember his weekly baseball telecasts, will ever forget Ol' Diz, all three hundred pounds of him, ambling up the rope ladder to the broadcast booth, or stuffing popcorn in one hand while guzzling pop from the other, or preparing to belt out his rousing trademark ballad, "Wabash Cannonball."

Dizzy Dean died in July of 1974. Though in recent years he had slipped from the national spotlight, his impact had endured, most markedly in the style and legacy of laughter he left behind. Surely, one mused, Diz would go on forever, baffling partisans and critics alike, embellishing even the most mundane of themes. Yet now he was gone, and his death was nationally mourned, a final tribute to the unhip, uncultured yet beloved Ozark boy made good.

What was there about Dizzy Dean which so endeared him? Immortalized in his own time, the subject of prose and verse, Ol' Diz became part man, part legend, part myth, each adored by the masses. All that despite an education which ended in second grade. "And I wasn't so good in the first grade, either," he once recalled.

15

Dean was a product of his region and times; indeed, he came ultimately to symbolize them. The son of a migratory cotton picker, Diz was a rawboned scrapper from the dirt farms, rough and ready and slightly tattered. He became a hero to the Depression downtrodden, escaping what they had not, living what they could only dream.

For a memorable period in the mid-1930s, Dean was baseball's greatest pitcher, its most alluring gate attraction. Yet even the records of the era do not do his life justice; Dean's influence became more pronounced in later years. And to the end, when Ol' Diz was buried in the small town of Bond, Mississippi, he retained the common touch.

"His philosophy was doing a fella right," said brother Paul, overshadowed always, who combined with Diz to form one of baseball's most famed pitching duos. "He never saw a man he didn't like or respect, and there weren't many who didn't respect or like Dizzy. Those qualities are God-gifted."

For Dizzy Dean, the public often masked the private; the two were hardly inseparable. Privately charitable and publicly flamboyant, unschooled yet wise to the ways of the world, for forty years he was a figure around whom fame fit comfortably and controversy raged.

Few could remain distant or impartial. To some, Dean was the supreme braggart and pop-off, the unwitting clown; to many he was a first-rate showman, a figure of Bunyanesque proportions. Few could deny, either, that Dean was financially enriched, or that his national renown had endured long after his playing days had ceased.

"He was Dizzy Dean, with enormous charm and color and appeal," is how announcer Red Barber described him. "He was smarter than a fox. I think he always knew what he was doing and what he was saying, and I wish I had the money he has made and saved. He had it buried in tomato cans all over Mississippi."

Dean's money, however, had not made him the idol of millions, nor had his education or pitching feats. What made Diz so beloved, and so ridiculed by those who despised him, was what he echoed: the plain, unpolished yet triumphant country boy, perhaps a final vestige of an America gone forever.

Ol' Diz pitched for the St. Louis Cardinals during the 1930s, helped make their rollicking Gas House Gang a household word, then departed the playing ranks to become a broadcaster. Stories about him abounded, many more fiction than fact, many more the product of writers' fertile minds than Dizzy's equally facile tongue.

One tale concerned an incident in 1930. Ignoring curfew, Dean bumped into a Texas League president at 4 a.m. "Good morning, Mr. President," Dean is supposed to have said. "So the old boy is prowling around by himself tonight, eh? Well, sir, I'm not one to squawk. Us stars and presidents must have our fun."

Another incident arose when Dean, born in Lucas, Arkansas, began giving sportswriters different locales as his place of birth. "I was helping the writers out," Diz explained. "Them ain't lies, them's scoops."

Oft-told though these stories were, Dean's naked, unadorned manner was even more revealing, especially when Diz spoke to America on television. Dean was total ad-lib; each broadcast was marked by the spontaneity even polished scriptwriters would have found difficult to approach. And how Dizzy Dean could mangle the King's English.

As a television announcer, Ol' Diz fractured the language so badly that school teachers arose in protest. A new lexicon of baseball terms evolved. To Dean, a runner didn't slide, he "slud." A fielder hadn't thrown the ball, he had "threwed." Ol' Diz would grandly announce, "The runners are now returning to their respectable bases," and laughter would erupt in living rooms across the country.

Whenever a weak-hitting pitcher was at bat, Dean invariably jested that "He has an eye like a hawk." Then, just as regularly, he'd belt out his version of "Wabash Cannonball." And America loved him for it. Perhaps Diz knew all along what he was doing, just as Barber claimed. Yet the novelty was untarnished; Dizzy Dean was as appealing in 1974 as he had been in 1934.

More so than Ruth, or Stengel, or Gehrig, Dizzy Dean was pure Americana. That was the essence of his appeal. He spoke of an earlier era; his bearing was of a simpler, less abrasive age. To be sure, Dean could be insufferably vain. "I may not have been the greatest pitcher ever, but I was amongst 'em," he was fond of saying. Part egotist, part gambler, with the gall of a brass monkey thrown in, Dizzy Dean was a man of many dimensions—and all were overshadowed by the folksy, down-home charm which made Diz a long-running hit with Middle America.

The turbulence and social unrest of the 1960s never really touched Ol' Diz; "Who the heck is Raquel Welch?" the Great One once asked. To Dean, the Age of Aquarius was less than home terrain; his life leaned more toward Gene Autry and Roy Acuff and Pepper Martin's Mudcat Band, each a remnant of decades past. He was an enduring relic, steadfast and unchanging. For those who feared that nothing would remain unaltered, Dizzy Dean offered contrary proof.

The times, they were a-changing, but Ol' Diz hadn't, and truth was that it hardly seemed to matter. Still present were the always memorable mannerisms, the laughter, the bravado which had invariably marked his personal veneer. And present, too, was America's ardor toward him, undimmed by the intervening years.

Many had laughed at Dean's antics on the field. The more television-oriented focused on Dizzy's theatrics in the broadcast booth. "This was the magic of Dizzy Dean," broadcaster Buddy Blattner said the day after Dean died. "He became a legend to thousands of people who didn't know if Dizzy had thrown left-handed or right-handed. And didn't care. He knew what people wanted to hear."

One year before his death at sixty-three, NBC brought Diz back for its first 1973 Monday night telecast, and he went on to completely dominate Curt Gowdy and Tony Kubek, its two regular announcers.

There was Ol' Diz cracking jokes right and left, repeating lines as funny then as they had been ten years before. On May 21, 1973, the laughs flowed fast and free. As usual with Dizzy Dean, the ball game came alive.

Where did Dean live? Gowdy asked him.

"Why, in Bond, Mississippi."

Where was Bond?

"Oh, 'bout three miles away from Wiggins."

Then where was Wiggins?

"Oh, 'bout three miles away from Bond," Diz replied.

Only Dean could get away with a sequence like that. "They'll never be another one like me," Ol' Diz often said. And as was his custom, Dizzy Dean was right.

II

Baseball was Dean's perfect forum. For more than a century the game has been at once solitary and inclined to humor. The extrovert has habitually thrived in baseball, where intimacy reigns and players stride alone across the field. "How can you identify with a guy three hundred pounds or seven feet tall?" Bill Veeck asked. "Baseball is the only sport the common man can relate to." Another devotee, writer Roger Angell, has marveled at baseball's sandbox appeal, even in the most august of parks. "You can actually see the players' faces. You can almost know what they are like."

This has been baseball's mystique, the ability, the visceral need of Americans to empathize with their heroes. Football players are too hulking, too distant, too heavily masked by helmets and pads to attract the personal loyalties which baseball spawns. Basketball's giant figures are too far removed from the common man's element; hockey's too far from the American past. Yet baseball endures and prospers, the most graceful and artistic of American sports, and ultimately the most beloved.

Critics who spurn baseball as slow and tranquil, out of step with the violence which mars our times, fail to grasp its enormous impact on the masses. Baseball's solitary grace is not obscured in a bedlam of bodies, or in a jarring crash near the goal, or in a madcap scramble near the backboard. Its grace exists to be seen, not clouded, and those who excel on the field or in the broadcast booth magnify that artistry. In baseball, the solitary performer prevails, especially when his last name is Dean.

Ol' Diz shared baseball's capacity for humor. Even in the midst of a World Series, few seem to approach it with any degree of solemnity. Bullpen pitchers exchange barbs with bleacher residents, players joke with and insult each other. Humor is not treated as treason.

A natural comic of Casey Stengel's caliber would have gained a foothold in any sport, but perhaps only in baseball could he have become a household word. The same was true of Dizzy Dean. Baseball's creed is all its own; tension is anathema. "Not too hard, not too easy," Stengel frequently exhorted his troops. For six months baseball is played almost every day; any person who tried to stay emotionally primed for each game would go mad, or to the minors, whichever came first. Baseball comedians are as necessary as they are renowned.

And what a comedian was Ol' Diz. His character was ideally suited for baseball, and baseball's character helped him become what Curt Gowdy labeled an "American legend." By nature, Dean was suitably carefree to survive the ups and downs, the streaks and slumps, the lengthy pauses between times at bat or pitching starts. Clever, amusing, folksy and loose, Dean adopted and cradled the baseball mentality as his own.

Dean was one of a select group of baseball players whose reputation did not exceed their actual worth. The stark fact is that Yogi Berra, for all his malaprops and supposed warmth, was never much more than a mundane wit, his humor largely molded by Joe Garagiola. Satchel Paige was much less the folk philosopher than the illiterate pitcher who happened upon an adoring press. And Bo Belinsky, Hollywood-made and manufactured, saw his fawning public desert him even before his left arm did.

Unlike Bo and Satchel, Dean's image was largely self-formed. Totally extroverted, supremely confident of his role in life and ability to prevail, Dean delighted in the hurrahs which came his way—and ushered them to his door. America loved him for his outrageous and artless behavior, qualities which shielded the mind that made him exceedingly comfortable in succeeding years. Like Joe Namath and Denny McLain forty years later, the Dean of the early 1930s made public turmoil his means of capturing America's heart, or at least its rapt notice.

The gambler image affected them all. Namath guaranteed that he would win the 1969 Super Bowl, then did. McLain made a brief but tumultuous career of conning the public and himself. Dean won at cards, at golf, at baseball and pranks. "It ain't bragging if you can back it up," he was fond of saying, and for decades his life mirrored that phrase. Despite his riverboat style, though, Dean's manner was also marked by the rustic, almost innocent demeanor Diz recurrently displayed.

Fiction, critics said, often outlasted fact with Dizzy Dean. One reason why, of course, was that he seldom turned the other cheek when a chance for tall tales appeared. One incident speaks volumes about Dean's conquering ways with newsmen, as well as the idolatrous treatment sports figures then received from the nation's press. The episode revolved around conflicting reports that raged in baseball circles about Dean's enduring propensity for self-serving, headline-seeking oratory.

Not long into the 1934 season, Dean rode the rails to Brooklyn, where the Cardinals met the Dodgers in sainted Ebbets Field. On Diz's first day in New York, three writers visited Dean in search of a story. As he eventually told Roy Stockton of the *St. Louis Post-Dispatch*,

Dizzy Dean joins Roy Acuff in a chorus of the "Wabash Cannonball" during the 39th birthday celebration of the Grand Ole Opry in 1964. Dizzy was acclaimed the nation's number one country music fan.

"I give 'em each a scoop, Roy, so that their bosses can't bawl the three of 'em out for writing the same piece."

As Dean later resurrected what occurred, Tommy Holmes of the since defunct *Brooklyn Eagle* entered Diz's hotel room, wanting to know where Dean was born. Dean told him Lucas on January 16, 1911. Shortly after Holmes' departure, New York's Bill McCullough appeared, "and doggone if he don't want the same story." So Dean obliged, varying the prose somewhat. When McCullough left, he did so with the assurance that Ol' Diz first saw light in Bond, Miss., on February 22, "which was giving George Washington a break."

Roscoe McGowan of the *New York Times* came next, seeking the same background sketch Holmes and McCullough had sought. "I gave him a break, too," Dean recalled, and labeled August 22, 1911, in Holdenville, Oklahoma, as the environs which hosted his birth. "Them ain't lies, them's scoops," Diz snorted in defense of his answers. All three writers rushed to print their stories, two of which were false.

Ken Smith is the director of the Hall
of Fame, Cooperstown, N.Y.

"Sure, we wrote up Diz pretty good," said Ken Smith, now Director
of the Hall of Fame, formerly a sportswriter with two old New York
papers, the *Graphic* and *Mirror,* "but that's what our readers wanted
in those early days. Baseball was so intimate then. We didn't knock
guys like they do now. That story about Dean and his birth dates was
true, maybe some of the others weren't, but in any case it was all right
with us.

"Ed Sullivan was my sports editor in the early thirties, before he
went on to other things, and he told me, 'There's nothing wrong with
being in a player's corner. That's how you sell newspapers.' And that's
what we tried to do. Baseball wasn't as corporate then; it was personal.
And Dean was the most personable of all; he was his own best press."

The dispute over Dean's origins slackened in his later years, but the
controversy surrounding his real name remained. America knew him as
Dizzy, a label he acquired from Army sergeant Jimmy Brought during
a 1920s artillery stint at Fort Sam Houston. Official records listed him as
Jerome Herman. And there were those who said Jay Hanna Dean fit
him best.

"My name is Jay Hanna and not Jerome Herman, and I got it in
Lucas, Arkansas, and let nobody tell you different," he concluded a
news conference in 1971. Despite Dean's disclaimers, Diz helped
continue the disquiet with an oft-told tale about an event that occurred
when he was seven years old. A close neighbor in Arkansas, having
recently lost his son, saw his grief partly lifted when Ol' Diz changed his
formal name to that of the man's dead youth. Jay Hanna Dean became
Jerome Herman.

"All the neighbors really liked me," Ol' Diz modestly reminisced, "and especially so a man who had a little boy my age. Anyway, people sometimes wondered whether he thought more of his son or me. Well, the boy got sick, all of a sudden. My name was Jay Hanna and this kid's was Jerome Herman. Eventually he died, and his dad, he just grieved and grieved. We felt awful sorry for him.

"Anyhow, his dad was in a sorry state. So I went to him and says because I thought so highly of him I was going to take on the name of Jerome Herman. His dad got better, and I've been Jerome Herman ever since then." Until, of course, Dean turned the tables and became Jay Hanna once more, adopting the name his wife had used since they first met.

Chapter Two

Sandlots and Cottonfields

I

No matter what name adorned him later, there was little humor evident in Diz's formative career.

Heir to poverty, fathered by an itinerant sharecropper who traveled the South picking cotton, Ol' Diz was born Jan. 16, 1911 in Lucas, Arkansas. His mother died when he and Paul were little more than infants. His father, Albert Dean, drove his sons from one Arkansas, Texas, and Oklahoma field to another in a ramshackle truck. Numerous small locales, Holdenville and Lucas among them, boast even today that Dizzy Dean chopped cotton there.

As a child, lack of money, interest and stability at home forced Dean's early departure from school; the elder brother took to the cotton fields instead. By 1922, at age eleven, Diz—rising at 5 a.m.—often picked more than three hundred pounds of cotton a day. When the Army proposed a three-year term six years later, then, Dean quickly obliged. After all, the service corps offered free meals, clothes, shoes, and a chance to play baseball, not necessarily in that order. The Army and Dean were hardly a match designed in heaven, but each survived the other, and Diz left in 1929 with his pride intact, his demeanor unimpaired, and "the first pair of shoes I ever owned," courtesy of Uncle Sam.

With his Army tenure nearing its end, Dean quickened the process. One hundred and twenty dollars enabled Diz to leave the service, a widespread practice in the peacetime 1920s. "I bought Diz out with the money I'd earned," said Paul, still reserved and quietly articulate. "I had enough money I earned picking cotton that I could buy him out of the Army and still have some left. You see, my Dad hired out to pick for three and a half years and I suppose we had as much money as anyone else then. Everybody had pretty rough going during those days." Not much rougher, though, than rival hitters of Dizzy Dean would soon endure. Out of service, Diz joined the San Antonio public service company so that he could pitch for its baseball team. There he first attracted the notice of Don Curtis, a scout for the Cardinals' Texas League farm club in Houston, by reeling off sixteen victories in a row. Curtis quickly signed Dean, a feat which required little prodding, and one of baseball's most improbable careers began.

"Man, can you imagine getting money to pitch," Diz wondered aloud as the 1930 season dawned; the world, or what he knew of it, was his. At a tryout camp in the Cardinals' Bradenton, Florida, spring training site, St. Louis general manager Branch Rickey watched Dean strike out three batters on nine pitches. Despite the fact that he had never even seen a major league game, Ol' Diz proclaimed he would lead the Cardinals out of the wilderness to a World Series crown, a goal the Redbirds would almost reach. "Judas Priest," Rickey said later, "I think Dean was right. He probably would have put us over."

Instead, Dean was shipped to St. Joseph, Missouri, the Cardinals' Western League team in what was then baseball's most prolific, envied and ultimately imitated farm system. His debut on April 20, 1930, gave portents of dramatics to come. Dean struck out eight, saw his club score two runs in the bottom of the tenth inning to edge Denver, 4-3, and started the Western League's first recorded triple play. Before one of his first starts he telephoned a rival manager, saying, "This here is Dizzy Dean. Yep, I'm back in town and I can hear you gnashing your teeth, brother. Just thought I'd call and tell you I'm gonna pitch against your club this afternoon and hold them to two or three hits." Dizzy Dean, a man of his word, however inflated, "held them" to two.

Despite a woeful club behind him, Dean drew rave notices from the Western League. He won seventeen, lost eight and led the league in bizarre antics and I.O.U.s. At one time during the season he rented rooms at three addresses. Frequently he asked batters where they wanted him to throw the ball, a practice which underscored his infant but budding reputation as a lovable eccentric who flaunted rules and endeared himself in the process.

One vignette typified his madcap ways. Dean, going the wrong way on a one-way street, was signaled by a car's horn to veer off to one side of the road. Mistaking the horn as a challenge, Diz began a wild chase which extended for six city blocks. Only when the pursuing car neared him did Dean realize the driver inside was St. Joseph's Chief of Police. When next they met, Diz greeted him with, "Hiya, chiefy boy. How you doing?" Whatever his other faults, Dizzy Dean was never one to hold a grudge.

Dean's newly-found renown followed him to Houston, where he was promoted on August 5, 1930. During the next month, Dizzy pitched in fourteen games, compiling an 8-2 record, and molded an image which *The Sporting News* said "may make some of the older heads down Texas way stroke their chins as they watch Dean in action." Dizzy spent only four weeks in the Texas League before being kicked upstairs to the Cardinals. While he was there, even so, Dean seized more of the limelight than did many veterans who had played in Houston for years.

His theatrics began the morning after Ol' Diz dazzled the home folk and teammates with a 12-1 victory in his initial Houston encounter. Dean stunned the Buffs' president, Fred Ankenman, by walking into his office and making apologies for his performance. "I'm awfully sorry," he said. "I promise if you'll give me another chance, it'll never happen again. Can you imagine them bums getting a run off me." Dean was hardly in peril of being deprived of another chance, not with his fastball. And while sheepish prose from Dizzy Dean was not precisely what Ankenman expected, he was no more prepared for what occurred several evenings later.

Behind Dean, Houston was far in front of Ft. Worth when Ol' Diz staged some base-running antics that ravaged the club's usually unflappable manager, Joe Schultz. With a runner on first base, Dean smashed a drive down the left field line, normally worth a double. Dean turned the first base bag, then inexplicably retreated. On the next pitch St. Louis' most valuable pitching property in America bolted for second. Dean's impromptu act crossed up everyone. The Ft. Worth second baseman and shortstop froze, either asleep or too surprised to move. The catcher's throw sailed into center field. Dean completed his slide, righted himself, then tore around the bases and scored, returning to a bench on which Schultz was now enraged.

"Dean," he screamed, "what were you trying to do, kill yourself? Did you think you got the steal sign on that pitch or what?" Without pausing, Diz winked and calmly replied, "No, but I just knew I should have made second on that hit, so I decided to get there somehow and even things up." Dean's rationale did little to reassure Schultz, but after September anxiety was no longer required. St. Louis, Houston's parent club, called for Dizzy Dean—and Ol' Diz was minor league no more.

Still several hundred miles from New York, where the Cardinals were to play the Giants, the Great One headed East. On the way to Manhattan, Diz tried to route himself through San Antonio, his current hometown. "I need several shirts before going to the big city," he explained. So concerned was Dean about his attire that only when convinced that shirts could be purchased (and washed) in New York, did he agree to forego San Antonio and report promptly to the Cards. Legend had it that Jay Hanna believed in keeping his shirt on, and a clean one at that.

Dean took charge in his major league debut, a 3-1 victory over Pittsburgh on the last day of the 1930 season. He allowed the Pirates only three hits, two by Pie Traynor, and quickly sealed matters in eighty-one minutes. Even more telling was an exchange which occurred as Dean warmed up before the game. "What about Dean?" St. Louis mayor Victor Miller asked Cardinal manager Gabby Street. "Is he going to be as good as everyone says?" Street laughed and said, "I think he may be a great one, but I'm afraid we'll never know from one hour to the next what he's going to say or do." To which Ol' Diz might have added, had he been listening, "Podner, you ain't a-woofin.'"

After downing the Pirates, Dean bemoaned the fact that "them bums got three hits off me." He watched the Cardinals lose the World Series in six games to Connie Mack and his Philadelphia A's, then drifted back to St. Joseph, where he told assembled fans, "Show me another pitcher in the majors who ain't never been defeated." Dean had only recently signed his 1931 contract, estimated at a lowly $3,000, but already he was telling writers to "soft-pedal the Dizzy Dean stuff and start in calling me the Great Dean.

"I guess I can live on my salary next year," he said. "A big reason is that the Cardinals made me stay with a guy named Joe Sugden all the time I was with them this year. Joe, he's a mighty good guy, but his idea of a good time is getting up at seven o'clock every morning and going to bed at ten every night. In two years I'll be of age and maybe Mr. Rickey won't think I need a nursemaid then.

"I intend to stay around for about a week here and then I'll go down to San Antone and live with the folks this winter. I ain't planning to do any work. Right after Christmas, I guess I'll start spring training. You see, I've got a sixteen-year-old brother that I'm going to take to camp next year. And next to me," Diz concluded shyly, "I think he'll be the greatest pitcher in the world."

Dean was not quite as heralded as his conjecture portrayed, even though he told a reporter, "If you want any pictures, you can write me at San Antonio. Don't need an address, everybody knows me." Nor was he ready to assume the mantle as "the greatest pitcher in the world." Within the next nine months he would become embroiled in spring training turmoil with Gabby Street and be banished to the minors. He would unleash an unchecked spending rampage which forced Rickey to restrict his financial means to one dollar a day. And he would stumble upon one of the most fortunate events of his life, a June 10, 1931 marriage to Patricia Nash, Houston store clerk who agreed to lend Diz two dollars for their wedding license, but refused to approve his favored ceremony site—home plate.

By 1932, though, Ol' Diz had the tides irrevocably behind him. The Gas House Gang would soon sweep across the American summer, marching without pretense or apparent fear against the economic woes which scourged the plains. The team was eclectic in its skills, virtually irresistible in its allure, and leading the march was Dizzy Dean. "Dizzy is the sort of bird who loves to beat a supposedly tough team and then pass the feat off with a nonchalant remark, like 'Them clowns can't hit a medicine ball,' " wrote *The Sporting News* in 1931, adding prophetically, ''It may be that Dizzy Dean will prove a mighty handy guy to have around before the next few campaigns are closed.''

II

Only in the small towns of America, far beyond the cities, in the prairies and the provinces, could Dizzy Dean find a perfect echo. These people were his natural allies; at heart, he would always be a small-town boy. His idiom was their idiom, his culture their culture, and they, above all others, understood him. When Ol' Diz talked about human love, he meant it. When he spoke of the heart-bond which linked black and white, the broad, enduring smile illuminated his entire face. And they, too, were of the small town. Whatever else marked his life, and there was both good and bad, and plenty of each, his faith in America and what it had brought remained untarnished, unmarred by the cynicism which assaults our times.

Dean led buoyantly, with empathy, by the manner of his life. Scorned and ridiculed by those who envied his success, or thought his bearing overly bucolic, Dizzy declined to respond in kind. He gave out no vicious threats, no violent urges to cripple or maim. Those taunts he issued were fleeting, received more with laughter than with hurt. ''Diz was a kid to the end,'' recalled Pee Wee Reese, twenty years ago captain of America's parish team, the Brooklyn Dodgers, more recently Dean's partner on the CBS ''Game of the Week.'' ''Diz could get angry, but there was little mean in Diz. In his own way, and some never understood this, he was sensitive, even gentle, aware of others around him.''

For several years Phoenix was Dean's residence, but Diz picked up stakes in the 1960s and went home, returning to the Ozark spirit which profoundly influences the mid and lower-South. Here, far beyond the Alleghenies, far removed from the Establishment centers of Washington and New York, the old culture of America survives and prospers, much as it did when Dizzy Dean marched unevenly toward manhood— people who teach Bible classes on Sunday, who attend church suppers, whose taste runs more to Kate Smith than Sonny and Cher, who view the Eastern Seaboard as injurious to the moral values and social decencies of an earlier America.

This culture, which laid claim to Dizzy Dean, also accompanied his rise. Whether Dean lived in Bond or Lucas, or shuttled between San Antonio and St. Louis, the natives who surrounded him were largely alike. The forgotten Americans, political pundits termed them in the late 1960s. Overwhelmingly Protestant, predominantly Baptist, conservative in substance and style, towns like Bond and Lucas formed a backdrop for the Middle America many public figures chose to prize and cultivate, then proceeded to eventually betray. Ol' Diz was not moved to betrayal; rather, he kept the faith, and Lucas watched with pride. So, too, Booneville, sixteen miles away.

III

I drove south and east from Ft. Smith, Arkansas, through the Ozark uplands. Rustic even by Arkansas standards, graced by steep passes beckoning to the valleys below, the highlands remained unchanged by time and untamed by man. The road, poverty unfolding on either side, approached Booneville, 3,239 strong, the major city closest to Lucas.

Here, as along the road, lumber, sheds, and rusted pickup trucks surrounded the houses that often doubled as shacks. The names on the mailboxes told of families which went back a hundred years. Clean, small lawns, now grown haggard with winter growth, betrayed the reddish-brown soil which lay beneath. Porches with swings were everywhere. One expected that any moment Andy Griffith might appear, or that one would be taken aside and told that Ma and Pa Kettle began their meteoric rise in this Logan County Village.

I found Jones Robertson and his sister Ella Mae, two of Ol' Diz's childhood companions, living two blocks from Booneville's business district. Their home was a one-story structure made striking by its lack of pretense and its ragged veneer. On the front porch four chairs were neatly arranged. Ella Mae was now seventy-six and graying. "Booneville's people goes to church," she said pleasantly enough. "That's where we would have been 'cept you wanted to see us." To divert the Robertsons from Sunday services was to upstage the Baptist Church, implausible even for one of Booneville's own.

At sixty-six, placid and full-framed, Jones Robertson eased into one of the few chairs in his living room. He had about him the strength and presence of a laborer who shapes his craft with dignity and pride. Since childhood, Robertson had farmed, built ships, and worked on railroads—and spent his lifetime following the career of a man he had known long ago.

During the mid-1920s, the families of Dizzy Dean and Jones Robertson lived in the Ouachita Mountains. They lived one mile apart and nine miles from Belleville, population 330, dividing line of the Rock Island Railroad. "They were there before we were," said Ella Mae.

"The Deans had come up from Oklahoma in 1924 and moved to Belleville before us. That's about thirty miles from here. And they left a couple years later, but Paul stayed with us while they were gone. We meant that Paul should go to school, and in fact, he went to the same country place as Jones. Then Pa Dean came back and took him, and after that neither boy got much schooling."

"Why, Dizzy couldn't learn nuthin'," Jones exclaimed. "He was too full of fun. You couldn't get him to study a thing. Every Sunday morning—real early—Diz would come running down to our house. He'd have a glove and a twine ball. You know, we didn't have anything better in those days. We had two teams, the young players and the men, and we'd steal the first team's equipment whenever we could."

This is the first known picture of the entire Dean family, believed to have been taken in the early 1930s. Front row; (from left) Mrs. Dizzy Dean, A. M. Dean (father), and Mrs. Paul Dean. Back row; Dizzy Dean, Elmer Dean and Paul Dean. (International News Photo)

"I was the first to play baseball with Jay Hanna Dean," he said, "and Ol' Diz loved it. That's all he thought about. Somewhere he was off playing ball; that was his life. And you knew he'd be involved with the baseball someday, even if we didn't know he'd go so far."

"That's right," Ella Mae confided. "My brother Gus—Jones is the baby of our family—he formed a little team and trained those boys on the meadow right next to our home. Dizzy and Paul and all the rest. They'd come over each Sunday, 'stead of going to Sunday school and church, and they'd spend it playing ball. Course, they had all worked six days, and I suppose they thought church could take a back seat."

"Now, on the first team," Jones began anew, "Ol' Diz, he was the pitcher—and that darn Paul played shortstop. I was at second. Elmer, their younger brother, the one that done the catching, well, he was kind of off a little bit."

"He was retarded some," Ella Mae added. "Folks called him Poodle."

In 1929 Dizzy was still several years away from major league fame. Here, in San Antonio, Texas, he pauses for the first known photograph of Ol' Diz in baseball uniform.

"You had to give Elmer a chew of tobacco or something to make him catch good," Jones said, laughing. "He was a strange one. One day we had a hot game going, and I wouldn't give Elmer a chew. Well, he let the ball go by him, intentionally I think, and Dizzy said for me to do the catching. I did and Elmer went to first base."

A chuckle erupted in his breast. "I was about fifteen then and Dizzy thirteen. Diz really gave it to Elmer that day, but he stuck up for him, too. He was like that, you know. Diz was tough as a boot, always wrestlin' in school. You'd get Diz by the toe and try to break his foot, but he'd stay with her 'til he couldn't take no more. He'd holler when he had to, but he was tough. Diz wasn't mean, just crankified. And he had his fun."

Fun was a commodity which largely eluded Albert Dean during his stay near Belleville. Profiles chronicle him as a figure inclined to labor and disinclined to smile, one whose view of life was blackened by the misfortune which had befallen him. "Dizzy's daddy was stone-faced," Jones said. "He was good to us boys, never did bother us, but he didn't have much to say. He sort of carried a hurt inside. They were poor. Their mother died when the boys was young and their daddy raised them 'til he got married again. Course, a man cain't raise kids like if they had a mother. And they just sort of scuffled around amongst themselves, making do as best they could."

"Well," Ella Mae stated indignantly, "they had such a big family. When we knew them they had eight kids. Mr. Dean had the three boys, and his second wife, a woman named Parham, she had four boys and a girl, and one boy was a cripple. Money was awfully tight then— so their daddy just stayed home and worked. He withdrew into himself. Didn't mingle much. He had a lot on his shoulders, with his first wife and all. Maybe that caused the grief." But Diz never showed those traits.

"Poverty made him (Dizzy) more ambitious," Jones said. "When he got his chance, when he got in the Army in the late twenties, that's when he got started. Diz didn't have much education, but he was as good a speaker as I ever heard. I remember him once at Belleville after he and Paul joined the Cardinals.

"Paul—I remember him—he said, 'I can't speak in public, but that Diz would rather get on that platform than any man I've ever seen.' And Lord, just like Paul said, Dizzy talked at the Belleville banquet 'til everybody had to go home. It was getting dusk to dawn. That was in 1934, and Diz hadn't changed since I last saw him."

"Diz was a scrapper," said Jones, who then began to laugh. "Why, I recall one time I like scared them two boys—Paul and Elmer—to death. We was boxing, and we was having at it round and round. And Diz was making it so bad on me that I whirled around and hit him right in the pit of his stomach.

"I knocked the air out of him, and of course, it blasted Diz down and he couldn't breathe. I scared Paul and Elmer right to death." By now his laughter was almost uproarious. "They went squalling and said I killed him. Oh, brother, it was something.

"Yes," Jones continued, "Diz was a home boy and people really liked his gab. Sure, we remember him from those early days. Who could ever forget?"

There was less in life to remember today, the Robertsons agreed, or to enjoy, either. Even in Booneville, the turbulent ragings of the immediate past had made their presence felt. Was there no role left for country folk like themselves, they asked? The media pandered to urban, more erotic and violent mores. The politicians, they felt, had deserted them. Their country, which they still honored and revered, had reverted to alien interests who shared neither their culture nor their concerns. Ella Mae's manner became more quiet, Jones's austere and resigned. There lay beneath all they said a sadness which could not be silenced, an unspoken fear that the nation they loved had turned to betrayal, or at the very least passed them by. Benign neglect was their common dread. "We don't have the good times we used to," Ella Mae said slowly. "Even here, where all we have is good, quiet people, folks used to have time to visit. Now they don't. This country, it's just changed so much."

Even more than urban blacks, who used the 1960s as their forum for impassioned outcries against prejudice and its sins, the Robertsons and their rural brethren now bore the evils of injustice and neglect. Their indignity remained unlessened, their dilemma undimmed. For they had no adoring press to raise their banner, nor make known their demands, nor fill the Manhattan canyons with their echoes. Few could deny that these people were impoverished, or that they seemed embattled and alone. Yet poverty had altered neither their decency nor their stoic charm. There was a poignancy to their plight which underscored the dignity they brought to life and love.

I bid Jones and Ella Mae good-bye, leaving them with companion time, the unflinching foe. Several hours later, at a local restaurant, I ordered the coffee Ella Mae had offered me earlier that day. I was alone, left to remember Booneville and its "good, quiet people," left to feel the echoes of the lost America they once had cherished and now remained to mourn.

Chapter Three

Shadow on the Walls

I

Looking back, one of their greatest virtues was the name, coined when Willard Mullin unveiled a cartoon in the New York *World Telegram* during the early baseball days of 1935. Mullin's sketch featured two large gas tanks on the indigent side of some railroad tracks, with several ballplayers moving over into the good part of town, carrying big clubs instead of bats on their shoulders. The cartoon's title? "The Gas House Gang," of course.

The Cardinals' name indelibly etched their repute forever. In the 1970s the Oakland A's, every bit as rambunctious as the Gas Housers, distinctly more talented, won three World Series in a row. Like the Cardinals, the A's were composed of varied, volatile types. Yet who will wager that, forty years from now, Oakland will be remembered as vividly as the Depression day Redbirds. Those St. Louis clubs live on, and their Gas House label remains in large measure why.

"Swarming up from the Texas wheat fields, the Georgia cotton lands, the West Virginia coal mines, the Oklahoma cow ranges, the Ozark farms, the Gas Housers redramatized for the public that old traditional story about the talent of common men," sportswriter and drama critic Lloyd Lewis wrote thirty years ago. "They fit the historic pattern of the American success story, the legend of the country boy who, on native wit and vitality, crashes through, clear up to the top."

Dean crashed through, clear up to the top, all right. Perhaps his rise would have occurred during any era, no matter what the circumstances or when his career began. A Dizzy Dean might succeed in any age. His fortunes were irrevocably aided, though, by the town in which he made his debut, St. Louis, and the indomitable club he joined. The Gas Housers, they were called, and their antics were so outrageous that even the legendary Yankees of Murderers Row sought the shadows.

The Gas House Gang held St. Louis and the nation enthralled. They boasted enough characters to last most teams a lifetime; partisans claimed, not without merit, that the Redbirds were more lively than the other seven National League clubs combined. They were a blatant, cursing crew, managed by Frankie Frisch, well-schooled in prior rough-hewn tactics by John J. McGraw. Pepper Martin, Joe (Ducky) Medwick, Leo Durocher, the Dean brothers and Ripper Collins—they all made Gas House an unalterable tonic for an America which sought, even craved, figures to adore.

The Cardinals baited fans and rivals, provoked fights with teammates, brawled with umpires, kicked dirt at umpires, mocked league officials and embronzed themselves. They were the only team in baseball annals to form a band, the Mississippi Mudcats, which evoked more notice in hotel lobbies and night clubs than most clubs did on the field. They were one of the few teams to ever stir a full-fledged riot. And they were the only team which could boast about the public unfolding of Dizzy Dean.

He arrived during the Great Depression. Long, winding bread lines were in massive vogue. So were soup kitchens, pleas for one full meal a day, billboards which proclaimed, "I will share," apples for sale on deserted street corners. Herbert Hoover's legacy had already been defined forever; urban shanty towns of the unemployed down by rivers bore his name. "Hoovervilles," they were called. Men pounded pavement in futile search for employment. Winter days went unmarked by heat. The madcap antics of Prohibition had given way to such plaintive songs as "Happy Days Are Here Again."

For St. Louis and its environs, the despair was magnified. Although nearer Illinois than Kentucky, St. Louis has always borne a Confederate charm, a civility that lends itself more to the agrarian South—and the rural South had been ignored or exploited since the Civil War. Its farmlands, ravaged for generations, had seen the topsoil crumble and the hillsides erode away. To the West, out on the Great Plains and the prairies beyond, winds and drought had withered the wheatlands and buried farms in unending currents of sand. Tenant farmers, both black and white, bore the assault's full brunt. Poverty eclipsed even the barriers of race, a verity which made a lasting impact upon Dizzy Dean.

The Depression made Gas House a bond which could be shared by men no matter how lowly their individual straits. There was Martin, brash and brawling, deflecting balls with his knees, his chest, his head, roaring into second base on his face, his back, his belly hard and lean, exciting the multitudes with his tumultuous play. And Ducky Medwick, a notorious bad-ball hitter in the later mold of Yogi Berra and Roberto Clemente, a man who antagonized teammates, rivals, enemies, friends.

And Leo Durocher, aggressive, abrasive, scarred by life and impaired by love. And Rip Collins. And Mr. Frisch. And, of course, the brothers Dean.

To be sure, the Gas Housers were not nearly as skilled as myth-makers would eventually suggest. Durocher, as has long been his custom, grievously overstated the case when he labeled the 1934 Cardinals only slightly inferior to the '27 Yankees of Gehrig and Ruth. St. Louis clubbed only 104 homers and allowed nearly four runs a game. The Cardinals barely edged a crumbling Giant team in the season's final days. Without one Dean they might have finished in the second division. Without both Deans they might not have finished. Yet their fame endures, thanks in large part to the belligerence and speed which marked their style. Momentarily, at least, the Cardinals eased the burden which warped the impoverished throngs. Social critics argue, often persuasively, that the 1968 champion Tigers helped to cool the racial fires in Detroit, that the Red Sox of seven years later aided in subduing the hates which busing had inflamed. So, too, did the Cardinals of the 1930s help to deaden life's burgeoning economic fears.

II

Events moved swiftly in the spring of 1931, three years before Gas House reached its public crest. With the bases loaded and none out, Dean sauntered into a March exhibition game against Philadelphia and struck out Al Simmons, Jimmy Foxx, and Mickey Cochrane, future Hall of Famers all. St. Louis officials quarreled bitterly over the best manner in which to deal with Diz, a dilemma that surfaced all too frequently in later years. And the Lucas man-child was sent packing to Houston, having already vowed to win between twenty-five and thirty games. In fact, Diz was partly right; he captured twenty-six, but they all were won in the minor leagues.

"It was a sight," his manager, Gabby Street, recounted several years later. "I'll never forget that exhibition game against the A's. Diz was sitting on the bench—he'd been with us a little while—and he was already muttering.

" 'I just wish Ol' Diz was a-pitchin,' he said, just loudly enough so that I could hear.

"Well, I looked at Diz and screamed, 'So get in there and pitch, and I hope they beat your brains out,' " Street continued. "So what's he do? He ambles out there to the mound, a big smile all over his face, and strikes out three legends at bat. One thing about Jerome—silence did not surround him."

While controversy raged around Jay Hanna, one of baseball's true guiding spirits remained in the shadows, exerting his Puritan influence over the Cardinals and their fortunes. Like Babe Ruth, whose bat fundamentally altered the game's future course, and Larry MacPhail, brusque, abrupt and splendidly disruptive, who introduced radio and night games to his fellow owners, Branch Rickey nurtured and shoved baseball from its dark ages into a less barbaric era. Advocates termed him innovator, preacher, diplomat, historian. Critics labeled him bombastic, Bible Belt, calculating and cheap. Above all, cheap. Almost infamously so.

Thus Rickey's image emerged. A man of classical bent, one who openly professed his religious beliefs, who abhorred alcoholism and profanity, who steadfastly refused to attend Sunday games. These traits newsmen dutifully noted. So, too, did they notice his other qualities—the baroque, professorial verbal manner, the desire, perhaps conscious, to court and mislead reporters, the marked ability to outflank player after player in contract debates. It was with at least partial justice that sportswriter Dick Young labeled Rickey "El Cheapo," and that Pat Dean called him "a stinker."

Branch Rickey came from Ohio, graduated from the University of Michigan, then entered baseball, a profession he was to graphically change. While by the early 1930s he had become the game's leading general manager, his initial baseball thrusts notably failed. In four years with the St. Louis Browns and New York Highlanders, forerunners of the Yankees, Rickey batted a less than imposing .239. His managerial efforts were equally uninspired; with the Cardinals and Browns, Rickey failed to place higher than third. In 1925 he was fired. One year later his successor, Rogers Hornsby, won the World Series with essentially the same St. Louis club intact. But misfortune faded swiftly; soon Rickey's executive skills, previously masked, were among baseball's most envied and praised.

As Cardinal general manager, Rickey's paternal instincts drew him to the farm system, a concept he fostered until his club ruled the National League. His format was brilliant in its simplicity—establish minor league teams and stock them with young players. Quantity, not quality, was of early import. As players improved, they would advance up the corporate ladder. Their talent already proven, their skills honed by competitive play, eventually they joined the Cardinals. Sheer numbers comprised the crucial essence; as more players signed, chances improved for more to help the Cardinal cause.

The system made for shameless profiteering; more players in the St. Louis chain meant that fewer would command decent salaries, and Rickey's salary scale was among the lowest in the league. Despite Dean's enormous impact, he never drew more than $7,500 until the post-championship year of 1935. Rickey had done battle with Cardinals before, but it was Ol' Diz who focused national notice on St. Louis' raging salary wars. The first skirmish occurred in 1931, shortly after Dean strode into Bradenton and promised Street he would lead the Cardinals to the World Series crown.

Dean invariably forced you to take him on faith; rare were the times he failed to make true believers of those he confronted and faced down. Before long Street had converted, too, claiming, "Diz is one of the best prospects I've seen in years." Yet Dean must fight the fact that Florida phenoms are hardly novel. For years fans up North have heard about the "future Warren Spahn" who emerges every spring, or the belligerent who will eclipse Pepper Martin on the basepaths. Each year they hear about the teenage marvel who can't miss, or the shortstop who'll bypass revered figures like Chico Carrasquel and Marty Marion, not to mention last year's regular shortstop. "We've got a shot at the flag," every manager says while reading from his cliché manual, and the fans inevitably believe.

Opening day comes quickly enough, however, and with its arrival stark, harsh verities dawn. The new rendition of Warren Spahn has an arm less super than sore. The shortstop phenom begins to look less like Lou Boudreau and more like Don Buddin, the ill-fated Red Sox figure of the 1950s who made a career of making dazzling defensive plays, only to fire the ball twenty feet above the first baseman's grasping glove; Buddin in the shortstop hole was a sure sign for residents of first base box seats to race for cover. Spring training fantasy, while beautiful, can be cruelly fleeting. This, then, was Dean's task in 1931—to convince the skeptics, to make spring endure into August and September. There was always a touch of fantasy about Dizzy Dean, an aura which lent itself to myth and magic. But his fame was not cruelly fleeting; his impact endured, and before his career ended, Dean had won 150 major league games.

Though Street, realizing talent, felt free to praise Ol' Diz, other Cardinal officials demurred. Dean had been in Bradenton only two weeks when Rickey took to calling him "something of a nuisance." Disfavor arose from Dizzy's growing monetary plight, a dilemma caused partly by the Great One's exorbitant spending and partly by Rickey's penurious ways. By April the interest which two weeks earlier had surrounded Dean, the antics that amused Cardinal fans and players alike, had blossomed into incessant turmoil. "At the moment," wrote the *World-Telegram,* "Mr. Dean appears to be in bad with the Cardinal management, due to his mounting eccentricities, and there is talk he may be shipped down to the bushes. That would be very regrettable. Baseball can stand a few more Dizzy Deans around. They add a dash of piquancy to the show." Seldom bound by discipline, Dean now infuriated Street, previously among his most ardent backers. Then the focus shifted, as it would so often, to money and Rickey's distaste for it in anyone else's grasp.

Dean's woes widened as spring training progressed. When Diz, flaunting his manager's practice schedule, failed to appear for a March 31 session, Street promptly forbade him to enter the Bradenton training site. "High-salaried pitchers on my staff are obeying orders and trying to prepare for the pennant race and this kid can't stay here if he's going to disobey all my orders," Gabby said, adding, "If Dean is going to worry anybody this year, it'll be the manager of Scottsdale or one of the other farms."

The dispute, which Rickey strove futilely to minimize, became vintage spring training gossip by April 7. Dean's financial straits were now public record, almost seventy-five per cent of his $3,000 salary already spent. When Dizzy's $400 in March wages vanished, he began leaving a trail of I.O.U.'s behind him, ones which covered soft drinks, clothes, women, and any other items that suitably adorned his style. Eventually the bills reached Rickey, who consulted with Cardinal secretary Clarence Lloyd—and in concert they offered their answer to the world.

At a news conference, Rickey urged, or "broadcast orders to," as the wire services reported, area merchants to reject any further Dean transactions. Furthermore, Dean was to report to Lloyd every morning, submit to a financial oath, and present a slip of paper which read, "Received today, $1, Dizzy Dean." One dollar comprised each day's spending money, a classic case of Rickey orthodoxy. Branch was a devout disciple of pay as you go economics; he may have been one of baseball's reigning patriarchs, but Branch Rickey was a comptroller at heart.

Dean, of course, threatened to quit, a scenario he often adopted in future years. Unlike many of today's actors, however, who use retirement solely as a ploy to lure a salary increase, Ol' Diz nearly left the Cardinals; his feelings of betrayal were unfeigned. Only a two-hour session with Rickey convinced Dean to remain a Cardinal until at least October 15, 1931. "I had an offer from an independent team at San Antonio that would pay me $250 a month," he said, "and I felt pretty bad at the way Street and Lloyd talked with me. But after Mr. Rickey got through talking, I felt like I ought to tell Lloyd to make my allowance ninety cents a day or maybe six bits. That man has talked me right back from San Antonio." Impetuous to a fault, victim of vintage Rickey rhetoric, Dean's acquiescence ruined a trip to San Antonio and produced one to Houston instead. Amid the oratorical barrage which Rickey thrust upon him, replete with the melodrama that accompanied his appeal, the verdict's outcome was virtually preordained. The nearest Dean came to being a 1931 Cardinal were the daily newspaper box-scores, ones which reflected a St. Louis team capable of winning the World Series without him.

Several days later Dean balked again. One month earlier Diz had waltzed into Bradenton and boasted, "I'm a big league pitcher and I'm going to stick on this club." To which Street advised him, "Son, take it easy. If you'll listen to the Ol' Sarge, he'll convince the owners of this club that you're a big leaguer with your arm and not your mouth." For the present, though, Street concurred with Rickey. Both agreed that Dean should seek out the Texas League.

Diz refused to accept his demotion, once more vowing to retire. "Jerome," Street consoled him. "All of us in the organization feel you need another season in the minors. Go back to Houston and I promise you'll be back here in 1932." Diz relented, then saw Gabby accompany him to the railroad station, where he slipped Dean some currency, eagerly received and quickly spent. Twenty years later Gabby Street died. "He was like a father to me," Dean said then. "He always knew what our troubles were and we could share them with him. And I guess

Gabby was the only one who didn't call me Dizzy. I was just Jerome to that grand old man.''

For Dizzy Dean, spring training 1931 had been disaster. ''That taught me the lesson of my life,'' he said later that year. ''I went back to work again. Then I got married. Now you can tell people that Old Man Dean's boy is here to keep his mouth shut, most of the time at least, and keep on working.'' Dean's clashes with Street were caused largely by his desire to pitch frequently. In Houston those wishes were fulfilled. Diz won twenty-six games and lost ten, struck out 307 batters in 425 innings and compiled an earned run average of 1.53. He was named the Texas League's Most Valuable Player. He was easily its premier attendance lure. And he met his ultimate match in Patricia Nash.

As cautious with money as Diz was carefree, Pat Dean provided the practical influence her husband lacked since childhood. Aided by her presence, Diz was no less flamboyant than in seasons gone, no less inclined to theatrics, but at least he was less wayward in his course. Pat babied Dizzy and mothered Paul, and handled contracts for both. ''He's the easiest person in the world to manage,'' Pat said in 1932, sentiments which would have stunned Gabby Street. ''I handle the money and all I say is, 'Jay, we'll not buy this, it's too expensive.' And he agrees just like that. Anything is all right with him. That's why I'm his banker, his bookkeeper, his manager and girl friend.''

Estimates of Patricia Dean varied widely. Partisans termed her the perfect mate for Ol' Diz. The duo stayed clear of public domestic strife, these accounts insisted; she lent to the marriage a measure of solidity and calm. Others were less kind in their regard. They thought Pat none too selfless, inclined to overly protect Diz and block out his associates, prone to see the world as a conspiracy out to wound her husband. They also made fun of her intent to save $1,200 of his $3,000 salary in 1931.

''I didn't know anything about baseball,'' she said in later years, softened and more serene. ''That was Dizzy's business. But I do know how the money is to be got and what to do with it. When one member of the firm is lacking in practical sense it's a good thing the other member has it, and that's where I come in.

''I've heard cheers change to jeers almost in one breath. The higher you are the harder you fall; that's the law of gravity. Well, when the crowds started booing Dizzy instead of cheering him I wanted him to be able to retire gracefully with money in his pocket. You see, I was determined Dizzy would not end his career on a park bench.'' Dean was in no danger of that, not unless he owned the park in which the bench was found—and neither were his chances of staying a 1932 Cardinal imperiled. St. Louis had won the previous year's World Series, spurred by the dramatics of Pepper Martin. The pitching staff was aging, though, and Street realized that only Dean might keep the Cardinals afloat. Alas, neither Ol' Diz nor anyone else could reverse the tides, and the 1932 Cardinals stumbled home a dismal sixth, eighteen games behind the champion Cubs. Attendance fell from 608,535 in 1931 to 279,219. Street's status slid further.

All this was entirely unknown, of course, when Dean arrived at Bradenton in February, 1932 and said, "I'm not trying so hard this year to live up to my nickname, fellows. I'm 'a taking the game more seriously." The new, sober-sided Dean could be benevolent, too. "Babe Ruth was made a Boy Scout in Florida this month and took the oath to do a good deed daily," Diz proclaimed that same week. "Now I've promised the Boy Scouts one of my deeds will be to take them the baseball that I strike out Babe with. So I figure we're even in this here Boy Scout business." Dean concluded 1932 with an 18-15 mark, but shed his Boy Scout garb in June. With the Cardinals in Philadelphia, where a year before Herbert Hoover had been greeted with derisive chants of "Beer, beer, beer" at a World Series game, Dean abruptly left the team and boarded a train for St. Louis. Unless he could reach a mutually agreeable pact with the Cardinals, which meant a revised contract, Diz said, "I'm through." He wanted more pitching starts and the money they would mean.

"Those Cardinals, they save me for a Saturday or Sunday game to draw a crowd," he growled. "I won't be able to score enough victories working only once a week, and then when I ask for the money I'm worth next year they'll say I didn't win enough games. How can you win? I get only $3,000 a year, and I've won six games already. Add that I'm a good drawing card, that big crowds come out to see me wherever I pitch, and I should be getting $7,500. Things are getting so bad that they won't even give my measly check to my wife. Now that's gratitude to her."

Dean's monologue closely matched another he issued the previous month, when Diz demanded to be traded or sold. To both outbursts Rickey turned a deaf ear, adopting an unusual reticence. Silence adroitly suited his cause; the 1932 Cardinals were doomed in any event, with or without Dean, and Diz could not afford to abstain for long.

The day after saying, "I'm through," Dizzy Dean bowed to the inevitable. "I am sorry I left the club like I did," he said, at owner Sam Breadon's request, in a letter to Street. "If you'll give me a chance to pitch in Philadelphia tomorrow and again in New York Wednesday, I will show you how games should be pitched—and won. Dizzy Dean." Shortly afterward, Pat Dean vowed to accompany Dizzy on his Eastern excursion. "It has nothing to do with his threat to quit," she claimed. "I'm doing this because it'll be cheaper to travel with Jay. Why, our long-distance bill for the last Eastern trip was $36. And besides, if I go along, it'll keep him away from those slot machines."

Had the Cardinals' 1932 scenario been as eventful as Diz's off-field antics, their attendance might have risen, but mediocrity prevailed. St. Louis moved briefly into contention in early August, then collapsed, leaving only Ol' Diz to partially salvage the season. He failed, but not before some laughs evolved.

One of the most memorable episodes came when Diz and a New York writer drove into a filling station. Dean looked at the pump for several

Dizzy Dean relaxes and prepares to take off his uniform following another winning effort on the mound.

moments and finally said, "That's always puzzled me. I don't see how they do it."

The writer wondered what Diz meant.

"It puzzles me how they know what corners are good for filling stations," Ol' Diz continued. "Just how did these fellows know there was gas and oil under here?"

Fortunately, at least for Dean, rival hitters were less enigmatic. During 1932 Diz compiled a 3.30 earned run average and led the league in strikeouts and innings pitched. He also became one of baseball's most oft-discussed figures. "A lot of people are under the impression that I'm a troublemaker," he complained, "but the only trouble I've ever had with the club was about money. And because a guy goes to bat about his 'dough-day' you can't call him crazy. Maybe you could if he didn't." Dean won over most of his teammates, naturally, many of whom were repulsed at first by Diz's erratic ways, a trait they felt would cripple Cardinal pennant hopes. Even first-division prospects soon faded, though, and interest shifted from Dean's role on the Cardinals to his impact on America, an import which slowly widened as the weeks unfolded and autumn neared.

On July 23, growling about an earache, Dean remained in St. Louis while the Cardinals barreled east to Cincinnati. Dean said he was ill; Cardinal physician Robert Hyland said no. "I don't care what he says. I'm hurting," snapped Dean, who failed to add that a deputy sheriff in Cincinnati was prepared to slap him with an overdue legal suit; the "earache," predictably enough, vanished when the Cardinals left Ohio.

Dizzy's charade yielded instant comic relief; when laughter at last subsided, focus shifted to still more Dean theatrics—unfurled at a rodeo two weeks later in St. Louis. Diz delighted spectators and appalled Western purists in the crowd. Instead of calf-roping while astride his horse, Dean first dismounted, then captured and tied up the calf he was trying to rope. Only afterward did he remount, having forever altered a once immutable profession. With Dizzy Dean, the barriers had a tendency to come tumbling down; whatever he touched did not remain unchanged for long.

Dean's propensity for stirring emotion had been vividly evidenced several weeks before. Less than a month after his celebrated twenty-four-hour walkout, Diz knocked down Dodger catcher Clyde Sukeforth with a fastball. The next pitch hit Clyde in the head. While Sukeforth collapsed, his Brooklyn teammates rushed onto the field, primed to brawl. Sukeforth was the most diminutive of Brooklyn players, and the most inoffensive, too, imposing neither in stature nor at bat. Dean's acquittal in a subsequent league report served only to further embitter the Dodgers, for Diz allowed no middle ground, and Brooklyn assuredly was looking for none.

"That was like Dean, hitting the smallest player on the team," said Sukeforth, now seventy-five and recently retired after nine years as New England scout for the Boston Braves. "Sure, it was intentional.

He was capable of doing almost anything. Part of it was ham; Dean was a born actor. And he said a few things that made sense; you couldn't deny Diz his humor. But we didn't like him much, and boy, after I went down, some of our guys ran him off the field. They chased him into the dugout, he was running so fast.

"We respected Dean, don't mistake me. He was an outstanding pitcher with remarkable control. But he was strictly fastball, a lot on the order of Robin Roberts years later. No breaking stuff at all, though he did develop a decent curve later on. I always thought Carl Hubbell was the better pitcher. Every time the two hooked up, Carl beat him. When Hubbell's screwball was on, you couldn't hit him."

Sukeforth never hit Dean much, either. He now lives on the coast of Maine, indulges in the sport he loves—"There are some great blue fish up here, just appeared a couple years ago"—and flees from how he is remembered best. In 1951, Sukeforth was bullpen coach of the Brooklyn Dodgers, a club favored by talent and cursed by fate. The Dodgers led New York, 4-2, in the ninth inning of the National League's decisive playoff game. Brooklyn called for a relief pitcher; Sukeforth must make the choice. "Erskine is bouncing his curve," he said, "and Labine seems tired." Ralph Branca thus answered the call. Bobby Thompson hit Branca's second pitch into the lower left-field stands. The Giants won the pennant. Sukeforth was fired and wrote an article for *Look* magazine, "Why the Dodgers Blew the Pennant." He was never able to help them blow another.

The Dodger assault of 1932 helped to unveil the holy wars Brooklyn and St. Louis staged in years ahead. Some of baseball's most lionized athletes, Stan Musial, Marty Marion, Pee Wee Reese and Jackie Robinson among them, clashed yearly as their two clubs contested for National League supremacy. The Cardinals in Sportsman's Park, Brooklyn in Ebbets Field, formed a rivalry whose intensity in the 1940s and 50s approached even the hallowed Dodger-Giant subway series. Though mutual loathing between the teams was in its infancy when Diz plunked Sukeforth atop his skull, Dean did little to subdue the incipient fires. He approached Street before a 1932 doubleheader against the Dodgers and said, "Let me pitch both games, Skip. These chumps are the easiest in the league to beat. I can whip these bums twice without even breaking a sweat." Halfway relenting, Street let Dean pitch the second game, and Diz complied with a win, 6-4. By season's end, after Brooklyn had outlasted the Cardinals, edging them by nine games, Dean bid the Bums so long and turned his notice to other clubs. "They ain't going to be a problem next year," said Diz, hardly endearing himself to manager Max Carey and crew. "Other teams will be our worry."

The Dodgers were not alone in their distaste for Diz. Concern had mounted, in fact, that Dean was preoccupied with proving himself against too many clubs. "If Dean continues at his present rate, he'll burn himself out in a couple of seasons," warned sportswriter Tom

Meany, "but if he works at a normal pace, he will be one of the league's best pitchers for the next ten years."

Diz faded before another ten years had passed, caused chiefly by injuries which forced him to alter his pitching motion; in the autumn of 1932, however, Dean's prowess on the mound was on the upswing, his public renown almost uneclipsed. With only six months of his major league career elapsed, Dean was not quite baseball's finest pitcher—Carl Hubbell deserved that label—but he was "amongst 'em." And as Dean so often chanted, "Brother, you ain't seen nothing yet."

III

By 1933, though baseball has long been slow to fully promote its leading lights, Dizzy Dean had already become a household word. "That's amazing for two reasons," Dan Daniel wrote in January, 1933. "First, because Dean has only been a major leaguer for one season. Second, because the baseball magnate for the most part is a very stolid and unimaginative fellow. Essentially he is a promoter, and yet he lacks all appreciation of the balleyhoo art and its possibilities." Despite baseball's remarkable resurgence in the 1970s, when it thrust football's National Pastime assertions aside, Daniel's critique is still valid today.

Ol' Diz knew intuitively how to cajole and use newsmen, how to influence them for his own means. Long before it became a focus of raging debate, Dean realized the exorbitant power, however well-meant or perverse, of the American media. "Okay, but make sure you've got plenty of photographers," Dean once replied to a stunt request. "That's all I care about."

In 1933 Dean was surrounded daily by photographers, most of whom were more intrigued by his pitching skills than Diz's off-field exploits. In response, he adopted a low profile for most of the season, hoping to conquer the National League and sharply uplift his $5,000 salary. Few, save perhaps Rickey and Breadon, disputed Diz's contention that he had already become the bulwark of the St. Louis mound staff, or that he should be entitled to a hefty raise. "I want $15,000 when '34 rolls around," he stated. "That's right. And while I don't want to take credit for drawing all the fans who see our games, I believe I draw most of them on the days I'm scheduled to pitch. That's B.O. (box office) appeal!"

No Dean season, obviously, could be entirely calm; several 1933 incidents assured America that however much Dizzy tried, the extrovert in him would not remain perpetually submerged. A notable episode occurred June 6, with Diz and the Reds' Paul Derringer brawling in full view of a Cincinnati Ladies' Day crowd. After exchanging barbs, the two started to wrestle, then were pinned to the ground by the Cardinals' Dazzy Vance as both benches cleared. Dean's teammates were less than placid, either.

Once Diz loaded the bases against the Pittsburgh Pirates at Forbes Field, that marvelously scenic park which closed in 1970. A high pop fly was lifted to short left field, falling safely in front of Joe Medwick's lackluster efforts to reach the ball. When Dean reached the Cardinal dugout, several steps ahead of Medwick, he turned on the unexpecting soul. "Great way to hustle," he snarled.

"Listen, you do the pitching, big mouth, and I'll take care of out-fielding," Medwick shouted.

Not halting stride, Diz replied, "I'll give you a punch in the mouth," after which a fight followed, one quickly checked.

Several innings later Medwick smashed a grand slam home run, a titanic blast landing in adjacent Schenley Park. Medwick returned to the bench, found the drinking fountain, loaded his mouth with water and began to wash Dean's shoes. "See what you can do with that load," Medwick said, and the two were fighting once more.

Medwick's affection for fists was an ideal way to silence the Master. "Dawgonnit, that Medwick don't fight fair at all," Dean often complained. "You argue with him for a bit and then he beats you before you've even had a chance to speak your piece."

Several weeks elapsed. The Cardinals began to slump. Diz missed an exhibition game and Street levied a fine. When Gabby returned to Sportsman's Park, Dean asked if he would reverse the decree. "If I shut out Brooklyn this afternoon," Diz inquired, "how about giving my money back?" Slightly nonplussed, Street hedged his reply. Help-less against Dean's incentive, the Dodgers lost out, 1-0, and so did Street's fine. L'affaire Brooklyn did not prompt Gabby's ouster, but neither did it arrest his decline. A late-season collapse and plummeting attendance (down 383,000 in two years) made nearly certain Street's eventual fate.

Before Street was axed, replaced by Frank Frisch, Dean set a major league strikeout record. On July 30, Diz struck out seventeen Chicago Cubs in an opening-game victory of a doubleheader, 8-2, at Sportsman's Park. His feat shattered the previous mark of sixteen held by Frank Hahn, Christy Mathewson, Rube Waddell and Nap Rucker, and was climaxed by three innings in which Ol' Diz struck out the side. Dean finished with a flurry, fanning six of the last seven batters he faced. "I should have done better," he said afterward. "My fastball wasn't breaking just right." Diz's endeavor lifted his 1933 total to 152, slightly behind the 164 recorded in the American Association by brother Paul.

One month later Rickey announced that Paul would join the Cardinals in 1934; another contributor to Gas House glory neared his debut. A player who had already arrived was shortstop Durocher, whom the Cardinals acquired from Cincinnati in June. With Leo's presence a steadying infield influence, Pepper Martin excelled at third base and his hitting unexpectedly rose.

Neither Martin, nor Durocher, nor Dean, nor the promise of Paul, could salvage the Cardinals' fallen hopes. After vaulting into the National League lead in early June, St. Louis finished fifth, nine and a half games behind the world champion Giants. Not even Ol' Diz's twentieth victory of 1933, which came over Brooklyn on Sept. 13 and of which he said, "It was just a breeze," could rescue Gabby Street.

"The players are fighting for Gabby," Daniel wrote as June reached its close. "Street knew some time ago that if he did not pull the Cardinals out of the slump, he would be asked to retire in favor of Rogers Hornsby." By September Street was out, Hornsby not in. Instead, St. Louis turned to the man players derisively called "John J. McGraw Jr.," the Fordham Flash, abrasive, Frankie Frisch.

Six years earlier Frisch had come from the Giants to St. Louis in exchange for Hornsby, a trade which stunned Cardinal partisans and prompted the St. Louis Chamber of Commerce to officially condemn Sam Breadon. Since then Frisch had silenced his critics, hitting as high as .346, batting in as many as one hundred and fourteen runs, leading the Cardinals to three pennants and one World Series. Now, as manager, he must lead in quite another way, and 1934 would afford him a tumultuous forum on which to display his wares.

IV

Born in Lucas two years after Diz, Paul Dean quickly fashioned a charisma that blended privacy, warmth, and innocence. He began as an amateur league shortstop, then was scouted as a pitcher in 1930 by Don Curtis, who had signed brother Diz to a Cardinal contract the previous year. During the next two years Paul Dean advanced to Houston, Springfield and Columbus, then made the jump to St. Louis in 1934. Despite his station in life, serenity proved elusive. For Paul was a gentle and sensitive man, one easily hurt, and despite his prowess on the field, often felt that his skills were slighted or ignored. "Paul almost got sent down in '34," said *St. Louis Post-Dispatch* sports editor Bob Broeg. "I think if he hadn't been Paul Dean, he would have been gone. But they stayed with him—they wanted the box office appeal of a brother act—and Paul finally came around. He was in deep trouble before that, though, and I'm sure he knew it."

The presence of Ol' Diz, momentarily, at least, saved Paul's career. "The Cardinals kept trying to build up Paul," relief pitcher Jim Mooney of the 1934 Cardinals said, "but for my money he couldn't carry Dizzy's glove. He was just a thrower." Tex Carleton, also of the same club, agreed. "Paul was nowhere near the pitcher Dizzy was." The most cutting estimate of all came from Detroit shortstop Billy Rogell, who hit against Paul in the 1934 World Series. "I'm seventy-three now," he said, "and I still think I could hit against Paul Dean in his prime. I'd knock his brains out."

Perhaps with gratitude toward Diz came also remembered grief. "Why," Paul said at his home in Springdale, Arkansas, "I beat Carl Hubbell four times in 1934. Diz didn't beat him once, but nobody talks about that. And for the life of me I don't know why." Regrets aside, Paul spoke proudly of his brother. "We looked out for each other. We were inseparable. That's why so many people keep asking me why everything's written now about Ol' Diz, period. Not about me 'n

Paul Dean, long past his pitching career, now lives in Springdale, Arkansas. (Springdale News Photo)

Paul, Dizzy and me. All they write about is Dizzy Dean. Why can't it be like old times? Just answer me that.

"Take a movie that was made about Ol' Diz, 'The Pride of Saint Louis,' you know. It wasn't much of a success," Paul claimed. "Heck, it stunk. But if they'd gotten hold of those New York and Hollywood writers and talked some sense into 'em, if they'd made the picture about the Dean brothers—notice, I said brothers—why, people would have stood in line to see that picture. They would have gone in three times and then gone back for more. That's what I mean. Those New York writers always louse it up. The real story was Diz and me, just like Diz always said."

In 1935, Paul again won nineteen games and held out for $8,500. Pressured by Breadon and Diz, Paul relented and signed for $1,000 less. Never again would Dean be able to bargain with resolve; the following season an arm injury occurred which ruined his career.

During his holdout in 1936, Paul's weight ballooned fifty pounds upward from its normal 185. "Frisch, I guess, was determined to get me into shape," Dean said. Once Paul signed his contract, he pitched almost every other day in spring training. When the season began he was inserted into the regular rotation, still brutally overweight. The exertion eventually told. Early in 1936 Paul pitched a complete game, then hurled six innings in relief the following day. "It was the twelfth inning," Paul recounted. "I felt a sting in my arm. The next day I went to throw the ball in a pepper game and couldn't hardly throw."

Paul Dean, winner of forty-three major league games at age twenty-three, would win only seven more.

"I maybe asked for what happened," Dean volunteered. "Frisch didn't cause my problems. Like Diz, I just loved to pitch. I had a love and affection for the game. That's the difference between then and now. Kids don't have the desire today. They're not as hungry.

"Let me tell you—we were hungry. I'll promise you that. And we had to be, because we were paid so poor. The owners really poured it on us. Now the players pour it on the owners. They're getting paid back for the way they treated guys who really loved baseball. That's why I'm still for the players, overpaid though they are.

"I've had a lot of letters from people who wonder why Diz had to die and leave us. That's God's will, though, and you can't fight that. I know this—there ain't no way I'm going to be separated from Ol' Diz. Not for long at least.

"You know something," Paul continued, smiling, "when that judgement day comes a-rolling in, we'll be back side by side. Ol' Diz and me are going to be back together again."

Chapter Four

Tumult and Applause

I

Dizzy Dean's propensity for bravado was never more evident than in March of 1934. St. Louis had fallen before a Giants' assault the previous season, when summer crested, rippling and hot. Yet here was Dean six months later, ridiculing the world champions and canonizing himself. "It will take about ninety-five games to win the pennant, and the Giants can't take that many," Dean pledged, and in fact they won ninety-three. "That's why we'll win." Brother Paul had not thrown a major league pitch. Diz had never won more than twenty games. Yet here was Dean pledging, "Me and Paul will win between forty-five and fifty games this year, you guys can bet on that," and in fact they won forty-nine. How many games would Ol' Diz win? "Why," he answered wryly, "all the games that Paul don't."

Dean's claims were meant for public consumption, and they were indeed consumed. Dizzy's saving grace, though, like Joe Namath of forty years later, was his refusal to take himself or his image too gravely; bombast aside, both men reveled in the light and whimsical approach, endearing them far beyond solely athletic roles. Dean never became a caricature of himself. Diz strove for self-esteem, and he tried to sell himself, but he rarely sold out. Perhaps there was too much of the common soil in Dean, and the confidence which arose thereof, for him to lust after public adoration. Self-assured men do not need to stridently posture; Dizzy Dean could laugh at himself. "Yesiree, Ol' Diz had hisself some good life," he said in the early 1970s, "and I did it by just being Ol' Diz.'' Deeds spoke for themselves. ''It ain't bragging if you can back 'em up,'' and Diz could invariably back them up. Especially in 1934.

The Giants' Frank O'Doul, who said about Diz's 1934 vow, ''In spite of what Mr. Dean says, I believe it would be a good idea for the National League to hold the race anyway,'' was among those amused by Dizzy's unending gall. O'Doul's flaw was not in dismissing Dean's motives, which were to miff the Giants and uplift a then undermined Cardinal cause. That Dean would have understood. His, and New York's ultimate error, became the dismissal of Dean's ability to realize his boasts, or the effect his rhetoric had on St. Louis teammates.

''The Cardinals don't have a chance,'' Giant manager Bill Terry sniffled, and he and O'Doul were not alone. The Cardinals were quickly relegated to also-ran contention, rebuffed by their critics and ignored by their fans. Attendance had plummeted in 1933; another seasonal plunge might endanger the St. Louis franchise. Instead, the totally unforeseen occurred, and one of baseball's most memorable seasons unfolded. ''I hear we're picked to finish sixth or lower,'' Frisch said in March. ''That's all right with me. I wouldn't care if they picked us to finish last. If everybody got to thinking that we might give them a surprise.''

Dean's manner one afternoon gave portents of what 1934 might entail. During an exhibition game, where strategies are curtailed and players platooned at will, where scores are counted and then discounted, the Giants belted Diz for seven runs in a single inning. Dean was so enraged that he retaliated in full. Seven consecutive Giants were plunked with Dean fastballs. In an *exhibition* game, no less. ''They ain't going to beat the Master like that,'' Diz fumed.

The seventh batter was Terry, laconic and aloof, protective of his players to a fault. Four years earlier Terry tied a National League record with 254 hits; he would bat .354 this time around. Today, however, the unflappable Terry was notably upset. Not believing what he saw, Terry pranced out of the batter's box, glared at catcher Bill DeLancey and snapped, ''Is Dean crazy? What's the matter with you guys?'' Next he asked umpire Cy Pfirman to quell Dean's ire. If Terry was annoyed, Ol' Diz was incensed. ''Had Terry come charging out to the mound, Dean would have known how to respond,'' recalled Ken Smith, who covered the Giants regularly. ''But here was Bill asking Pfirman to stop the knockdowns. That provoked Dean even more. How could he fight an ump?'' Terry's growling brought him little profit; after striding to the plate, he was hit by Dean twice, once on the pitch and once when the ball bounced up and deflected against the Giant's neck. Diz was also bounced, thrown out of the game by Pfirman. Afterward Frisch remained silent; never would he order Dean to abort his knockdown mode. For the Gas Housers, baseball was war, exhibition or not, and their riotous ways continued into the regular season, when the real conflict began.

The Cardinals broke with a rush, winning twelve of their first fourteen home games. Even though many of its seats were unoccupied daily, Sportsman's Park was a marvel, both for the Cardinals and their fans. Cramped, warm, slightly homespun and lovably familiar, it reeked with memories and boundless nostalgia. Seats were hard, comforts uncommon, and parking was perpetually minute. Yet few were the seats which offered a poor view of the playing field; even the least expensive ticket made for intimate sport.

A double-decked grandstand extended fully along both foul lines. A roof hovered over the right field pavilion. Left field stood 355 feet from home plate, a hefty shot even for power hitters. Right field was a more accommodating 310. To reach the center field bleachers required a prodigious blast of 426 feet. Foul territory was scarce, the Cardinal bill for foul balls lured to the stands was immense. Already more than fifty years old when the age of Gas House dawned, Sportsman's Park was a cynosure around which the Midwest met; coming to the ballpark was almost like coming home. A country-fair aura prevailed, born of intimacy and spurred by convention, and the Cardinals' start in 1934 served to underscore that trend. Here was a baseball park, solely and without exception, not a circular, sterile coliseum where football thrives. At Sportsman's Park, where fewer than 35,000 patrons could attend, the rural touch existed and baseball reigned. So, too, did the Cardinals in 1934.

For two months the Cardinals were a team triumphant. From April 29 to June 12, Dizzy and Paul won six straight games apiece. The Deans appeared in thirty-one of the Cardinals' first fifty-two games, boosting St. Louis in the standings but prompting fear that the two would tire as autumn neared. Conjecture raged not about who was the National League's finest pitcher, but rather which Dean brother warranted that claim. America had never seen their likes before, and not a few observers gave the upper edge to Paul.

"Paul's fastball seems to have more of a hop than the one Dizzy throws," said Ol' Diz's old rival, Clyde Sukeforth, perhaps not the most impartial of souls. "Paul had two strikes on me when I batted so swiftly that I thought he pitched both of 'em at once." On any other club, Paul's rookie brilliance would have been unrivaled, but he was still Dizzy's younger brother, and the Cardinals rallied behind Ol' Diz. On May 21 the Cardinals invaded the Polo Grounds, that bathtub-shaped ballpark on the Harlem River banks, and before thirty-five thousand they ravaged the Giants, 9-5, staking the elder Dean to a nine-run lead. "My players are willing to hustle," said Frisch, at home in New York, where he had helped the Giants win four successive pennants during the 1920s. "They're more than willing. They're positively determined." Absent was the ridicule heaped on St. Louis barely two months before.

June came next, and with it strife and strike, controversy and mounting losses. The afterglow of a misused, Dean-dependent pitching corps tore at the Cardinal calves. During spring training Paul Dean had staged a minor holdout, then signed his rookie contract for $3,000.

On June 1, without warning, Ol' Diz refused to wear his uniform in Pittsburgh, saying "I won't throw another ball," unless Paul was given $2,000 more. That money, claimed Dizzy, making only $7,500 himself, had been promised Paul by Rickey in March—and Diz now threatened to strike. "I'm underpaid, but my brother is worse underpaid," he said, making ready for the salary wars which would follow the 1934 season. "I'll take the rap myself, but my brother must have the $2,000 extra or we don't pitch."

Though the Deans had compiled eleven wins between them, Rickey was disinclined to yield. "Dizzy is just popping off again," he said. Publicly, Breadon viewed the matter with more alarm, and Paul was soon appeased; Diz's strike was aborted, peace preserved. Harmony proved far more elusive. For few clubs are at once harmonious and beaten, and the Cardinals' June swoon stamped them as eclectic losers, vagabonds whose picaresque skills could not offset a glaring lack of pitching depth.

Paul (Daffy) Dean warms up in 1934, his rookie season with the St. Louis Cardinals. (International News Photo)

Within three weeks the Cardinals tumbled from a perch atop the National League to four games behind New York. The slippage was startling, even Dizzy and Paul were unable to wholly hold back the tides. On June 26 the Giants slammed St. Louis, 10-7, dropping the Redbirds into third place. The Cardinals were 17-21 without the Deans, 20-4 with them. Reports abounded that Frisch would be fired if the slide continued; only New York's inability to squash all contenders denied the rumors their full effect. With the Cardinals in decline, Dean's notice inversely rose. Life greeted Diz with echoes of applause, each crescendo more vocal than the one before. He was the champion of the grandstand and bleachers. Cardinal executives, Rickey excepted, became hesitant to dampen the free spirit who drew national notice their way. National League publicists, showing rare theatrical acumen, began to blare Dean's billing above the Cardinals'. Paid promotions in daily papers, burying the fact that St. Louis would play Chicago, bannered the game as Dizzy Dean vs. the Cubs—and the same was true, if far less pervasively, for brother Paul.

Incidents arose which magnified the mystique. Once Dean visited a children's hospital in St. Louis. Ol' Diz autographed books, casts and scorecards, told how he threw the curveball and "fogger," his trademark phrase for the Dean fastball, and asked patients if he could better their lives. "Anything at all," he chimed. "There ain't no exceptions for you kids."

One boy, "Bless him," Dean said later, put forth his choice. "Strike out Bill Terry for us this afternoon," the child said, and the ward patients took up the cry. "Strike out Terry," they chanted. "Do it for us. We'll be listening on radio."

Why always Terry and the Giants? Diz mouthed to a companion, who heard Dean tell the patients, "I'll do it. I'll pitch this game for you guys. And if I get the chance, I'll strike out Bill with the bases loaded."

The finale quickly followed. The Cardinals led, 2-1, as New York batted in the ninth inning. With two out, two men singled and another walked, the last, tiny Hughie Critz. The bases loaded, up comes Terry; who could ask for more? "I hate to do this, Bill," Dean said as Terry ambled toward the plate, "but I promised some kids in a hospital today that I'd fan you with the bases full. That's why I had to walk little Hughie." On three pitches Terry struck out.

Within several weeks Terry became embroiled in another Dean vignette. As impersonal in bearing as Diz was vibrant, as terse as Dean was verbose, Terry was a perfect foil for the Master; the fact that they were two of baseball's most skilled performers, each of whom played with a contending team, served merely to underline their conflict. Even so, Dean liked Terry and often paid him visits on the road.

The Cardinals were in New York, a Giant meeting underway, when Dean crashed into the clubhouse. "You'll have to get out of here," Terry shrieked. "We're holding a meeting."

Dean replied, "What you talking about, Bill?"

"We're going over the Cardinal hitters."

"That's all right, you go ahead," Diz reassured him. "You can't learn me nothing about them; I already know all their weaknesses."

The Cardinals received few other midsummer laughs. Except for Dizzy and Paul, who themselves writhed from aching arms, Cardinal foibles merged on the mound. Only the Deans kept St. Louis close. On June 27, Ol' Diz edged the Giants, 8-7, and received $100 for appearing on a post-game program; that sum, paltry by today's standards, comprised almost half a month's salary for an average Cardinal. In mid-July Dean won his ninth consecutive game, and seventeenth of the year, 4-2, over Boston. A victory on July 16 lifted his record to 18-3; exuberant St. Louisans, confident their club would somehow overcome New York, envisioned an "All-Western" World Series between the Cardinals and Detroit.

By July 26, Jay Hanna had vanquished the Giants four times without a loss. For six weeks after June 16, Ol' Diz remained unbeaten, then suffered his fourth loss on July 28, a date made infamous when Dean said his most memorable moment had come not from baseball, but from a rendezvous at a Ft. Worth airport with Will Rogers and Mae West. On August 7, the Cardinals' one hundred and third game, Diz downed Cincinnati for his twentieth victory, expected now for months. "There's a lot more wins where these came from," he claimed, and autumn would prove him right.

Brash and unyielding, Dean ideally suited the Cardinal mold. Cursed and reviled by rivals, Frisch led a turbulent, combative crew. Martin pawed the earth in frenetic style, inciting quarrel with teammates and opponents, playing with silent hurts; once Pepper stayed in the lineup for days despite a broken finger. Bill DeLancey brought skill and courage. A fine catcher, even more vituperative than Frisch, he gave no ground save to tuberculosis, the disease which curtailed his career. Medwick clung to conflict, once giving pitcher Carleton a black eye because Tex was slow to leave the batting cage, then a year later knocking out another pitcher, Ed Heusser, after Ducky had been called "a loafer." Durocher, too, played with spirit and lust, though he largely spurned the obscenity and vocal barbs which won him fame in succeeding years. Despite his Medwick misfortune, even Ol' Diz was drawn to combat, his assaults wholly verbal and cast as taunts. To players who anchored a hole for their back foot in the batter's box, Dean became hostile in intent. Motionless he would stand, nodding his head, until the hitter's ritual was done. "You all set now?" Diz screamed. "You finished? Well, get a shovel and call for the groundkeeper 'cause they're going to bury you right where you're standing." And invariably the next pitch knocked him down.

Nineteen thirty-four began the Cardinal heritage of fearless strife, a tradition which outlasted almost every other club's. When the Gas House Gang grew old, Rickey called upon the hundreds of Depression youths who graced his farm system. Up came Stan Musial, escaping the timeless poverty of Donora, Pennsylvania, and Albert (Red) Schoendienst, he of Germantown, Illinois, and Enos (Country) Slaughter, who heightened the Gas House penchant for genuine, almost violent desire. Slaughter played with the Cardinals from 1938 to 1954, then was dealt to the New York Yankees. There he pulled a side muscle, prompting manager Casey Stengel to ask how soon Enos could play. "How soon?" Country said. "Right now. Ain't nothin' but a little meat torn away from the rib cage that'll mend itself in no time." Slaughter's credo was mean and unflinching; injuries were to be discounted, not dwelled upon.

During the mid-1960s came the Cardinals of Orlando Cepeda and Bob Gibson, the cheerleader and the loner, who combined with Lou Brock and Curt Flood to reaffirm the courage of '34. "That club was tough, but so were we," Joe Garagiola said of his 1946 world champion Cardinals. "We were fearless. Anything you did, you felt you were ahead of the game. Not that you'd been in the trenches necessarily. But you were so glad to be back (from the War). You'd hear rumors. 'Wait 'til you see this or that guy.' Harry Walker told us some war stories. Then he warned us about his guy Ewell Blackwell with his sidearm fastball. Man, we didn't care. Let us at him."

For the 1934 Cardinals, Depression was the motive which made them expend their full measure of strength. For the Cardinals of twelve years later, the necessity to somehow forget World War II, to wipe its memories clean, prompted the impelling drive of Musial and Slaughter, small-town boys who sought desperately to make good. For the Cardinals of Cepeda, a Puerto Rican, and Gibson, Brock and Flood, all blacks, bias and its attendant grief caused their urgings to succeed. Depression, war, and injustice were traits not unique to the Cardinals; St. Louis teams, though, seemed able to undercut them, to lessen their enduring force. Baseball became a means of upward mobility and social ascent, of escaping the past and its inflamed convention.

The Cardinals have claimed their share of color, too. No team which boasted Slaughter and Garagiola could prove unduly dull. The championship teams of 1967 and '68, led by Cepeda and Gibson, were tabbed El Birdos by Missourians, who loved their skills and comeback flair. Gas House's appeal was slightly more bizarre; it reeked, in fact, with juvenile humor and rowdy charm. The Gang disrupted hotel lobbies with their antics and carried workmen's tools on the road. They carted fiddles and harmonicas, washboards and guitars, and enlivened long train rides with favored songs. Bill McGee played the fiddle, Martin played guitar. They played when the mood obliged them or the crowd desired—in the clubhouse, dugout, railroad station or train. The band lured a harvest of headlines, and Frisch, as urbane as he was short-tempered, a highly sought banquet speaker, reaped them as well.

"I had the good fortune to manage a terrific ballclub," Frisch would begin his post-dinner remarks. "I am possibly the only manager who carried an orchestra. We traveled with more instruments than we did shirts or anything else. . . . And there is the placard as we got off the train—The Gas House Gang plays here today. A tremendous picture of the Mudcat Band; down in the corner is a little picture of Medwick,

over there is a picture of Dean. I walk in the ballpark and here is a microphone and seven seats for my orchestra.''

Music composed only one means of Cardinal color; Dean and Martin saw to that. During exhibition games they often located the park's public address system, then went on to enchant spectators with their down-home version of the unfolding action. On tempting July afternoons, with heat searing the ballpark girders, the temperature nearing 105 degrees, Diz and Pepper latched onto paper and wood, then built a fire before the dugout. Armed with blankets, they mocked the summer sun while squatting, Indian-mode, around the fire. Once the two wrestled for an hour in the St. Louis clubhouse, their match ending minutes before Dean faced the Dodgers. Perched at hotel windows, they took delight in throwing bags of water within striking distance of sidewalk victims. Martin would look for a fan which cooled the hotel lobby, then approach it with sneezing powder enclosed in newspapers. When Martin opened the paper, the powder escaped into the fan; within minutes the lobby was deserted. Ofttimes, Pepper and Diz waited until a formal luncheon began at their hotel, then placed smoke bombs in cars parked along the curb. Next they stood guard until the guests started their engines. When the bombs exploded, and visitors rushed to reenter the hotel, Dean and Martin greeted them in fireman uniforms purchased earlier that day.

Strike three! Dizzy shows his stuff as the Cardinals down the Detroit Tigers in the 1934 World Series. (UPI)

One morning a near-riot ensued. Collins, Martin, and Dean rented construction overalls and tools, marched into a banquet room and began to survey the walls. A lavish meeting was already underway. "We're redecorating the whole place," Collins told the assembled throng. "Can't you tell? Go right ahead with your speeches. You won't bother us."

Defiant on the field, the Cardinals were unruly off. Humor and immaturity merged. "Musial said that the ways of players had changed greatly since he played," Bob Broeg told me, "and he came along a little while after Gas House ended. He said comedy was broader, cruder then. The players were more rural, they had less education. And if that was true of his era, it was surely even more so of Dean's."

Neither charm nor color, nor the pranks which marked their times, allowed the 1934 Cardinals to easily oust New York. Collectively more skilled than the Gas Housers, capable of extending their lead, New York seemed always destined to triumph. Frisch's major concern became the Cubs and their late-season surge; St. Louis journals warned that even second place might elude the Cardinals.

"Frank was worried, but no matter what people said, we thought we could still catch the Giants. When you had a guy like Diz, no matter how crazy he was, you knew you had a chance to win." At seventy-four, soft-spoken and retired, a resident now of Binghamton, New York, Gas House pitcher Bill Hallahan vowed that historians would fondly remember Ol' Diz. Perhaps more so, he said, than would his own team-mates. "Diz was great and I liked him—so colorful, so eager to help the club. Frisch didn't even have to order Dean to go and throw in the bullpen. He did it anyway, I swear, sometimes just by instinct."

Hallahan hesitated. "Maybe I shouldn't say this," he said, " 'cause I did like him, but some of our guys didn't care much for Diz. It wasn't that he got preferential treatment from Frisch. Hell, Frank wasn't that way. And most of the players didn't know what went on in the front office. Rickey kept a tight lid on. But the writers, they were all over Diz. He got the ink, and some guys, they didn't like it. Not a bit."

Wild Bill laughed and gestured. "I'll tell you the way I felt. When you have a person that says, 'I can do this or that. Just watch me,' that's being a braggart. But when you say that and keep doing what you say, that's something. And Dizzy did it all the time; I've never seen anything like it since."

While Ol' Diz crowed, the Giants swaggered. The previous season that sinewy lefthander from Missouri, Carl Hubbell, he of the peerless screwball, had won twenty-three games, ten of them by shutouts. This year he would win twenty-one and lead the league with an earned run average of 2.30. Mel Ott and Bill Terry, both of whom swung from the left side, combined to form baseball's most formidable offensive duo, now that Ruth and Gehrig had been shattered by the Babe's eclipse. Ott and Terry teamed for 43 home runs, 35 by Ott, and drove across 238 runs. The Giants outhomered St. Louis, 126-104. They scored only 39 fewer runs and allowed 73 less. They were clearly the superior team—and blessed even further, it seemed, when Dizzy and Paul were suspended in an August 14 incident that stunned the Cardinals but ultimately turned the pennant chase around. "It was weird," Ken Smith recalled. "People thought the turmoil would kill St. Louis. I did, too. But when the Deans were faced down, it gave the Cardinals the lift they needed, the lift they hadn't had."

Decisive in their effect, events took hold on Sunday, August 12, when the Deans lost a doubleheader before thirty-six thousand at Sportsman's Park. His team floundering, rumors of his impending departure ripe, Frisch grew outraged when Ol' Diz and Paul missed a train for Detroit, site of an exhibition game the following day. A year before Street had yielded to pressure from above, reversing his stance on Dizzy and cancelling the pitcher's fine. Frisch would prove far less pliable. Now six games behind New York, willing to force the issue, Frisch fined Diz $100 and Paul half that amount. Though the Deans had won thirty-three games and lost eleven, Frisch stomped into the Cardinal clubhouse on August 14, informed Ol' Diz of the dual fines and told him to take the field.

"You can't fine me," Diz protested, tearing his uniform from the neck down, then seizing other uniforms to do them equal harm.

"Oh, can't I," Frisch cried. "Well, you're fined, you and Paul, and this fine is going to stick."

"If that fine sticks for Paul and me," screamed Dean, now suitably enraged, "then we're through with the Cardinals. In fact, I'll show you what I think of this organization," and with that he was off and tearing again.

Between uniform rips Dean panted, "This is sure swell treatment you're giving a fellow who has tried to pitch the Cardinals to a pennant. I won't pay that fine and I'll speak for my brother Paul—he won't pay either."

Dean started for the clubhouse door. "Where are you going?" demanded Frisch, moving toward him.

"Don't stop me," Diz replied.

"Well, it's all right with us if you never come back," shouted Frisch.

Dean slammed the door behind him and raced into the Cardinal executive quarters. Demanding his pay, he was asked to "come back pay day," which was August 15, tomorrow.

"I won't be here tomorrow," Diz retorted. "I'll be on my way to Florida. And so will my brother Paul," who had followed to the rear, presumably lending moral support. As the two prepared to leave the clubhouse, they were slapped with notices of indefinite suspension, courtesy of Breadon, Frisch, and Mr. Rickey.

"Something had to be done," mused Frisch several hours later. "Other players on the club have been fined for doing things they shouldn't have, and they've taken their fines. No players can be bigger than the game, or bigger than their club. There will be discipline on this club, even if we finish last, which, of course, we won't." Without the Deans, naturally, neither would they finish first, a fact few realized more vividly than Ol' Diz himself.

"We're going on a fishing trip to Florida," Diz insisted as August 14 ended, "that is, if we have enough money coming after they take those fines out of our pay. Of course, it's possible the Cardinals will return the fines when they find out how badly they need us. A lot of folks don't think Frankie Frisch can afford to lose his two best pitchers, of which I'm one."

Told of Dean's remarks, Frisch held firm. "The hell I can't lose those guys," he huffed. "I'll pitch Bill Hallahan, Walker, Carleton and the two old men (Jesse Haines and Dazzy Vance, the latter acquired from Brooklyn), and we'll win." Critics praised Frisch in print, but few doubted his eventual retreat. Frank would crumble, they said, when the Cardinals began their fold; Breadon would not allow Frisch's pride to subvert the World Series receipts he craved.

The Deans remained in St. Louis the next day, shoving to the shadows their Florida excursion. "The Cardinals can't get by without us," Diz said. "We'll wait here."

Breadon, though, would not relent. "The next move is up to the

Deans," he said. "I'm standing squarely behind Frisch and will offer no concessions to the rebels." Rickey, following suit, rallied behind his manager. So did Cardinal players, recently grown disenchanted with Dean's celebrated billing and unaccountable ways. So, most surprisingly, did Cardinal fans, who vilified the folk hero they once groveled to adore.

Nine months earlier Dean had lured an overflow throng to Washington University, where a field house crowd of 9,500 witnessed his first cooking lesson. Dean prepared a turkey for roasting, then started to bombard the audience with eggs. "Watch it. Duck. He's gone crazy," the visitors screamed. A mad scramble ensued. Only when the eggs began to bounce did their true substance appear—pure rubber. The audience roared; this was their Dizzy Dean, lovable and eccentric, master of the madcap innocence they revered. St. Louis had worshiped Dean's comic touch, a quality of which he, also, was proud. What the public now saw, and decidedly despised, was Ol' Diz's almost transparent arrogance, a belief that he could hold the Cardinals hostage in the midst of a pennant race, ransom becoming an erasure of his fine. Dean misjudged the extent to which he could manipulate team and town; for perhaps the only time during his turbulent career, he was a stranger, even here in St. Louis, seeking home and friendship.

All this was lost on Dizzy Dean; within the next several days his fortunes continued to ebb. When Dean received his semi-monthly check, he found a $36 bill for the two uniforms he ripped. "I don't think that was nice," Diz told reporters. "I was mad and lost my temper when I tore the uniforms, but they weren't destroyed. They could have been mended." Dizzy's plaintive pleas went ignored, as did his cure for the Cardinal uniforms.

Even after Dean returned, Breadon said, the fines would remain. "And he'll come back," the owner stated, "when he accepts club discipline and rules." Diz replied that he and Paul would never cringe. "We'll stick around until August 23," he said, the date the Giants came to town. "It takes Diz and Paul to stop those guys," Diz continued, "then we figure the Cardinals will make overtures to us to regain their lead." On August 15, contrary to Dizzy's hopes, Breadon said the Deans' refusal to surrender would cost them dearly; for every day suspended, Dean would forfeit $50 salary, Paul $20. Frisch disclosed that Pepper Martin would be used on the mound. Rickey stayed silent. Ol' Diz waited and sulked.

The following afternoon both suspensions were officially announced. "Mr. Breadon and Rickey have strongly backed me in this matter, giving me a free hand," Frisch said after an hour-long conference with Ol' Diz and Paul. "The fines imposed will stick. I do not propose to be dictated to by two ballplayers, even if it means losing my job." Faced with a united front office, the Deans' last, ultimate gamble rested upon the Cardinals' ability to collapse. But rallying behind Frisch, St. Louis won seven of eight games in their absence; the Deans, incredibly, had become expendable, and so, also, their cause. "For a time the fans were amused by the antics of Dizzy, and his leading brother Paul into scrapes with him," Dan Daniel wrote after the August fiasco passed. "As a matter of fact, the customers thought it was just a lot of clever publicity stuff. Now the supporters of the Cardinals are tired of Dizzy, tired of his charades."

With Dean's defenses crumbling, on August 16 Diz asked for truce. "I don't want to lose any more money," he pleaded. "How about it, Paul? I'll pay part of the money you've lost." Paul at first was hesitant, asking Frisch to revoke the fines. Then he, too, bowed to the inevitable, only to find that mercy was not among the lexicon of favored Rickey terms. "The front office doesn't want us back at all," Diz complained bitterly. "When we saw them yesterday, they asked us why we didn't go down to Florida for the fishing trip we first talked about." While Ol' Diz withered, Rickey chanted, "Ten more days off the payroll," and Frisch concurred. Money was not the sole commodity they sought to strip from Dean; dignity was yet another.

One day later Paul Dean was reinstated and charged $120. Meanwhile Diz traveled to the Chicago office of Kenesaw Mountain Landis, baseball commissioner since 1920, who pledged to conduct a probe into the affair. "I want to get back to pitching baseball," Dean mourned. "And I'm willing to do anything necessary to straighten this thing out." Within seventy-two hours Landis flew to St. Louis and held closed court. "The judge said no writers would be allowed into the hearing," veteran writer Ray Gillespie said, "but the first thing he did when he entered was open the vent above the door. We heard the whole shebang." For four hours the Deans exchanged barbs with Breadon, Frisch, and two St. Louis lawyers. One of the hearing's comic parts concerned Dean's shredding of his uniform, once in anger, the second time to oblige wire service photographers. Another memorable moment came when Diz denounced the Cardinal offer to employ brother Elmer, then a peanut vendor in Houston. When Elmer arrived in St. Louis, Dean charged, he was taken to Sportsman's Park and given peanuts there as well.

Vignettes notwithstanding, the outcome was preordained. Though some made much of Landis' rapport with players, he was still the owners' commissioner, beholden to their votes. The suspension was lifted and Ol' Diz allowed to return. His impromptu revolt cost $486, more than fifteen per cent of Dean's 1934 salary—$100 in fines, $36 for uniforms torn beyond repair, $350 in payroll wages lost. The Great Strike had ended in abject failure. Even with those who loved him most, it was difficult to be generous in judgment, or deny that Diz had lured ridicule his way. It was now up to Dizzy Dean, whose club was still far behind, to bring his season to climactic peak, to show what he could do.

"Failure was something very foreign to Diz," Buddy Blattner said, "and it stunned him. He'd always had such overwhelming ability that he was able to back up everything he said. I think this is why the adversity in 1934 cut him so deeply. I remember Diz and Carl Hubbell's great duels, for instance," Blattner recalled. "Once Diz was in New York and he was interviewed. 'I'll tell you, podners,' he said. 'They get me one run tomorrow and I'll beat them.' And this is when the Giants were really good. The next day forty thousand fans packed the Polo Grounds, where the dressing rooms were directly in center field and elevated. When Diz came out forty thousand people stood and booed. And booed. With each passing inning they booed some more. Diz would raise his arm defiantly and they'd boo even louder. Well, the game finally ended, a shutout for Diz, and the whole park stood and roared in tribute to him. The old place about collapsed. But that was Diz.

"He had a master's degree in both pockets out there on the mound," Blattner said "And he had a powerful personality; one he could turn on like a light. Like all the great thesbians, you put them on a stage and they come alive. Before the floodlights came on they couldn't even say their name. Diz was like that. When he walked out to pitch, he came alive. I mean, the whole world was his."

In August of 1934, that world had collapsed. Properly contrite, aware that his teammates harshly opposed his strike, Dean returned to St. Louis a chastened, if not more humble, man. There he began the most astonishing deeds of his major league career, heroics which would forever cloak him in a mythic mold. His fortunes, elevated again, endeared him to Breadon, who figured to lose $100,000 unless the Cardinals won the pennant; and Frisch, whose latest rumored successor was Columbus manager Ray Blades; and Rickey, now three years without a pennant.

"Rickey never was all that fond of Dean," said an associate who was close to him during the 1930s, "partially because Diz often called him Branch. He preferred the title Mr. Rickey—it was more imperious. Rickey liked ceremony, especially when it focused on him. But he liked winning even more, and Dean helped him in a way all the pomp in the world could not approach."

Ol' Diz's post-strike debut was not without ceremony of its own; he took the mound August 24 and left it one hundred minutes later, a winner once again. Dean blanked the Giants, 5-0, by now haunted by *deja vu*; the victory, Diz's twenty-second, was his fifth consecutive over New York. "Dean was nearly invincible," Frisch rejoiced, a scenario that became commonplace as September's pennant drive began.

Blessed with Indian summer, the Cardinal cause seemed nonetheless lost. Diz and Paul would not suffice; what St. Louis required (and ultimately received) was an extended Giant losing streak, one to rival the 1951 collapse of the Brooklyn Dodgers, who blew a thirteen and one half game lead in the season's final six weeks, or the Philadelphia Phillies of 1964, who held a six and a half game cushion with twelve games left and still managed to fold. A September 15 article in the *World-Telegram* gave evidence not only of Dean's efforts to provoke the

Giants, but the less than polished sports prose of the 1930s, too.

"Dizzy Dean tried to put the black-cat jinx on the Giants yesterday," the piece started, "but they held him off at the portal of the dugout. While making his way to the St. Louis bench, Dizzy saw the sinister feline wandering under the grandstand. Before Mr. Cat could dash into the dugout Dizzy grabbed him and brought him on the field. With a broad grin the Diz bore the meower toward the baliwick of the world champions. But they saw him coming and threatened him with violence or something.

"So he took Mr. Whiskers back under the stand, and there he waits to see which way the pennant goes. When interviewed by Dizzy the cat said he had been spending the summer at Yankee Stadium." The Giants were immune to black magic, but not to bumbling efforts of their own, and as October neared, their collapse gained substantial, then irrevocable thrust.

September 21 crystalized the Giant plight. At Ebbets Field for a doubleheader against the Dodgers, Ol' Diz threw a three-hit shutout in the first contest, yielding his first hit in inning eight. A no-hitter followed in the second game, one whose finale Pat Dean refused to watch. As Paul Dean toiled during the ninth inning, Pat covered her eyes with a fur piece every time a ball approached the plate. "Dizzy showed us more stuff than Paul," Dodger manager Casey Stengel insisted afterward, "but Paul just burned the ball in there and our boys couldn't connect." From the subliminal shadows Diz made one of his most oft-quoted remarks. "The only thing that makes me mad," Diz said, "is that Paul didn't tell me he was gonna throw a no-hitter. If I'd 'a known that, I would have throwed one, too."

Before the game, Frisch had held his usual clubhouse session, giving advice on how to combat rival hitters. "Keep the ball high and outside on Leslie," Frank began. "He'll hit it over the fence if you get it inside."

"That ain't how I pitch him," Dean replied. "I don't give that guy nothin' but low inside stuff, and he ain't got a hit off me yet."

"Now about Tony Cuccinello," Frisch, undaunted, said. "Nothing but curves for him. He owns a pitcher like Vance. Tony'll hit a fastball into the left field corner every time you give him one."

"That's mighty peculiar," said Ol' Diz. "I never have bothered to dish him up a curve yet, and he's still trying for his first loud foul off me."

Still unfazed, Frisch continued to detail the Dodger lineup. As each hitter's name arose, Frisch advised Dean to pitch him one way. Diz countered with quite another.

"This is a silly business, Frank," Dean said. "I've won twenty-six games already this season. So, as I see it, it don't look exactly right for an infielder like yourself to be telling a big star like me how to pitch." Finally flustered, Frisch must have marveled at Dean's penchant for ousting rivals from the attention he craved. Yet several hours later, brother Paul would upstage Ol' Diz, a novel feat in any year.

Within the next week, having lost six of their last seven games, the Giants' once commanding lead dwindled to one-half game. New York's final two encounters were at home against the Dodgers, whom Terry had mocked earlier that year, asking, "Is Brooklyn still in the league?" St. Louis had three games left, all with the Reds at Sportsman's Park. Frisch announced that Ol' Diz would combine with Paul to hurl the final weekend's games. Granted, he had little choice; most of the pitching staff had unfailingly flopped. Even among Cardinal supporters, who had religiously avoided Sportsman's Park all year, the demand for tickets grew heated and intense. Dizzy Dean won the opener against Cincinnati, tying the race; three weeks earlier St. Louis trailed by seven games. Paul then stymied the Reds, 6-1, while the Giants were losing once more, giving the Redbirds first place, their first residence there since July. Sunday, September 30, would presumably end the season and decide the race. A crowd of 35,274, most of whom hoped to see Dizzy seal the pennant and win his thirtieth game, jammed and elbowed its way into the Cardinal yard. More than forty-four thousand flocked to the Polo Grounds to see the final act of the Giants' tragedy unfold.

New York bowed out first; even with Hubbell ushered in to relieve, the hapless Dodgers won, 8-5, giving the final lie to Giant dynasty hopes. More than nine hundred miles to the west, master of the scene before him, Ol' Diz paid the scoreboard no heed. Exhausted but redeemed, the scars of August over and done, Dean blanked Cincinnati, 9-0, making the Cardinal pennant margin by two games.

When Bill DeLancey clenched a popup to end the game, Diz scrambled toward him, grabbed the ball in his glove and sauntered into the dugout, evading the fans who surged on the field. The Cardinals had won nineteen of their last twenty-three games. The Deans had pitched in five of the final six. "The key came on September 5," Frisch maintained. "That's when I told our club it ain't over. 'Fight to the finish,' I said, 'and if you do I'm telling you fellows that we won't be beaten.' Tell you the truth, though," Frank confided, "I didn't think we could win it myself." That he did was due in large measure to the brothers he had shamed a month before.

Meanwhile Detroit rejoiced. Twenty-five years had passed since the Tigers last clawed their way to an American League pennant; now, in October of 1934, the Cardinals were coming north for the World Series. Two hundred thousand ticket requests vied for forty-seven thousand seats at Navin Field. When the Series ended, the Tigers losing, four games to three, St. Louis owned a triumph, bitterly earned and brilliantly conceived, that not even Detroit could long begrudge.

Dizzy Dean gained credence from the times in which he first performed. Television had not been invented by 1934; radio, though operative, was still not available to the masses. The number of weekly magazines and daily papers rose upward yearly; nearly six times as many existed as do today. How a player was described, the manner in which his actions were detailed, had a telling, indeed decisive, influence on the final memories imbedded in millions of American homes. Ol' Diz flourished in that climate; as Paul Dean and a score of others affirm, the press was decidedly on his side.

Bespectacled, convivial, an associate editor for *The Sporting News,* Ray Gillespie traveled with the St. Louis Browns and Cardinals from 1924 to 1951. Though one of the nation's first accredited baseball reporters, a member of the Baseball Writers of America Association since 1922, Gillespie belonged to that rare breed of diamond personnel —one who failed to regard the past as sacrosanct and unmarred.

"I've always made it a habit to forget what's gone before," Gillespie said in St. Louis. "I live in the present, the future, if you will. That's the trouble with the game today—its owners dwell on the past. There's nothing wrong with present-day baseball; Lou Brock, for example, is one of the most exciting players I've ever seen. Shuck off the past, it won't do you any good." An enviable pose, but one which the mention of Dizzy Dean might change.

"Can't say that I mind talking about him," Gillespie said. "Diz was a newspaperman's dream. Every day he'd give us some new story, a novel experience to write about. It was incredible. I'll never forget what happened just after Paul came up in '34; the two Deans were going wild. So one day the managing editor of our paper, the old *Star-Times,* called me in. He'd been reading some of my stories.

" 'Hey, what is this all about?' he demanded, and he was a big, burly guy. 'What is this man's right name?'

"I answered him, 'It's Dizzy.'

"He looked at me and said, 'Don't you know we could be sued?' He was really mad.

" 'Well,' " Gillespie continued, " 'I don't think Dizzy knows.'

"The managing editor looked at me and said, 'I'll be honest. I'm beginning to be skeptical about you guys. These things you say Dean does—they're impossible. Nobody would do them. I can't believe this Dean is that dumb.'

"So I told him, 'Wait a minute here. He's not dumb, he's smart.' And then I said, 'How would you like to meet him?' I figured that would silence this guy quick."

Gillespie shed his glasses, then began anew. "A day or two later the Deans came in. Well, our managing editor really let them have it. At first he didn't believe their story at all—I guess he thought they were a fraud. He started asking questions, really digging. Finally he asked, 'Well, Diz, what's your background? What nationality are you?' He figured that would fox them out.

"Diz looked at him and said, 'Gee, we're just Southwest boys. I guess you'd call us Americans.'

" 'No, no,' the managing editor said. 'What's your heritage?'

"Paul spoke up and said, 'Diz, I'm not sure, but I remember our parents saying we was Presbyterian.' "

Gillespie laughed loudly. He was neatly tailored, an immaculate sort who belied the ancient image of sportswriters as an accursed, brawling bunch incapable of behavior verging on the couth. "Dizzy really grabbed this town," he said. "Everybody in St. Louis, and I mean everyone, was his fan. I used to say he was as good as he wanted to be. He had more gall than anyone I ever saw. I remember one incident vividly. It happened the day in 1933 that he struck out seventeen men to set a new National League record.

"We were sitting on the bench before the game and I asked Diz, 'How do you feel today?'

" 'Oh, I feel great,' he said.

" 'Boy, it's hot today, though,' I mentioned to him.

" 'Man, I like it that way,' Diz said, laughing. 'I feel like I might just go out and set a new strikeout record.'

" 'You're kidding me,' I said.

"Dean snapped back, 'Do I ever kid?' And danged if Diz didn't do what he said he would.

"In 1934," Gillespie said, "who could ever match what happened? I was with Dean at the World Series when we went to Henry Ford's home outside Detroit. And Will Rogers was with us, too. He was an admirer of Dean. All the way out to Dearborn, Ford's home, Rogers was preparing Diz and Paul for the meeting. Will kept saying, 'I'll take care of the introductions.'

"Anyway, we were to have breakfast at the Ford Hospital. When we finally met, Rogers made a big to-do. 'I would like you to meet Dizzy Dean and his brother Paul,' Will said formally to Ford.

"Ford responded, with just as much dignity, 'How are you, Mr. Dean?'

"So what does Diz do?" Gillespie asked. "He looks at Ford and booms out, 'Hiya, Henry.'

"Well, everybody was shocked, but Ford kept his composure and asked, pleasantly enough, 'What is the outlook for my Tigers?'

"And Diz, he roared, 'Well, it don't look so good. My brother Paul's going to pitch today. I'd say you're in trouble.' "

"There was a lot of the showman in Diz," Gillespie said. "We were great friends. He'd kid you and you'd rib him right back. 'You guys sit up there in the press box and all you do is eat sandwiches,' he'd tell me. Once he came out on Braves Field and threw a ball into the press box. Diz said, 'That should wake you up.' "

Ray Gillespie was a writer of recognized talent, a man respected for the quality of his craft. He was also calm, refined, almost courtly in his ways. Sam Muchnick, another writer who traveled with Dean, was neither courtly nor refined. He was, however, gruff, rotund, industrious and a promoter of no small skills. Like Ray Gillespie, Muchnick was soon drawn to Ol' Diz and the turbulence he lured.

"We were close," said Muchnick. "I met Diz when he first came up in 1930. We ran around together, we'd go to gyms and watch the fighters. Diz was a riot to be with, not that he was irresponsible or anything.

When he was getting a dollar a day, he'd go down and treat the club to a round of cokes. Blow it all there. No wonder he was popular. And not that he was well educated, either.

"Show you what I mean," Muchnick pledged. "I recall in 1932 Diz had to take a physical exam. I had a Model A Ford at the time, and we went to the doctor's office. Diz went in and I waited for him outside for quite a while. Finally he came out and he won't say nothing.

"We got in the car and started driving. At last I say, 'What did the doctor say, Diz?'

"Diz just sat there. Finally he said, 'I don't know what's wrong with that guy. He wants to do me in, to take care of me for good.' He looked at me and said, 'He wants to take it all off. All of it. Did you ever have that done to you?'

"Well, I told him, tongue in cheek, 'Yeah, Diz, it was done on me, but I was only eight days old, so I don't know if it hurt or not.' "

Muchnick attacked his cigar and roared while reliving the exchange. "Poor Diz, he didn't know what circumcision meant," he said. "People would have taken advantage of him if it hadn't been for Pat. She could control him something fierce. She was the motherly type who always looked out for his well-being. Pat knew Dizzy for what he was—a big, ungrown-up kid."

Muchnick joined the *St. Louis Times* sports staff in 1925, leaving seven years later when the paper was purchased by the cross-city *Star*. "This has always been my home," said Muchnick in his downtown St. Louis office, "and I've always had a soft spot for baseball. This is real Cardinal country, you know. The team has promoted well. We've had good announcers who helped build the tradition. And a good press helped, too. The boys have been informative and factual, but they haven't tried to cut players up.

"Hey, I'll tell you about Ol' Diz. He was some broadcaster. Cosell says he calls 'em like he sees them, but Dizzy did it first, and a lot more honestly. If he thought a player stunk, he said so. And he said a lot; Diz remembered his friends. Even when I was out of baseball, and couldn't do him any good, he'd come up to me and say, 'Hiya, podner.' Diz was a good man."

So, in his distinctly amiable way, was Sam Muchnick. Like Gillespie, he sought out and befriended the game's leading and lesser players; "It wasn't a cardinal sin then," he said, "to write a good story about the guys who played." Though he fled newspapers in 1932, becoming one of America's most influential wrestling promoters, he held a nostalgic yearning for the life which had been his. "Those were good times," he said. "Not for an old guy like me, but for the young, like I was. Then you've got the world by the tail." Muchnick smiled, sadly, it seemed, as he rose from his desk. "You seen Broeg yet?" he asked. "No. Well, you'll love talking to him. He has a memory and a love for dates that'll knock you out."

From the St. Louis 'sports fraternity,' labeled as such by Ken Smith, Bob Broeg has wrung affection verging upon awe. Nationally known for his weekly column in *The Sporting News,* the author of seven widely-heralded books, recipient of the University of Missouri's medal for distinguished service to journalism, Broeg became sports editor of the *Post-Dispatch* in 1958. "I took over from a marvelous writer," Broeg said as we sat amid the cluttered desks and bookshelves which invariably mark newspaper quarters. "Roy Stockton was my idol. Of course, he'd been the original chronicler of the Gas House Gang. Even though I think writing on the whole is better today, and I probably write better day in, day out, than he did, I've never seen the day I could touch Stockton on his best day. He was a gem."

"The times were right for Dizzy Dean," Broeg began. "The country needed heroes. I remember when I took tickets at Sportsman's Park in the mid-thirties. You wouldn't draw flies all week, but then came the Sunday doubleheader. You know, Breadon was condemned for playing two games on Sunday. He actually started the practice—and people called it synthetic. But by 9 a.m., when the gates opened, the whole upper section would become instantly filled with brown-bagging out-of-towners. Why did they come? Because they were almost certain to see Ol' Diz pitch. The Cardinals staggered it that way. And they really pulled them in from the hinterlands."

"This," I argued, "is when the Cardinal allure had its inception."

"Yes, but you have to remember why St. Louis' impact on baseball then was so great," he counseled. "In the thirties, in fact, up until twenty years later, this was the majors' westernmost club. You could almost say it was the most southerly, too. So the Cardinals had all this area to themselves, and their spiritual following was considerable.

"I clearly remember Bob Feller in Iowa and Mickey Mantle in Oklahoma—they both told me years later that the big event of their young lives was when their fathers mustered a couple dollars to bring them to St. Louis for a Cardinal game. And that was characteristic—this was the focal point of an entire part of the country.

"Let me give you an example of the Diz I knew. You remember Clarence Lloyd, the secretary who gave Diz a dollar a day? Well, he played nursemaid to Diz and Dean didn't like it. Yet many years later, when Clarence was eighty and almost destitute, largely because he'd been so generous toward others, he wrote a moving letter to Stockton saying, 'I guess I lived too long.' So we started a fund—Stockton and Frisch and Sam Muchnick—and we came up with $7,500. Diz pitched in $500 of that.

"Well, did Pat give me a lecture on the phone. She said, 'You know Diz is a soft touch. We're already taking care of a former major leaguer,' a fellow by the name of Gene Moore. The point is that Diz was a big enough man that he came to the rescue of a guy he had reason to dislike, almost to detest."

Between them, Dean, Martin, and Frankie Frisch created almost volcanic turmoil. Many were the barbs they took delight in exchanging.

''You have to remember,'' he warned, ''those insults were laden with humor. Dean used to tease Frisch unmercifully, and Frank would scream back, but Frisch was amused more than he let on. And humor was less refined, cruder then. Diz fit right in. Why, in the 1940s Walker Cooper on the Cardinals would tie your tie in so many knots you could never get it undone. That's the way their laughs went.

''Martin, like Dean, loved to razz Frisch, who would invariably respond in a huff. Once Frank was haranguing the Cardinals in their clubhouse. It was like a morgue. Finally Pepper, in the nasal twang of the Southwest, said, 'Frank, can I ask you a question.'

''Frisch said, 'Yeah, what?'

'' 'Frank,' Pepper began, 'I was just wondering if I ought to paint my midget auto racer red with white wheels or white with red wheels.'

''With that,'' Broeg concluded, ''Frisch laughed and said, 'Aw, get the hell out of here.' I mean, the meeting broke up right then.''

Heading for a downtown restaurant that Dean himself had favored, I repeated Gillespie's contention that current players were selfish and too monetarily inclined. ''Wasn't Dean cut from the same mold?'' I asked.

''No,'' said Broeg, ''Diz was pretty much a team man—and he could be easily swayed. Take this. In 1934 Jesse Haines, the Cardinal pitcher, was in ill health. He was also very old. Late in the season Dean and Frisch had a fight and Diz refused to put his uniform on in New York. By this time the Cardinals had a real chance to win the pennant. Well, Haines deliberately stalled around until everybody had taken the field. Then he began on Dean, and he really played ''Hearts and Flowers.''

'' 'Diz,' Haines pleaded. 'Ol' Pop sure could use another World Series check. I'm in bad shape, you know.' Oh, he played it to the hilt—super maudlin—and Ol' Diz never had a chance.

''Finally,'' Broeg related, ''Dean said, 'All right, Pop, god dammit, Ol' Diz will do it for you, but he won't do it for the Dutch bastard (Frisch).'

''And he put his uniform on and went out and beat the Giants. Haines followed him out and winked at Frisch and said, 'Now, Frank, don't say a damn thing.' Frisch had put Pop to the whole scene.''

''Yes,'' said Broeg, ''those 1930s, they were a sight.''

III

Even more than most cities, none of which escaped its sweep, Detroit bore the indignity of Depression. Banks closed. Assembly factories slowed, all but coming to a halt. For thousands of unemployed auto workers, ''Brother, Can You Spare a Dime?'' verged less on romantic prose than a dirge which sounded daily. For the baseball Tigers, hard times proved nearly lethal. In 1924, spurred by Ty Cobb and aided by contending status, the Tigers drew more than one million to the green fortress known as Navin Field. Nine years later attendance had fallen more than seventy per cent, to 320,972; in five years under Bucky Harris, Detroit placed no higher than fifth.

Then, in October of 1933, Mickey Cochrane came to Detroit from the floundering Philadelphia A's. He came for $100,000 and he came to play. Self-made and taught, Cochrane led the Tigers on the field and off, shoving mounting bills and overdue rent into the Depression shadows. He hit .327 as the Tiger catcher and managed the club as well. Detroit won 101 games and the 1934 American League pennant. Attendance surged upward and controversy soared. The Tigers were a splendid, riveting team. They boasted four future Hall of Famers—Cochrane starred at bat and in the field; Hank Greenberg, earnest and unsure at first base, hit .339 and clubbed across 139 runs; Charlie Gehringer, smooth and silent at second, batted .356; Goose Goslin finished at .305. Six regulars hit above .300. Pitcher Schoolboy Rowe, an unimpressive 7-4 the year before, rebounded to win sixteen straight games and compile a 24-8 record. Tommy Bridges climbed from 14-12 to 22-11. Rookie Elden Auker chimed in at 15-7 and Firpo Marberry was 15-5. Small wonder that baseball was fun again at Navin Field, or that Detroit exulted.

Like St. Louis, Detroit is one of America's great baseball towns, though minus its civility and Southern charm. Where St. Louis is serene and leisurely, the Motor City is boisterous and brash; Detroit lays claim to many of the nation's longest strikes, one of the nation's highest crime rates, the worst American riot of the Twentieth Century. Detroit is blue collar and union-oriented, lunch-bucket and hard hat. Yet Detroit is benevolent, too; few cities in America contribute more annually to charity. And Detroit is loyal; what other city in America would turn out one million strong in 1975 to watch a baseball team that won fifty-seven games and lost 102, one that groped its way through a nineteen-game losing streak? Just as the Tigers of 1934 brought trolley cars to a halt along crowded Woodward Avenue, so did the champion Tigers of thirty-four years later help subdue the guerrilla spirit which cursed their city. "This is a town," wrote columnist Joe Falls, "that in seventy-five years has developed a true passion for a boy's game and a love-hate relationship for the men who play it." Detroit thrives when its Tigers win, or even contend for a pennant, and that passion was rarely more evident than in October, 1934.

All summer the nation's pages had been replete with Dizzy Dean— Ol' Diz squabbling in the Cardinal front office, doing public penance before Landis, Dean on the mound, in the dugout, off the field. His antics, now slightly repetitious with crowds grown accustomed to Dizzy's routine, beckoned irresistibly to the patrons of Detroit, who waited to be enthralled. "The Deans are something new to Detroit, which, unlike the Senior Circuit or two-club cities, never saw them in action," one newspaper account began. "This town is dying for a look at the Deans. Gaping crowds stood outside the hotel this morning, waiting for a glimpse of Dizzy and Daffy."

God was in his heaven and Dizzy Dean owned Detroit. The Series lured George Raft and Shirley Temple. Will Rogers and Joe E. Brown came to town. So did William Frawley, whose fondness for baseball was such that in the 1950s, during his halcyon days as Fred Mertz on the television series, "I Love Lucy," he demanded a contract clause which allowed him a week's leave to attend the World Series. "I just wanted to see for myself," said Frawley in 1934, "if there really was a Dizzy Dean. He sounded too good to be true." Even Babe Ruth, his dominance of baseball at an end, became a Series fixture, trying vainly to recapture the limelight which now belonged to Dean.

"Boys, I know just what you want me to say," Diz advised the assembled Series press. "You want me to pop off, do a lot of bragging about me and Paul. Well, I ain't gonna brag. All I'm gonna say is that I aim to plow the ball through there, and Paul here is gonna fog 'er through. This series," he concluded, "is already won, but I don't know by which team."

Dean reveled in his glory. Utterly contemptuous of the American League, derisive in his posture toward Detroit, Ol' Diz displayed the monstrous gall that prompted Rickey to exclaim three years earlier, "Judas Priest! I never heard a ballplayer talk like that before in my life. Do you know what he said to me? 'Mr. Rickey,' he said, 'I am worth all the money I'm asking. You pay me what I want and I will put more people in your ballpark than anybody but Babe Ruth.' " Rickey would not pay what Ol' Diz sought, not yet at least, but Dean had already upheld his part of the compact. America flocked to watch him perform in October of 1934; the Babe could no longer equal his appeal.

Toward the Tigers, Dean taunted, "What kind of a club is this, anyway? There must be better clubs than Detroit, even in the American League." Before the first game the Cardinals stole a quick look at the interior of Navin Field. With the Tigers in the batting cage, the field cluttered with writers and photographers, Diz bounded from the dugout, bedecked in street clothes. He took off his coat and hat, located a bat, then strode to the plate and cried, "Let a man hit that can hit." Dean smashed several pitches, some of which landed in the bleachers, then wandered toward Hank Greenberg, whom Diz would abuse unmercifully in the Series to come.

"See that? That's how to hit the ball, Moe," he laughed, using the oblique anti-Semitism then common among major league players. Diz asked what kind of bat Hank intended to use. Greenberg meekly lent him the club, which Dean lifted, studied judiciously and returned. "Throw the bat away," he said, "I'm a pitchin'." During batting practice Dean's bat accidentally sailed into the Detroit dugout. No one was hurt because no one was there. The Tigers were assembled for their clubhouse meeting, to which Diz said, "If they're thinking, they're as good as licked."

An hour later, while Dean was warming up, photographers asked Diz to pose with a tiger skin, replete with tail and head, hung around him. Dean obliged delightedly, insisting upon impromptu burlesque. As the tiger skin hung aimlessly around him, Diz launched into an unpatterned jig, gestured to onlookers, picked up several baseballs and fired them wildly and at will. Next he grabbed the skin by its tail, whirled the

Dizzy Dean (left), Tiger pitcher Schoolboy Rowe (center) and Paul Dean (right) pause for a moment before the second game of the 1934 World Series. (AP Wirephoto)

hide above his head and flung it toward the clubhouse. "We'll twist those Tiger pussycats," roared Diz, and indeed he did.

Wanting to avoid matching Roe against Ol' Diz, Cochrane started graying Alvin Crowder in the Series opener. Dean countered with an eight-hit effort, then apologized for not pitching a shutout. Five Detroit errors, two by third baseman Marvin Owen, and four hits by Joe Medwick gave the Cardinals a victory, 8-3, and a 1-0 lead in games. Afterward Dean laughed, "Did you see how that Marberry, when he came in to pitch, threw his leg up in the air. He looked like something that just came out of a fresh egg!"

The combative fervor of the Series had already been instilled. "It happened in the first game," Butch Yatkeman, the Cardinals' equipment manager, recalled. "Jo Jo White of the Tigers crashed into Frisch real hard at second base, really blasted him, and that stirred everybody up.

"Durocher came over to him and asked, 'Frank, do you want me to take care of White?'

"Frisch said to him, 'Hell, no, I'll do it myself.'

"So the next time White came steaming into second base they both covered. Durocher slammed the tag on his head and Frisch slammed the glove in his stomach. Oh, it was tough. And nobody enjoyed it more than Ol' Diz.''

Despite their opening loss, the Tigers were still favored, but the tides quickly shifted away. "I told you before this started that those Deans would win all four games," said Casey Stengel, avoiding the disjointed Stengelese which later became his trademark. "You should have known I ain't no Little Ned from the Third Reader." The Tigers had stirred Detroit, livening its tempo and pulse. Now the spirits were silent, struck mute by Dizzy Dean.

"You take somebody like Pearl Bailey," Ken Smith said. "Everybody knows her, no matter where she goes. She's an international big shot, and the same was true of Dean. Kings knew him. Presidents knew him. So did Joe Blow in Poughkeepsie." So did Henry Ford in Detroit, who made effective use of the hottest property around. Athletes have always been in great demand, accessories to be displayed and flaunted. Washington, D.C., officials are prone to praise their football Redskins, hailing them as the kind of men who make America great. Frank Sinatra has long made much of his alliance with Leo Durocher. During Willie Mays' years in New York, Broadway performers clamored for his supposed friendship. Sports figures are prized commodities, invaluable if adroitly merchandised, and even critics never doubted Ford's ability to promote.

On October 4, 1934, Henry Ford marketed Ol' Diz. A limousine brought Dean from Detroit to Dearborn, from where Jay and his wife journeyed to Ford's Greenfield Village School. There Diz spoke to students, regaling them with some of his well-versed yarns. The episode lured reams of press notice, enough, indeed, to justify the $100,000 in broadcast fees Ford had budgeted for Series radio exposure. When Dean's lecture ended, students asking vainly that Diz be allowed to stay, a police escort from Dearborn to Navin Field enabled Jay Hanna to arrive moments before the second game began. Once there, he soon wished for absence.

The Cardinals broke in front, 2-0, then saw the Tigers surge from behind to win, tying the game in the ninth inning, winning three innings later. Rowe, of whom Dean later said, "That Schoolboy had better know his lessons, because I'm plenty tough as a teacher," mastered the Cardinals, yielding seven hits, only one after the third inning. The next day Paul Dean, his case as always understated, quietly moved the Series St. Louis' way, allowing eight hits but stranding thirteen Tigers to triumph at home, 4-1. "I'm just a semi-pro beside Paul," Diz chortled, hardly bemoaning the fact that Greenberg had struck out twice in the third game with the bases loaded.

When Dean finally escaped the rush of reporters, men who pursued Diz daily whether he starred on the field or sat idly on the bench, he left the Cardinal clubhouse and fled Sportsman's Park. As Dizzy tried to hail a cab, a sprawling limousine pulled near. The two men inside asked Dean if he wanted a ride back to his hotel, the Forest Park. "Sure, pals," Diz said. "Why not?" He was partially inside the car when Breadon, spotting America's most balleyhooed athlete from the Cardinal executive offices, screamed from the window, "Dean, get up here now!" Chancing nothing, Breadon next dispatched an errand messenger to fetch Ol' Diz.

"Do you know those men?" demanded the Cardinal owner, wan and anxious when Dean appeared at the desk.

"Naw, they was just fans, I guess," Dean said, prompting a heated Breadon homily on the danger of suspect friends. The Cardinals never charged formally that Diz was potential kidnap fare, but they issued no denials, either, and the incident was seized upon by newsmen, who treated Dizzy like a unique and endangered soul. Breadon assigned bodyguards to patrol the ground outside Dean's hotel room. They were to accompany Ol' Diz to and from upcoming Series games, an escort of which the Master was inordinately proud.

"A lot of them Hollywood big wheels don't get none of this," he boasted to a teammate. Dean introduced his protectors by name to baseball writers, adding in a stage whisper, "That guy, he's guarding just me." Eager to avoid further Dean insults, a desire which proved wholly vain, the Tigers skirted the issue. Tongue in cheek, Cochrane denied he was involved in the alleged kidnapping, confiding, "The idea, of course, has my complete approval." Many of Diz's teammates, not so discreet, mocked the entire incident, and Dean himself seemed amused. City authorities, however, were more concerned; a probe into the episode began. This despite no evidence to support any but the most plausible finding—two fellow travelers who wanted to vicariously aid the Cardinal cause, and in a most innocent way.

Breadon was still enraged when Frisch, now ahead two games to one, gave Diz another day off, saving him for the potentially crucial fifth encounter. The gamble reaped few benefits. Though Auker was rapped by St. Louis for four runs in as many innings, he recovered and pitched a shutout from the fifth inning on. Meanwhile, the Tigers pounded five Cardinal pitchers for thirteen hits and ten runs, aided by five St. Louis errors. The affair was loosely played and professionally devoid. Greenberg earned momentary redemption from what would become a dismal World Series (Hank struck out nine times) by lashing two doubles and singles that drove in three runs. At third base the normally reliable Martin made three errors. The Cardinal plight was such that Dean, albeit in a reserve role, reserved most of the theatrics for himself.

With the Cardinals behind, 4-3, in the fifth inning, Dean was inserted as a pinch-runner for slow-moving Spud Davis. That Diz suggested the change speaks volumes for the deference toward him which even Frank Frisch displayed. Runners were on first and third with one out; only a double play could close off the inning and keep the game untied. Ol' Diz, who fancied himself the complete player ("Man, could I hit that cabbage,'' he said of his batting prowess), edged carefully toward second base. Martin, at bat and wanting to hit the ball in the air for a sacrifice fly, followed with a ground ball toward second baseman Gehringer instead. With Durocher, the tying run, tearing for home, Gehringer shoveled the ball for the force out to shortstop Billy Rogell, moving quickly across the bag. Rogell leaped to avoid Dean, barreling toward second base, and threw high and hard toward first. Instead of ducking, or sliding around Rogell, Diz leaped high to block the throw. The ball bounced off his forehead and deflected into right field.

Dean collapsed to the ground. Usually imperturbable, Pat Dean cried silently for solace. Albert Dean, who before the game said of Dizzy and Paul, ''These children ought to be mighty proud to have their picture took with me,'' rose from his seat and peered toward a fallen son. For one of baseball's rare moments, as when outfielder Fred Lynn's colli-

An injured Dizzy Dean is helped by teammates after breaking up a double play in the 1934 World Series. Frank Frisch is shown kneeling behind Dizzy. (NEA Service, Inc.)

sion with an outfield fence stunned a sixth-game World Series audience in 1975, the outcome of a game assumed secondary import. The fact gnawed that even in a boy's game men could become crippled or deformed. Dean was carried off the field, unconscious and cheered by thousands. When he regained cognizance, Dean's first words were, "Did they get Pepper?" That they did not was of little matter.

"Diz wasn't hurt bad," Paul said afterward. "All he was doing was talking, just talking."

"What did he say?" a sportswriter asked.

"He wasn't saying nothing," Paul replied. "He was just talking."

The Series was even, 2-2, and Ol' Diz must pitch tomorrow. "Ain't no bother," said Dean. "Nobody's going to stop Ol' Diz with a simple hit in the haid," and as though to underscore his claim, a St. Louis newspaper placed above its injury article the double-edged headline, 'X-Rays of Dean's Head Show Nothing.'

When Dean next entered the Cardinal clubhouse he rubbed his head and drawled, "Where was the bodyguards of mine yesterday? That was one time I sure could have used 'em." Ol' Diz quickly found he could use some batting support, too. In the fifth game, an affair which lasted less than two hours and lured a throng of thirty-eight thousand to teeming Sportsman's Park, Tommy Bridges held off Dean and the Cardinals, 3-1, sending the Series back to Detroit with the Tigers in front, three games to two. The Tigers, having shattered the invincible Dean, were now heavily favored. Yet Gas House bravado remained. The Cardinals continued flinging barbs at Cochrane, so exhausted from a taut pennant race that he spent his Series evenings in a hospital. A minor Cochrane injury led one Detroit daily to label him, "Our Stricken Leader." Cochrane had driven himself and his team like a man possessed, but the ill-effect eventually rebounded his way. "You on your deathbed yet?" some Cardinals shouted, alluding to the provincial headline. Many taunts were less than gentle. Almost all were ruggedly obscene.

The Tigers shortly became even more infuriated. Pitching bravely, pitching decisively, with no skilled help available in the bullpen behind him, Paul Dean kept the Cardinals alive with a pulsating sixth-game victory, 4-3. In the eighth inning Diz stood in front of the St. Louis dugout, mocking Greenberg, imitating his stance at the plate. Afterward he entertained writers with an expanded rendition of the X-ray story. "They didn't show nothing," he chuckled, "just as I suspected. And you know I went out and had some sort of tests made on my noggin, and I come out one hundred per cent except that the left side of my head, where I was cracked, was even more perfect than the right side."

The Series' largest crowd, 44,551, had jammed Navin Field to witness Game Number Six, one they expected would be the final encounter. But Schoolboy Rowe appeared with a swollen pitching hand, a condition he never fully explained. Rowe yielded ten hits, three of them by Durocher, whom the Tigers derided as the "Big Out" all during the

Series, and the Cardinals scored a seventh-inning run to force a seventh game. Cochrane was now bereft of pitchers; neither Rowe nor Bridges could start. He must go with Auker, formidable, talented but a rookie nonetheless. For his part, Frisch must choose between Bill Hallahan and a weary but exuberant Jay Hanna Dean.

An aging craftsman, Hallahan had pitched eight impressive innings in the Series' second game. "I did pretty good," he reminisced four decades later, vowing, "and I would have done even better in the seventh game." Three years earlier Hallahan had won two games and saved another in the Cardinals' victory over Philadelphia, Connie Mack's World Series farewell. He was rested and accustomed to crisis. He had proved his mettle in what media house men persist in calling the "October Classic." And Ol' Diz was tired. Dean had pitched eleven times in September, winning seven games and saving three. During the last nine regular-season games, Dean hurled four complete-game victories, three by shutouts, including his thirtieth victory. Already he had pitched twice in the Series; if started in Game Seven, he would throw with only one day of rest.

Dean's credentials, however, were imposing, almost unreal. He had compiled a 30-7 record and 2.65 earned run average. He led the league with 195 strikeouts. He was baseball's most fabled pitcher, having bested his critics all year, and Diz wanted the chance to triumph again. "I won't be able to hold my usual press conference tonight, fellas," he told writers after the sixth game. "I got to go back to my hotel. I need all my sleep and rest, so that I can pitch the seventh game." The reporters laughed and nodded, on Dizzy's cue, but Frisch was less easily convinced. Perhaps even a tired Dean was preferable to Hallahan or anyone else; the Cardinals were concerned, nonetheless, that Dizzy's ardor for night life might hurt him in this, the most important game of his career. Frisch hinted to several writers that Hallahan would pitch the seventh game, then waited for Dean to react. He had not long to wait.

Enraged that a lesser figure might replace him, Dean confronted Frisch in the clubhouse showers. "Dammit, Frank," Diz screamed. "You wouldn't dare pitch any of those bums tomorrow, not after I've brought you this far already. You won't need any runs tomorrow. I'll shut them out. You know, I ain't failed you yet," a claim which merited no rebuke. After pleading for the starting call, Ol' Diz pledged to retire early that night, a promise which delighted the Fordham Flash. "All right, Jerome, but no fooling around," Frisch counseled. "And remember, if you win that game tomorrow, it can be worth $50,000 to you and more over the years." To which Bob Broeg added, "For a pitcher earning what Diz was, fifty grand had to sound, well, just grand."

There have been many tumultuous World Series games, and "that game tomorrow," the seventh of the 1934 classic, ranks among the most memorable. Superlatives depend largely upon one's perspective. Boston partisans claim the sixth game of the 1975 Series, when Carlton

Fisk's twelfth-inning home run downed the Reds, 7-6, and stirred emotions from Bangor, Maine to Narragansett Bay, remains the most dramatic of all World Series games. Pittsburgh fans opt for 1960s final game, when Bill Mazeroski's ninth-inning blast beat New York, 10-9, for the Pirates in a contest which oozed with melodrama. Brooklyn pays homage to 1955, when Johnny Podres vanquished the hated Yankees at last.

Entire World Series remain unforgettable, worthy of recall and nostalgia years after the act itself. The 1960 World Series was a riveting affair. So was the 1947 Series, when the Dodgers and Yankees staged a madcap set of games. The Red Sox and Reds were both gifted and ambitious in 1975, and their classic left America limp. Much of the 1934 World Series was also tautly played and closely contested, many of its games won with distinction and lost with honor. The Series' final game was neither taut, nor close, nor deluged with honor. It was, however, bizarre. Uproarious. And undeniably stunning.

October 9, 1934 began innocently enough. Once on the field, Dean posed for pictures with Will Rogers, the cowboy humorist who echoed his inflections of the Southwest. Diz waved at fans and obliged the writers clustered around him. He reassured Frisch and implored his teammates, and soon made manifest that this afternoon in Detroit would be inextricably linked with him forever.

Readying to warm up, Dean neared Auker, the submarine-throwing lefthander. Diz paused, arms behind his back. He chuckled, shook his head and said contemptuously, "You don't expect to get anyone out with that stuff, do you, podner?" To say Auker was unnerved would be to understate the case. "Are you going to pitch this guy today?" Dean yelled at Cochrane. "You guys must have given up." Diz resumed his laughter and continued. "This guy's nothing. He's a joke. Why, my slowest stuff is faster than that." Such rhetoric hardly endeared him to Cochrane, any more than did the damage Dean and the Cardinals inflicted sixty minutes later.

The game scoreless, Dean led off the third inning with a weakly-hit drive to left field. Goose Goslin pranced leisurely toward the ball, assuming, as did almost everyone else in the park, that a single would content Ol' Diz. Dean knew otherwise. ("We pitchers have to be great athletes," he once said, " 'cause so much depends on us. We can't be bums at bat or on the bases.") Ignoring the screams of coach Buzzy Wares, Diz spurted around first base and started for second. Stunned at Dean's abandon, Goslin fired an erratic throw to Gehringer, who readied to slap the ball on Diz, sliding toward the bag. But Dean eluded the Silent Man's tag; his hook slide brought the crowd to its feet and the Cardinals to life. Martin followed with a grounder to first baseman Greenberg's right, a ball which might have produced a double play (or at least a force out) had only Jay Hanna remained at first. With the Great One perched atop second base, Greenberg was forced to stop the ball backhanded, then reverse his momentum, wheel and throw across his body to Auker covering the first-base bag. Never a truly accomplished fielder, Greenberg hesitated, unsure whether to feed the ball to Auker or make the play himself. He did neither, and Martin was safe. So was Dean at third. "Great play, Moe," Diz shouted. "You're the best player we've got."

Three years earlier, Martin had run wild against Cochrane and the A's, stealing five bases, one short of the Series record, and gaining fame as The Wild Horse of the Osage. Now Pepper galloped again. With Cochrane behind the plate, Martin stole second base. Jack Rothrock was intentionally walked, loading the bases. Money player Frisch, nearing the end of his career, followed with a drive down the right field line, fair by inches, clearing the bases and staking the Cardinals to a three-run lead. Exit Auker, who bore Dean's taunts as he trudged toward the dugout. Schoolboy Rowe, pitcher of nine innings the previous day, took the mound in Auker's stead—and the Cardinals pounded him with neither mercy nor remorse. Three hits and a walk led to two more runs, filling the bases and bringing Ol' Diz to the plate. This time Dean chose finesse, topping the ball for a single down the third base line. His two hits in an inning tied the World Series mark. Before the inning ended, and Cochrane yanked Rowe for Tommy Bridges, the Cardinals scored seven times. Dean was triumphant. The crowd was morose. Frisch was a genius and the Tigers were done.

As the score mounted, so did the abuse which Ol' Diz dealt out. No one was immune, least of all Greenberg. Dean laughed at the Tigers and mocked them from the mound. He postured, grimaced, and bowed to the stands. In the fifth inning Frisch stormed toward Diz and threatened to remove him from the game.

"Aw, come on, Frank. You wouldn't dare take out Ol' Diz when he's pitching a shutout," Dean said.

"The hell I wouldn't," said Frisch, now furious. "Just try me. Just lost Greenberg. Just try me." Greenberg promptly struck out, his eighth time in a Series which brought him massive but largely unfair shame as a man who crumbled under pressure.

One inning later came the event which lent to the game its irretrievably violent tinge. Ducky Medwick crashed a booming triple. As his slide concluded, Medwick's leg slammed into third baseman Owen's chest. For Owen, the World Series had not been overly inspiring. The Tigers' final-game deficit, now nine runs, and Medwick's defiant wont compounded his unrest. He braced for trouble. Medwick, unleashing a punch that did Owen little harm, willingly obliged.

When the Cardinals were finally retired, Medwick resumed his place in left field. His arrival was greeted by a response which shifted between disorderly and obscene. Medwick was hailed with a pop bottle landing several feet away. Another bottle followed from the bleachers. And another. Then came the fruit—oranges and apples, bananas and pears—all aimed for Medwick and the frustrations he mirrored. Why grandstand denizens had fruit available to them, no one has yet explained. Medwick refused to retreat and the barrage continued. On the field came ground crew laborers to subdue the litter; with their arrival the tumult ceased. Moments later the onslaught continued and again Medwick stood fast. Finally he and Owen were ordered to Judge Landis' box, located near first base. Frisch and Cochrane attended, too. So did Bill Klem, the umpire behind the plate.

"I asked Owen if he had provoked the assault. He assured me he had not," Landis said that evening, warding off acid criticism from the nation's press. "Then I ordered Medwick off the field. We had a ball-game to continue." With Medwick banished, the bombardment ended. Much to Detroit's chagrin, the game began anew; three innings later the Cardinals would be champions of the world.

A year earlier Dean had been asked to define his greatest day in baseball. "Every time I hold a ball in my hand and put that suit on," he replied, merging a touch of Horatio Alger and Tom Mix. "That's been my biggest day." Now all the great days crystallized in the ninth inning of the seventh game.

With one out the Cardinals led, 11-0. Greenberg was once more at bat. As he shuffled to the plate. Dean took several steps toward the Detroit dugout. "Hey," he called to Cochrane and his silent crew. "Ain't you got no pinch-hitter?"

Again Frisch raced to the mound. "Just what are you doing?" he demanded. "We got a lot at stake."

Durocher then joined the assemblage. "Come on, Frank," Leo prodded. "Let Diz here have a little fun."

"Yeah, Frank," Dean added. "You're a great guy, but you worry too much." When play resumed, Greenberg struck out, the third time that game. Moments later the game ended, a shutout for Dizzy Dean and one of baseball's most improbable chapters complete.

Afterward in the clubhouse the liquor and applause began. Dean entered to a phalanx of cameramen, reporters, and radio personnel. Sifting through the bedlam, Ol' Diz searched out Frisch, slumped in feigned exhaustion on a chair. "You know, Frank," Dean said, "you should take things easier, or first thing you know, you'll have a heart attack." Thirty years later Frisch's seizure gained national notice; though he finally recovered, Frank always whimsically placed the blame on Dean. Here, in 1934, Frank merely smiled and dreamed of winter's peace. Five minutes later Diz posed for pictures, wearing a pith helmet and holding a rubber tiger doll. He started to chew the tiger's tail, then shook hands with everyone in reach; few were immune from Dizzy's grasp. Next he thrust his arm around Will Rogers and said, "What'd I tell ya, guy? I knew we'd whip them Tigers."

The tiger doll neared ruin as Ol' Diz twisted its head, mangled its tail, used it for rhetorical effect. "I said I'd pitch a shutout today and I did," Dean defiantly told the writers clustered around him. "I never felt tired and even if I was I wouldn't say so. If I was beaten I wouldn't have any alibis. The Cardinals got a great club, and it's not the kind of a team that would make excuses if it lost. And that's more than I could say for the Tigers. My brother Paul beat 'em a great ballgame yesterday and all you've heard since then have been alibis from them.

Frank Frisch and Ol' Diz embrace following the final game victory of the 1934 World Series. (Wide World Photo)

It ain't right, but we showed 'em, huh, Paul?''

Several feet away, another player whose worth was evident sat staring at his locker. "I don't want to talk about it (the clash with Owen) if I can help it," Joe Medwick, a pipe dangling from his mouth, declared. "I just got out there to hustle, to play, to win. About all I can say is that I'm sorry it happened." Ducky had hustled and Ducky had won. So, too, had Martin, Frisch, the brothers Dean, and captain Durocher. Dead End Kid, manager martinet, me 'n Paul and Leo the Lip.

Within hours of Medwick's ejection, the St. Louis business district was cluttered with bodies and ad-lib bars. Liquid flowed, confetti reigned, parties dotted urban blocks. The exploits of the 1934 Cardinals produced delight, pure and uninhibited. They also served the ancillary purpose of uniting the populace against the spreading shadows of social blight. Music, fine restaurants, an intimately arranged downtown area, a revival of business and revival of pride—all marked St. Louis' growth in the years which followed 1934. Yet to many St. Louisians, the import of baseball outshone them all, and never more than in the season of Gas House, when a group of flaming, disruptive men crossed the dividing line between stardom and the stuff of which legends are made.

For Dizzy Dean, the Series of 1934 was a God-sent prize; he became the nation's predominant sports figure, willing to be merchandized, able to command almost any wage. During the next five months Ol' Diz earned more than $40,000 for endorsements, personal appearances and banquet speeches; memories of Dean's barren background were fleetingly shunted aside. Poverty was out, the gold rush on. A flood of Dean-related products was unfurled. Consumers could buy a Dizzy Dean candy bar, Dizzy Dean overalls, a Dizzy Dean shirt and Dizzy Dean watch. His name was imprinted on fielders gloves, on baseball shoes, on uniforms and hats. Dizzy and Paul received $5,000, a higher fee than even Ruth had gained, for a one-week vaudeville stint at the Roxy Theater in New York. The script was written by Dan Parker, sports columnist for the *Daily Mirror,* and included some eminently forgettable lines.

Announcer: "Well, boys, how do you feel after your big stage act?"
Ol' Diz: "I feel like a load 'a wood."
Daffy: "What do you mean, like a load of wood?"
Ol' Diz: "All broke up."
Announcer: "Well, Diz, what do you think of Christy Mathewson?"
Ol' Diz: "They tell me he was a great pitcher, too."

Despite the abundant corn, New York critics praised the show. Diz defended his vaudeville debut, saying, "All me 'n Paul is trying to do is get back some of the money Rickey cheated from us." Rickey declined response, mindful of the contract skirmish ahead. Meanwhile the Deans began a frantic barnstorming tour, accepted practice then in the absence of competing autumnal sports.

Along with Martin, Dizzy and Paul joined the Bushwicks, a New York semi-pro team, and played the Black Yankees before fifteen thousand at Dexter Park in Queens. "Here was a freezing cold night, and both Deans were pitching. Well, everyone in New York came out to see Ol' Diz pitch," said Ken Smith, resorting to fringe hyperbole. "The Deans had pitched the night before, and Diz threw his arm out at Dexter Park. But he had to go around like that. After all, he wasn't paid much during the regular season," a dilemma which Ol' Diz would soon confront.

In Kansas City a turnaway crowd packed Muehlebach Field to witness Jay Hanna oppose Satchel Paige. In Milwaukee five thousand disgruntled fans demanded refunds after the Deans curtailed their promised pitching stint. In Newark and Pittsburgh huge throngs greeted America's most noted duo. In Columbus Dizzy said he and Paul would win sixty games in 1935, a goal they never neared, and in late October Dizzy Dean was named Most Valuable Player, an honor made memorable by its total lack of surprise.

All year Dean had provoked outrage among his opponents and glee among his neighbors. Now the outrage was muted, the applause sustained. "He may have been the greatest pitcher I ever saw," Wild Bill Hallahan once said of Diz. He surely was in 1934.

IV

From 1930 to 1939 Billy Rogell played shortstop for the Tigers. Few doubted his courage or questioned his worth. He started fights with rivals and held his own with friends. When he retired in 1940, intimates urged him to run for the City Council in Detroit. He ran and won, and has been winning ever since. To politics Rogell brought the same abandon which marked his baseball career. Deference never graced his repertoire, but a gruff, almost obsessive honesty did. He seemed to cherish his image as an aging yet rebellious militant, authoritative amid permissive times, a defiant who spurned compromise and caution.

Rogell never batted .300 over a full season, never hit fifteen home runs in a year, never made himself hallowed as a shortstop of flair or distinguished range. He thrived, however, on what Leo Durocher later called "intangibles," and fought with a fervor which seemed to set the 1930's apart from any decade that came before or since. "Damn right, we had a different attitude then. I wanted a job. I had to work," he said. "That was our attitude. Now, Christ, it's practically spelled out how you can cheat the country. I tell 'ya, the American people has lost their guts."

He was an opinionated man. "We loved baseball, I say that sincerely," he said, "and we played tough. We'd yell at teammates. If they weren't hustling, we'd jump on them quick. You bet we did. And we played for nothing. I only got $12,000 in 1934 and 1935. Jesus, today, these guys knock in fifty runs and they make a fabulous salary. And for what? For being mechanical men." His voice had sharply risen. "Babe Ruth made $80,000. Guys are making three times that much now, and they couldn't hold a candle to him.

"A lot of us came along too soon. You know, I played in the major leagues for ten years and I don't get a pension—didn't start until '47. Now I don't need a pension, but a lot of players who played in my time do. After a guy leaves baseball, nobody seems to give a damn. And that's wrong. The attitude of these guys today, well, they don't care about us old-timers. What the hell, when I was playing, I was happy to see old-timers come into the clubhouse because he'd been a man responsible for my being able to play ball. Today you go into the damn ballpark, they don't even want to talk to you!"

He was a proud man "We had a hell of a club in 1934 and '35," he proclaimed. "Course, I won't say we had a better club than St. Louis did, the year they beat us in the '34 Series. But our infield drove in 462 runs alone that year, which is the most driven across by any infield in the history of baseball. Listen now—in the history of baseball. But very little is said about it.

Billy Rogell played shortstop for the Detroit Tigers in the mid-1930s. Left, as he was then. Right, as he is now.

"Why's that? Because you watch network TV and there's Joe Garagiola talking about his Cardinals and Tony Kubek babbling about his Yankees. All Kubek ever talks about is the Yankee club he once played on. You'd think no other club ever existed. It really gets nauseating. Well, Kubek can hardly talk, so you can't expect him to interpret much.

"We beat his beloved Yankees but good in those thirties, and they were the real Yankees then, not the shoemakers they have today. We won the pennant fairly early in 1934, even though it hurt us in the Series that followed. We were too relaxed. And the next year we didn't win so early, and we didn't take the Cubs lightly in the Series. So we won. Actually, I thought the Cubs of '35 were a better team than St. Louis the year before, but that's baseball. We just peaked too soon against the Cards."

He was reflective, too, beneath the rhetoric which verged on excessive and made diplomacy foreign. "Dizzy Dean," he pondered, "knew how to blow his own horn. And he knew what he was blowing. I've looked at a lot of pitchers. Grove, Gomez and all those fellers. Walter Johnson, too. Diz didn't have to take a back seat to any of them. Dean would have made it in any era." He paused for emphasis. "Any era," Rogell repeated. "Christ, now he'd knock the bats out of some of these guys' hands. You can't go back, of course. It's silly to even try. But I'd like to see these big shots today swing at Dean. They'd be lucky to get a good foul off him. I don't mean to downgrade baseball, don't mistake me. There are some good players, all right,

Paul Dean, (left) and Dizzy Dean show off their grip during the 1934 World Series game between the Cardinals and the Detroit Tigers.

but Dean would beat them, just like he always did, just like he did us.

"Course, I always did say Dizzy was a lot better pitcher than his brother," Rogell continued, almost derisively. "What got me about the '34 Series is how Dean kept talking about Paul. That's all you ever heard about. I've seen loyalty before, but this was ridiculous. Hell, Paul was a runt compared to Diz. And the funny thing was that I could hit Dizzy but not his brother. Now how about that? Diz kept saying what a great fastball Paul had, so we'd look for it and look and look and never see it. And he beats us twice. But boy, even today I wish I could hit off Paul in his prime. How I'd love that."

Two American League players were involved in moments made memorable by Dizzy Dean. Earl Averill slammed a drive which broke Diz's toe in the 1937 All-Star Game, notably slashing Dean's career. And William Rogell, shortstop turned civic servant, fired a ball toward first base that struck a glancing blow off Dean's forehead in the 1934 World Series. "Right between the eyes I hit him," said Rogell, "and no one felt worse than me."

"It really bothered me," he conceded, "that poor sight being carried off the field. Of course, it was Dizzy's fault. He threw up his head in the way intentionally. Even said so. He wanted to break up the double play. And to tell you the truth, I never saw the play because I was coming to the bag at an angle. I caught the ball and threw. And Dizzy threw up his head. Actually," said Rogell, ever the competitor, "if I'd have known his head was there, I would have thrown the ball harder."

The Cardinals, Rogell admitted, were hardly deterred. "God, they hustled," he bristled. "Martin ran like hell. Medwick killed us. And old flannel-mouthed Durocher at shortstop, he played his heart out." The Tigers aided, too, with their seventh-game collapse, a debacle whose culprits Rogell seemed almost eager to name.

"Cochrane was the boss, but he blew it," he fumed. "Nobody but him. Here he starts a rookie in the final game of the Series. A *rookie*. Can you imagine that? Schoolboy Rowe could have pitched a while and Cochrane passes him by. That killed us, pure and simple.

"And then there's Goslin. Gees, when Dean hit that pop fly to left field in the third inning of that game, Goslin just stood there. And stared. He just froze. Well, I'd gone back for the ball, but when I saw I couldn't get it, I went back to second base. And all of a sudden here comes Diz tearing for second base."

"I never imagined he'd try for a double," he huffed. "Never in a million years. What let Diz make it safely was that when Goslin finally got the ball, he threw it twenty feet to the third base side of second. And even then I almost got him, but Dean made a beautiful hook slide. You know, we would have had him easy if Gehringer had covered the bag and I'd been able to take the relay throw and flip it to him. But where Gehringer was, I'll never know."

"It was pathetic after that," Rogell said. "I dream about it even now."

Chapter Five

Flourish and Farewell

I

A new year dawned and the nation grieved. Those Americans who despised Franklin Roosevelt, and they were far more numerous than the Eastern press portrayed, sorrowed at the New Deal and what it had wrought. Those whom life greeted less gently, who regarded Roosevelt as both redeemer and patron saint, anguished when the Supreme Court ruled invalid the National Recovery Act. Critics labeled NRA jobs menial and unneeded; boondoggles, they were called. But work meant dignity and food, and neither was abundant during nineteen thirty-five. Americans mourned, too, as Babe Ruth's career neared its poignant end. They grieved yet further as shops closed, wages fell and Roosevelt's full employment seemed a cruel and mocking hoax. Fear itself was the least of America's worries; the war which would revive the nation's economic fortunes remained six years away. Depression misery lingered, still able to afflict and curse.

The year, like much of the decade, was kinder to Dizzy Dean. Since October, 1934, cheers and ovations had encircled him. With fame came official pomp; content before to use hotel stationary, Ol' Diz now assaulted mail recipients with letters and envelopes reading, "Dizzy, Pat and Paul Dean, Deanville, Bradenton, Fla.," a practice Jay claimed "shows I ain't no business dummy." From Bradenton, Dean boasted that the Cardinals, once having won the pennant, would meet the Red Sox or Indians in the World Series. "We won't wait for a late start this year," he said in January, 1935. "Our youngsters now appreciate what pennant-winning baseball is, and how to play it." Of his own prospects, Dean was equally serene. "I'll be grand this year. I'm not going to sign for less than $25,000. That offer stands for two days and then I'm asking for five grand more. They'd better come up with the dough or else."

Dean surfaced in late January at Manhattan, where the New York Chapter, Baseball Writers Association, named him player of the year. Advised that he must address the writers' dinner, Diz asked if the word 'bums' was permissible rhetoric. His arrival prompted Frisch, also at the affair, to claim, "Diz ain't strange at all. And I wouldn't call him cocky, either. He simply believes in himself and, as you may have noticed, he is not backward about saying so." With Diz at the dais, Will Rogers told the overflow crowd, "Diz is worth all he can get. I know that, and so do you," sentiments which lured prolonged applause. Soon after, however, Dizzy met in closed conference with Breadon and Rickey, who insisted that Dean had already signed a contract worth only $17,500.

"Dean accepted terms several weeks ago," said Breadon, "and we will go to Judge Landis, if necessary, to enforce our agreement with Dizzy." Dizzy's denial, issued promptly, ran counter to reports emerging in New York newspapers which supported Breadon's claim; those rumors, Dizzy said, arose because of a contract between a food company and himself. The company demanded that Dean sign with the Cardinals before it would hire his services. To please them, Ol' Diz presently explained, he promised verbally to sign. Breadon's version differed—Diz had agreed to sign for $17,500; he must honor those terms. "Dean has no leverage," Dan Daniel wrote. "In baseball acceptance of terms, verbally or otherwise, is tantamount to signing a contract." The press supported Breadon. So did Landis and the prevailing times, which favored the owners and their penurious ways.

Dean, nonetheless, remained unswayed. "They think I'm fooling," Dizzy said, "but I was never more serious about nothin'. Everybody tells me I'd be a sucker to take less than twenty-five grand, and Ol' Diz is going to holler for that until he gets it." Several days later he threatened to quit. The next morning he demanded to be sold or traded. Rumors began that New York had offered $100,000 for the Master; Bill Terry, while denying them, cautioned, "I'm sure Sam Breadon could get that much."

On February 5, Ducky Medwick became a holdout. He wanted at least $10,000, or he would quit as well. "Club officials apparently believe," Medwick said, "that I can live for a year on the fruit and vegetables which thoughtful Detroit fans contributed during the last game of the World Series. Such is not the case." The situation bordered on camp comedy, with Dizzy Dean staging the laughs.

Two days after Medwick's vow, Dean arrived in St. Louis. "I'm fed up with the way I've been treated," he said. "I'm seriously thinking of getting out of baseball anyhow. I'm looking for a business and I may take the corner right across from Sam Breadon's place." That afternoon Ol' Diz adopted an old and perfected routine—complete reversal of stance with no apologies attached. He signed for $18,000, complete victory for Breadon and humiliation for himself. Embittered by the outcome, Diz put forth no sorrow, uttered no regrets. Instead, he acted as though Breadon had capitulated, not Jay Hanna Dean. To Breadon's "I want to congratulate you on that contract. It calls for a lot of money," Diz smiled and said, "I'm worth it. You know that. I'm just glad you could reach an agreement." Dean then pledged to win twenty-five games, and "me 'n Paul'll take forty-five."

The salary wars done, Dean's focus shifted to other, less pressing matters. In March he swaggered into Bradenton, trying to clarify insults he had thrown the Sultan of Swat. In late 1934 Ol' Diz had scored Babe Ruth, saying he should remain in the American League; with Ruth since sold to the Boston Braves, a charter member of Dean's own league, the Great One must sound retreat. "Let's get this straightened out," Diz said. "I've been on the pan for what I said. Maybe I popped off suddenly, but they got me wrong. I think Babe's as great a guy as there ever has been in baseball. I can't understand how the club owners of that league ever let the Babe get away. That's why I knocked the American League. Yes sir, tell the Babe for me that I'm on the square with him." Next Dean revealed he had bet Ruth the Babe would not touch him for a home run in their first four encounters, a wager Ol' Diz easily won. Incidents like these aside, Diz claimed he would adopt a "modesty platform" in 1935. "I'm only declaring myself a twenty-game winner," he said, again shifting his ground. "I'll be tickled to death to win that many."

Other issues erupted, too. There was always a familial affection between Dizzy and Paul; now another party threatened to encroach. Jack (Dopey) Dean, member of the St. Louis Browns, began telling writers that he was a first cousin to Ol' Diz. Dean's rebuttal was direct and indignant. "I don't know what nationality he is, but Dopey ain't no kin of mine," Diz said. "He sends me a telegram one day, telling me he's a cousin of mine—the next he sends me one saying I'm his nephew. Plug crazy, I calls it. I just ignore him. Anyhow, I don't mess with them second-division teams."

The Browns, understandably, were infuriated—and ditto for Bill Terry on March 21. "We want no part of Dean," he growled. "No fraternizing with him. He's not going to sit on our bench or sit in our clubhouse here or in New York or St. Louis. We don't want a fellow like that around." Terry's furor was provoked by a knock-down incident several days earlier; the Giants, having pounded Dizzy for seven runs, saw Phil Weintraub and Terry hit the dirt on eight consecutive pitches. "He's bad news," Terry said, "and let me underline the bad." For his part, Diz did little to calm the combative winds. During one spring training game he strode to the Giant dugout and asked if anyone could cash a check for $5,300, each player's World Series share on the 1934 champion Cardinals.

Terry, who placed Dean on center stage, was hardly alone; Floridians flocked to see the Master perform. In St. Petersburg, whose population barely exceeded ninety thousand, an overflow crowd of 6,476 jammed Waterfront Park to watch Dean confront Ruth and his Braves; the Yankees vs. Ruth had drawn only 4,726 earlier that week. "Dean has drawn the casual, as well as devoted, fans out," wrote Daniel. "Perhaps half the turnouts for Diz have come from persons who are new to the local ballpark. In all the hotel lobbies they have heard about the mystic Diz. Some of the kindly ladies think he is some sort of a baseball yogi, who can do the Indian rope trick, or make serpents hiss out of catchers' masks. He's packing them in all over the circus circuit."

On April 6, three days after Frisch fined him $100 for missing a train, Dean disclosed that 1936 would mark his final season, "that is, if I can have two more good years." Royally expected was the news that Pat agreed. "At the end of next season we expect to have $150,000 of our own. Figuring six per cent interest on that sum, we will have a yearly income of $9,000. We'll be able to live in luxury on that. You know, we don't go in for big money ideas." Neither, it proceeded to become evident, did Kenesaw Mountain Landis.

Austere and pungent, Landis eyed money with desire and distrust. Moral leprosy had tarnished baseball in 1920, the Black Sox scandal of the previous autumn first drawing public notice, and the Judge vowed adamantly that his sport would never be crippled again. When reports reached him presently, therefore, that Diz had accepted a $5,000 bonus payment, Landis summoned Dean to Chicago. The money, Diz said, came from Dick Slack, an East St. Louis furniture dealer, in return for Dean's guest presence on radio. Not wholly yielding, Landis approved the exchange, but warned that Dean "must accept no money from anyone on earth except your ballclub for your performance on the ballfield." The Good Judge was high priest as well.

"If anyone offers you money," Landis said, "I want you to promise me that you will kick him in the teeth. Will you do that?"

"Yes sir," Dean replied. "Yes sir, yes sir, but if someone offers me $3,000, can't I take it?"

"Not if you don't know what it's for," the Judge advised. "If it's for your activities on the field I want you to take a baseball bat and hit the man over the head that offers it to you. Is that clear?"

"Yes sir, Judge," said Diz. "It sure is."

Reaction from the media was hostile and swift. Columnist Westbrook Pegler best echoed the anti-Landis case. "This was strictly the old Chamber of Commerce routine," he wrote. "It was the sort of thing that Landis is paid for at a much higher rate than Dizzy Dean is paid for winning pennants. It was intended to impress the baseball customers with the piety of the baseball industry and to obscure the tyrannical meanness of a business which mooches its advertising in the guise of sport, lives on the sporting illusions of its customers and hires a resounding mane of an old-time news-maker (Landis) of the U.S. District Court to endorse its habits." Pegler's convictions came before their anointed

Ol' Diz (left), Frank Frisch (center), and Cardinal owner Sam Breadon (right) discuss the upcoming 1935 season at spring training in Bradenton, Florida (AP Wirephoto)

time; his vitriolic rhetoric scorned big business, derided motherhood and apple pie. Few, at least in 1935, dared to call baseball an "industry" or doubt its moral purity. Marvin Miller, player representative during the 1970s, would have christened him saint.

The Cardinals were also touched by travail; their regular season broke badly, Chicago giving signals of what September, 1935, might provide. On opening day the Cubs' Fred Lindstrom slapped a line drive which deflected off Dean and forced him from the game. "They'll pay for that," Ol' Diz mourned afterward, then recovered and rallied as April closed. Against Boston, Dean faced Ruth, struck him out and smashed a home run. "When you waltz one into the stands, it gives you a nice sort of a feeling," he said. "And when thirty thousand folks have come out to watch some other fellow like Babe whack your stuff in that fashion and then you turn around and do the whacking yourself it makes that nice feeling all the nicer." When Dean walked three Brooklyn Dodgers in an inning, forcing in a run later that week, those sentiments quickly faded; they paled even more when Dizzy's uproar over the umpiring produced his prompt ejection. And delight did not enwrap him when Philadelphia manager Jimmy Wilson said, "It's getting so you can't even get a hit off either of the Deans without getting beaned the next time out,'' after Ol' Diz dusted off three of his batters in the early stages of May.

Despite Dean's setbacks and rebuffs, *The Sporting News* was moved to label Diz ''the new gate God, the successor to the throne of public appreciation and idolatry.'' Dean, naturally, gave credence to those claims, saying, ''I'm lucky to be alive. I couldn't show my face in Florida this spring without a million autograph hounds pestering me. If I hadn't called a halt to it, I would have gone nutty.'' Spring's tumult made almost inevitable a lackluster start, but the Cardinals and Ol' Diz grew uplifted as June came near; St. Louis momentarily regained its pennant-winning form of 1934, and Dizzy unveiled ''Poppin' Off, by Dizzy Dean,'' a new one hundred and fifty-word feature which made its syndicated debut in five major newspapers. The Redbirds and Dean had played far worse at this time a year before; few doubted their capacity to pen another verse of autumn thunder, this time vintage 1935.

Yet June brought discord and jealousy, and when autumn came, Cardinal hopes had fled. On June 4 Dean did battle with Medwick at Forbes Field, the incident causing Frisch to threaten Diz with a $5,000 fine. ''You know what I think?'' said Diz. ''They're trying to get me in bad so they can take away a big chunk of the money my contract calls for.'' Frisch was less amused. ''Dean's lucky he didn't get a stiff fine or suspension as a result of the way he acted,'' Frank huffed. ''Pittsburgh was the climax. Imagine, telling Medwick he hadn't hustled. Dean thinks he can throw the ball past good hitters just because he's Dizzy Dean. That's not baseball. He can't play that way for me.'' Shunted to the rear was the adulation spring training had evoked.

Pressed by newsmen, Dean denied that cleavage had arisen between himself and Cardinal mates. ''There ain't no jealousy here,'' said Diz, who also forecast he would win twenty games and the pennant would be a ''breeze.'' When he added, however, that the Giants, not the Cardinals, would create the breeze, controversy flared anew. Two days later he begged the first of his summer pardons. ''I'm cooled off now,'' he reassured St. Louisians. ''I'm sorry about the whole affair.'' Despite the apology, Dizzy's tendency toward disquiet thrived. On June 7 Dean surveyed the Oakmont, Pennsylvania, golf course, site of the National Open. ''What's tough about this course?'' he asked. ''If I didn't have to throw that tomato for a living, I'd take this game up in a serious way and win all the championships. And this is one course I'd tear wide open.'' Those boasts brought few Pennsylvania plaudits, and two days later the home folk were no more kind. At Sportsman's Park a crowd of fifteen thousand pelted Ol' Diz with lemons when he took the mound against Chicago, then watched in silence as St. Louis tamed the Cubs, 3-2.

''Dizzy is learning this year,'' a *Sporting News* editorial read, ''that his outbursts are not meeting with the same tolerance and sympathy from fans as was the case last year. He's making the money now.

He has been well treated, not only by the Cardinals, but by the public in general. As a result, his outbreaks of temperament come with ill grace from one to whom the fates have been so kind." Rushing to underscore those charges, critics brushed aside Dean's record, 10-5, and ignored the fact that he almost solely had kept the Cardinals afloat. St. Louis' pitching had ignobly collapsed; Paul Dean was 6-7, others even further behind.

Cries of dissension widened. "How in the devil can Diz be in the best shape to play ball," a Cardinal teammate asked. "Vaudeville tours and what not; all winter running around endorsing this and that, never getting proper rest. Trying to be everything from a comedian to a traveling salesman, a sandwich salesman to an author—in fact, everything but a ballplayer." To which Diz replied, "That ain't so," and Frisch answered, "I've read that I'm sore at Diz. Why, hell, I play pinochle with him, and I don't play pinochle with guys I'm sore at."

Frisch's backhanded praise calmed the outcry, but soon he must defend Ol' Diz once more. In early July, before an exhibition-game crowd of over eight thousand at St. Paul, Dean sulked and cowered in the dugout, refusing to even appear. For the fourth time in two months Diz was widely denounced as arrogant and crude. "Oh, he just went into another one of his trances," Frisch responded. "This affair will blow over." Cardinal officials greeted Dean's petulance with magnanimity and kindness; the Great One, regrettably, stayed clear of either gratitude or joy. "I don't care if they didn't fine me," he said, "they're still a chain gang." Shortly afterward Dean issued another apology, prompting *The Sporting News* to state, "There is nothing wrong with a fellow who makes mistakes, but is willing to admit that he is wrong." Soon, however, Ol' Diz reversed terrain again, drawing near-blanket censure in the process.

Scheduled to throw out the first pitch of the Catholic Diocesan baseball tournament, Dean ambled into Springfield, Illinois, for the final game thirty minutes late. Told that pre-game ceremonies, starring Governor Henry Horner, had been delayed pending his arrival, Diz informed the reception committee they might be delayed even more. He wanted to eat, Diz said; all else would have to wait. "What about the Governor? an alarmed local denizen asked." "I'll be glad to meet him," Dizzy answered, but "his Excellency" should stay patient until then. "I'll get there eventual," Dean continued, "First, though, I gots to get some steak and potatoes." The game was already in its second inning— Diz was ninety minutes late—when he finally appeared.

While Diz's public rapport alternately rose and faltered, his prowess on the mound remained unscathed. On August 9 he downed the Cubs, 4-2, his nineteenth win and eighth in a row. "The Deans are not for sale," Rickey promised, "and they won't be for sale next year or the next." A week later Dean won again, beating the Giants for his third consecutive twenty-victory season. On August 26, and now winner of twenty-three, Diz said "the Giants are finished," and vowed he would win fifteen more. By early September, though, Dean had abandoned those hopes. His sole interest shifted to the pennant chase, which still embroiled New York, St. Louis and the Chicago Cubs.

The Cardinals led, as they had for weeks. When the Giants invaded Sportsman's Park on Sept. 12 for a four-game series which would be decisive in its import, New York trailed by three and one half games, the Cubs by two. St. Louis readied for what surely would be another Indian Summer surge. But Diz was tired, losing twice in the Giant series alone. Huge crowds, including a final-day turnout of 41,824, the largest single-game throng ever at Sportsman's Park, watched the Cardinals bow three times, yielding first place for good. Two weeks later Chicago clinched the pennant, clubbing the Cardinals, 6-2, and ravaging Dean for fifteen hits. Diz led the league in innings pitched (324), strikeouts (182) and victories (28) but the Cubs spurted to a four-game margin over St. Louis, eight and a half over Terry's Giants, who once more collapsed in the September rush. Chicago won an incredible twenty-one consecutive games.

Dean left St. Louis with a parting pledge. The Cubs would win the World Series, which proved unfounded, and he would soon start a barnstorming tour. "Then," he said, "I'm going down to Florida, catch about five hundred pounds of kingfish a day and teach some of those boys down there how to play golf." The eighteen-game post-season swing began serenely enough, Dean luring large crowds and the lion's share of applause, but memories of mid-summer impudence before long were revived. On October 17, annoyed by the sparse crowd which watched him perform, Diz stalked out of an amateur exhibition game in Chattanooga, Tennessee. "I can make more money playing poker on the train," he boasted. The game, arranged for charity, had attracted about three hundred and seventy-five fans. "It's not worth the risk of getting hurt," said Dean, "to pitch for a crowd like that." Public reaction was adverse and harsh. Again forced to apologize, Diz offered to pitch for free, the revenues to benefit local charity. The game's promoter, Chattanooga president Joe Engel, unequivocally refused.

"You'll never appear in my park," an Engel telegram read. "Your attitude and actions toward a most worthy cause is evidently exemplary of your inner self." To which Sid Keener, sports editor of the *St. Louis Star-Times,* added, "Dean is a great pitcher, but a bust as a good-will ambassador." Five months later Kenesaw Mountain Landis, master of Dean the preceding summer, wrote the episode's finale by taxing Diz with a $100 fine.

Privately dismayed, Rickey bequeathed to Dean his public blessing. Thirty of the thirty-eight Cardinals were for sale, Branch said, but Ol' Diz's station was secure. "I'd be crazy to trade him," Rickey said, "and whatever my other attributes, no one's ever called me that." Even so, Pat Dean called him "malicious" in February of 1936, one month after Diz celebrated his twenty-fifth birthday by buying her a four-passenger cabin plane. "There'll be no back-seat driving for me up in the clouds with Diz," she said then. "I'll let him take care of that while I personally handle the stick." Pat sought, too, to handle her husband's contract; Diz would hold out, she said, until the Cardinals met his new, revised salary demands.

Each year Dean threatened to leave his favored sport; this season's holdout was even more surreal and tortured than most. The Cardinals offered $18,500; Diz spurned compromise and chose instead contempt. "I'm shooting from the shoulder now," he said. "If they don't give me what I want, I'll retire and go into the furniture business. Listen, I could make as much as they offer in darn near a month from radio, barnstorming and furniture." Forty thousand dollars, Diz said, was his asking price. He scorned his bosses and scorned the team. Of Virgil Davis, St. Louis catcher, Diz claimed he would never pitch to him again. Davis countered by saying he would "knock Dizzy's block off" when next he entered the clubhouse, to which Dean retorted, "I'll be there throwing punches." Ultimately, of course, Diz signed an agreement to "pitch to anybody on the club, as long as it will bring St. Louis a pennant."

March, 1936 came and exhibition games began. Between taunts and press conferences, Dean took to the golf course, beating all comers and uplifting his wealth; Babe Ruth lost $190 to Ol' Diz alone.

On March 22 Dean signed for less than $25,000, terms which left Dizzy "satisfied" and Rickey "pleased." Dean returned to find the Cardinals no more predictable than before. "We could finish first or in an asylum," Frisch said, adding, "You go to the outfield, Diz, and run around until you drag."

"Well, just let me pitch batting practice, will you, Pappy?" Dean answered. "I like to hear you old bones crack."

Diz's holdout had not dulled his pitching skills, nor inactivity his appeal. In early April eleven thousand members of the Boys' Club of New York, ranging in age from eight to eighteen, answered the question, "If you could have the choice of all the jobs in the world, whose job would you want?" Most often named was Robert Ripley, author of the Believe It or Not cartoons. "He's so busy," said one respondent, "with his broadcasts, his drawings and his trips that he doesn't have time to get into trouble." Next in line were J. Edgar Hoover and James Cagney. Placing fifth through seventh were Franklin Roosevelt, King Edward VIII and Fiorella LaGuardia. Trailing Cagney, situated in fourth place, was Dizzy Dean.

The Cubs paid little homage on opening day, knocking out Ol' Diz in inning seven. While the hapless Dodgers also downed him, 5-2, on May 12, the game enlivened by a brawl between Stengel and Durocher beneath the Ebbets Field grandstand, Dean entered June with ten victories, the most in either league. Number eleven followed within two days, his seventh in a row, and Ol' Diz chortled, "I guess I ought to win forty games this year." By mid-June Dean had thirteen games to his credit and the Cardinals led the league. "Gee, they have almost as many people here as they do at the ballgame," Diz exclaimed from a balcony

Dizzy Dean and Babe Ruth tee off in January, 1936. Dean's weight was over 100 pounds lighter than it would become some twenty years later.

seat at the 1936 Democratic Convention in Philadelphia. "And those spectators down there, why, they get almost as much applause as I do in St. Louis." Dean reaped cheers in Boston, too; at Braves Field for the July 7 All-Star Game, he faced only nine batters in three innings. The National League won, 4-3, its first all-star victory, but Dizzy Dean was uncommonly reserved. "I can't understand why I didn't get a hit," he said. "Heck, I struck out. Anyone should be able to hit those American League pitchers. And as far as their sluggers, they ought to get down on their knees and give thanks they don't have to work in our league, where they'd see good pitching every day."

St. Louis pitchers hardly warranted that label, not with Paul Dean and Roy Parmalee weak and disabled. On July 11 Diz himself was shelved, injured by a line drive which slammed against his head. "Show me a pitcher who ends up in a good fielding position," Diz had often said, "and I'll show you a guy who ain't following through." Now, with New York's Burgess Whitehead at bat, the Great One made sure he 'followed through.' The ball off Whitehead's bat landed above Dean's right ear, deflected into left field for a double and turned Dizzy completely around. When Whitehead arrived at second base, he saw Dean on the ground, his body swung toward center field. Jay Hanna was sidelined for a week. "I was talking only recently about Burgess," Diz confided afterward, "and I said of him, 'There's a guy who might knock you right back into the minors.' But this is the first time I ever was hit hard enough to see stars."

Dizzy's return helped St. Louis revive. On August 10 the Master lifted his club past Chicago, 7-3, and back into first place; more than thirty thousand at Sportsman's Park watched incredulously as Charlie Grimm, Cub manager and resident comic, gave Redbird hopes an unexpected thrust. The game was decided in the first inning. With Billy Herman at bat, Dean abruptly raced toward the Chicago dugout. Tex Carleton, former Cardinal presently with the Cubs, leaped out to meet him. The two began to wrestle, were separated by the umpires, then were expelled from the game. Inexplicably, Grimm pleaded for both to return—Carleton, that day a benchwarmer, and Dean, who went on to mock the Cubs' goodwill. "My own notion," Daniel wrote, "is that Grimm was a sucker."

Publicly, at least, Sam Breadon said otherwise. "I want to thank you for the fine sportsmanship you showed this afternoon," he wrote in a letter to Grimm. "When you waived your rights and asked that Dizzy be allowed to continue in the game, you showed a fine spirit and consideration for the people of St. Louis who support baseball. The umpires told me that they would have had to expel Dizzy from the game had you not done the fine thing you did. You are a credit to baseball, your club and your home town of St. Louis." Tributes apart, suspicion lingered that Grimm had been, as Daniel ascribed, a 'sucker,' that charity in baseball was somehow misplaced.

By September the Cardinals needed charity and more. The New York Giants, victim of past autumn reverses, now stole the initiative and surged ahead. "Cardinal pitching," Tom Meany said, "consists of Dizzy Dean, no more, no less," and that would no longer do. On September 15, Carl Hubbell bested Ol' Diz, 7-5, boosting New York's lead to four and one half games. For once, cynics sneered, the Giants would avoid the Accordian Award, presented each fall for the season's greatest foldup. While New York gorged itself on the Subway Series, won by the Yankees, four games to two, Dean recounted the season past. Diz led the National League in complete games (28) and saves (11), compiled a 24-13 record, placed second behind Hubbell in wins, earned run average, winning percentage and voting for the Most Valuable Player award. "Carl's the best pitcher in the game, including Dean," said Diz, adding that he was already a holdout for 1937, "no matter what they have on their contract." So much for mutual compromise, and also for team morale.

"There are only four real players on the Cardinals," Dean proclaimed as October dawned. "The rest are real bushers, including Rip Collins." Collins, shortly afterward dealt to the Cubs, responded in kind. "This guy isn't half the pitcher Hubbell is," he said, slamming a table for rhetorical effect, "and you can't print that too strong for me." Echoing Collins, Rickey, who a year earlier had denied that Dean would ever be available, changed his pose as well. A "proper deal" might lure

Ol' Diz from Sportsman's Park, he said. The sunshine days were over, excessive security past.

Reports of Dean's impending sale cascaded across the nation's press. The Giants reputedly offered $200,000, a sum New York officials denied. "I'd sure like to pitch for the Giants," Diz said. "I think they could afford to pay a better salary. I like St. Louis, and I'd hate to leave my friends, but as the fellow said when the lion bit him in the pants, 'That's Africa!' " Dean burst out laughing. "Haw! How do you like that one? Joe E. Brown gave it to me. Wait 'til I spring it on Pepper Martin. He'll spray it over Oklahoma every time he goes to a Kiwanis dinner and makes a speech." The Cubs were rumored to have made an offer. Then the Reds. Then the Dodgers, impoverished and ailing. A report surfaced that the Pirates had bid seven players and $175,000 for Ol' Diz. "Sure would like to play in Pittsburgh," Jay Hanna sighed.

Turbulence became wedded to discontent. In October, en route to Florida with Pat, Diz ran his car into a highway guard rail near Birmingham, Florida. The accident, which thwarted traffic on the Bee Line Highway, occurred when Dean tried to kill a bee in the window while steering the car. Within several days Rickey admitted openly that Diz was for sale. It would require $400,000, he said, but "we feel a deal might be preferable instead. We feel the Cardinals would be better off with three or four good pitchers instead of only one star. Dizzy's not the one-man pennant winner he's supposed to be." Rickey tweaked his cigar, then continued. "This club won four pennants in six years before Dizzy joined us. Since then we've won one pennant in six years."

Dean exploded when told of Rickey's claim, slamming down his golf clubs, and stomped off a Bradenton course. "I'm tired of trying to win the pennant single-handedly," he said. "How could he expect me to, that Rickey? Only one pitcher besides myself won as many as twelve games last year. Why, the ballclub the Cardinals had the last two months wasn't any team at all. We even had a guy from the Piedmont League playing first base." Unperturbed by Dizzy's ire, Rickey tried to peddle his troubles away, but no club dared chance its total fortunes on a wild (if talented) eccentric—and prospects for trade slowly ebbed. Assuming the inevitable, that Diz would again return, Frisch said 1937's Dean should remain unbeaten. "I mean it," Frank declared. "Diz ought to win every game. Every one. Dizzy fouls up because he's so stuck on himself. He likes to show off by throwing the kind of fastballs hitters like."

As usual, Dean's focus was far more financially-tinged. He wanted $100,000, Diz said, "in view of the $400,000 price tag they put on me when they was prospecting. Think of the publicity they'd get for paying me such a salary." On December 20, 1936, however, even monetary matters held less than total sway. "I wanna wish everybody in this whole world a bright and happy Christmas. That's the old Diz's wish for everybody, including Father Branch and Uncle Sam. B. R. is my Dutch Father and Mr. Breadon is my Scotch uncle."

Both the Yankees' Lou Gehrig and the Cardinal's Dizzy Dean were holdouts at a spring training game in St. Petersburg, Florida, in March, 1937. (AP Wirephoto)

No remedy, least of all Ol' Diz's Christmas message, could hope to cure a nation plagued by rampant hunger, social strife and broadened fears of world upheaval. But millions of Americans chuckled, nonetheless; clubhouse turmoil, for all of Rickey's unfounded concern, had failed to diminish Dean's mystique, or the lasting affection with which the country held him. Though only twenty-five, Diz already owned one hundred and twenty-one major league victories; surely, fans thought, his ultimate total would approach any figure's who had come before or since. Incredibly, though, the salad seasons were over, Dean's playing career nearly done; the new year lured decline and injury, and before long Diz and St. Louis were intertwined no more.

II

From its inception, 1937 was distinguished by restless, tumultuous times. Americans watched with growing fear while totalitarian governments presided over Germany and Japan. Franklin Roosevelt embarked on a campaign to pack the Supreme Court, an ill-advised scenario which stripped away much of his public esteem. Shirley Temple's tender innocence lured thousands of families to abruptly resurgent theaters. And the Dizzy Deans exulted under the Florida sun, praising financial excess and shunning social restraint.

"We don't sign for less than fifty thousand," Pat declared. "We don't want to hear or see Rickey until he has a contract for that much in his pocket. Of course, he won't stay in St. Louis. He'll come down here and try to work us over with his sweet smile and mile-a-minute flow of oily gab. But he won't fool us. This time we're ready—and able—to tell him to go fly his kite." Momentarily, Dizzy's attitude was more subdued; the Cardinals would finish first, he said, if they yielded to his demands. If not, they would flounder and fall.

Dean returned St. Louis' first contract offer. He rebuked another, then a third. On March 11, with the club's training already underway, Diz rejected its latest bid, then saw the Cardinals depart for Havana and an exhibition series. Five days later, in a move which delighted Breadon but stunned reporters, Dean asked the Cardinals to authorize his retirement from baseball. "I will never pitch another major league baseball game," said Diz, who soon after placed his Bradenton home on sale.

To reporters, Breadon submissively agreed. "We cannot force Dizzy to remain in baseball," he said. "We will not attempt to get him to change his mind." Diz was startled; he had expected quite a different response. Outrage, regret, refusal—all these Dean had awaited. Not outright compliance. Breadon announced he would send a letter to Ford Frick, president of the National League, asking approval of Dean's request. The letter would then travel to Landis for ultimate concurrence, and with the Judge's signature Dean's career would end. Thoroughly outwitted, Dean relinquished hope; hours after vowing to never pitch again, he signed for $25,000. "Diz came out of his recent contract debate with so little glory and so much less loot than he demanded," Joe Williams would write, "that most of his airy bravado is gone. He's just another guy around the camp these days."

While few writers echoed Williams' severity toward Diz, accounts persisted that Dean's superb ability had at last begun to dim. "From the training base of the St. Louis Cardinals," one report read, "word comes that Dizzy Dean, the one-man broadcasting crew, is starting to lose his stuff, that he is no longer the supreme pitching artist." During 1936 Diz had fallen in winning percentage, from .700 to .649, in wins, from 28 to 24, and had failed for the first time in four years to lead the league in strikeouts. "Dean began to fade visibly last season," another article said. "His fastball wasn't jumping like it used to and his curve wasn't breaking with its customary sharpness. There are times this year when it looks almost like it is an effort for him to throw the ball."

Even more than most public persons, all of whom are assailable, voluble Dizzy Dean lay open to attack. Diz's skill and staying power, previously unquestioned, came under growing and frequent debate. Some critics, like Williams, scorned Jay's behavior. Several savaged him without remorse. Among the most acerbic was Jack Miley, columnist for the *New York Daily News*. "Dizzy is a big man now, especially between the ears," he wrote. "For a guy who was picking cotton for fifty cents a day a few years ago, Dizzy has an amusing idea of his own importance. Dizzy is full of prunes," Miley continued, "and my answer to him is—pfooey."

Unaccustomed to adverse, much less hostile, criticism, Dean reacted quickly. On April 3, after an exhibition game with the Reds at Tampa, Dizzy and his wife spotted Miley while preparing to board a hotel elevator. Within minutes Dean's only fight with the sporting press began.

"There's that Miley," Pat reported. Diz left the elevator and hailed their recently-discovered foe.

"I don't like the articles you've been writing about me," Dean shouted as he and Miley neared. "I don't want you to ever mention my name again. I don't want no $120 a month guy writing about me."

"That's fine," Miley screamed back. "I don't like writing about bush leaguers, anyway," and the fight was underway, engaging seven players in the melee. Before the finale dawned, Miley was slugged across the forehead with a pair of spike shoes and punched in the face. Dean was assaulted by Irv Kupcinet, a Chicago writer who rushed in to assist his fallen colleague. Kupcinet, in turn, was smashed across the left cheekbone, his face becoming swollen and badly bloated. Injured, too, was a floor lamp that sailed across the hotel lobby, breaking beyond repair. The Cardinals were charged with the fight's expenses.

Neither disharmony nor misfortune deterred Ol' Diz's course. He started the regular season with five victories in a row, halting spring rumors that his talent had mysteriously fled. On May 5 Dean captivated 1,500 students at a Harvard freshmen smoker. "We've been going tough," he told them, "but we were sure we'd have an easy time when we hit Boston . . . I am an unusual pitcher, you know, for, unlike the other great ones, I am a hard hitter." And a willing hitter, too, as the Giants found two weeks hence. Trailing 3-1, soon to lose his third straight decision to Carl Hubbell, Dean opened the ninth inning by decking Jimmy Ripple twice. On the third pitch Ripple attempted to bunt, hoping to draw Diz near first base and force a collision, but the bunt misfired and went foul. Ripple fared better the second time around, luring Dean to first and beating the throw. Crossing the bag, Ripple turned, swept past umpire George Barr and advanced toward Diz. He threw a punch and the fight began. Rebuked by Ford Frick the following day, Dean and Ripple were fined $50 apiece. "I have drawn up certain regulations," said Frick, "which have gone out to the club owners," penalties including fine, suspension and immediate ejection for any pitcher who sought to equal Dean's disruptive intent.

Rarely was Ol' Diz more a free spirit than now. On May 22 Dean pledged to boycott the All-Star Game. Two days later, angered by a balk call made the previous week, Diz countered with a sit-down strike. "You can't commit a balk if you don't pitch," he said, taking over eleven minutes to throw three pitches. While Durocher argued with umpire Beans Reardon, the game delayed, Ol' Diz squatted on the mound. His tactics infuriated opponents and bedeviled Frick. The next afternoon, Dean's zest for combat soaring, he traveled to Belleville, Illinois, where 1937's most embittered controversy arose.

Addressing a Presbyterian Church father and son dinner, Dean allegedly called Frick and Barr "the two biggest crooks in baseball," a quote Diz later steadfastly disclaimed. "All I did was discuss the balk rule," he insisted. "I said the rule as now called by umpires is a detriment to pitching and could hurt the game. What do Frick and his umpires know about pitching, anyhow? As far as the beanballs go, how can anybody say I deliberately tried to beanball somebody? Why, any pitcher can have a wild day." Neither balks nor beanballs, it was clear, incensed Ford Frick; what proved galling was the phrase "two biggest crooks." Ford's response was delivered by umpire Ernie Quigley, who approached Dean before a June 1 game in Brooklyn, armed with a letter of apology written solely by Frick. Diz refused to sign, saying the misdeeds cited were imagined and overblown, and later that day the Great One was suspended, banned "for conduct detrimental to the best interests of baseball."

"Quigley gave me two letters," Diz recalled. "One was the letter of apology to be signed by me; the other was notification of indefinite suspension if I did not sign. I refused to sign." During the last three months Dean had been involved in a publicized holdout, hotel fracas, beanball war, threatened All-Star boycott, balk controversy and indefinite suspension. Small wonder that Frisch remained adamant in his refusal to compromise, or that Ol' Diz was besieged during this latest in a season of madcap ventures. "I didn't say what I was supposed to have said at Belleville," Dean maintained. "So why should I apologize for it? All I said was that the rule book was unfair, and that's the truth. And no one can accuse me of trying to bean the Giants," though Diz never rejected the notion himself.

"I ain't signing nothin'. I didn't say anybody was a crook. There was plenty of people there who could testify to that. Shucks," he continued, grinning, "I was in a church, and I'd be likely to pop off like that in a church, anyway, wouldn't I? Course not."

Amid the rhetorical barrage, Frick refused to yield; only Dean, he said, could stop the suspension. "Diz can settle this quickly if he admits the errors of his ways, apologizes to the league for the things he has said or implied and puts it in writing," Frick told the press. "I've played along with him until I don't see how we can overlook his actions any longer. It gets to the question of whether Dean is bigger than the National League, and I don't think he is."

Dean thought otherwise, saying Florida was his next intended locale. "I'll loaf the rest of my life there before I'll sign," he vowed. "I can sit here like this and eat three squares a day all my life on the dough I have. This guy Frick wishes I didn't have it, so I would have to get down on my knees to him. Too bad for Frick I do."

Both star and supporting cast proved equal to their parts. Disowning caution, Dizzy vowed to sue Frick and the National League for $250,000, "that is," he said, "if they deprive me of making a living throwing the 'ol round ball." Murray H. Parres, a writer for the *Belleville Daily Advocate* and author of the "crooks" quote, confirmed to reporters Dean's slander of Frick. And the Reverend D. C. Boyd, pastor of the Belleville church where Diz's dilemma began, said he was uncertain whether the term "crooks" was used. "I thought his speech was a tremendous speech for baseball," he stated. "Let's leave it at that."

The tumult mounted and Dean stood fast. He would appeal to Landis, Diz claimed; failing that, he would sue. Denounced by newsmen, scored as arbitrary and unjust, Frick called a meeting for June 3; after a stormy three-hour conference, Ol' Diz was reinstated, his reputation cleansed. Jay Hanna signed 'nothing,' denying only the statements attributed to him in the Belleville press. The meeting with Frick, Gillespie said years later, had been boisterous and mean; once Dean shouted, "I will not sign a single thing," then stormed from the office and shouted, "The whole thing's off. I'm going back to my hotel and pack right away." The League President induced Dean to temporarily return, but Frick's hopes for victory (and face-saving) were first fleeting, then entirely vain.

"The opening gun was Frick's demand for Dean's apology," one story began. "The closing gun was Dean's refusal to apologize. In St. Louis, Dean's bigger than he ever was in his thirty-victory campaign." Frick had backed down, Dean prevailed. The following week Diz bested Carl Hubbell, 8-1, as 55,577 fans at the Polo Grounds grieved. Jay Hanna was 8-4 and the Cardinals clung close to the lead. Ol' Diz was front page again, the nation's interest once more renewed.

"Baseball's return to box-office popularity is, of course, mainly due to better times," wrote Lloyd Lewis. "But no account of its comeback can be complete without the award of great credit to one man—the stunning comic heroic Dizzy Dean—most famous of living pitchers. His personality rose to prominence in the lean years of baseball. Dizzy is always stepping into the breach that way, saving games which seem lost, turning mediocre scenes into thrillers, taking listless seasons and filling them with melodrama." Lewis, who himself leaned toward melodrama, now waxed poetic. "Dizzy has vitalized the game when the public was beginning to tire. He became the darling of the mob because he can make good the wildest, most laughable brags an athlete ever made, because he's honest, and because he's crazy about winning. In him lives again the bitter, profane, hellion lust for victory that McGraw and Frank Chance and Ty Cobb put into baseball."

Gone, almost wholly, were the rumors of Dean's failing skills, the soft-spoken innuendo which had marred his rites of spring. "Dizzy's hunger for victory," Lewis continued, "is so great that it has made him the first pitcher in organized baseball to be practically as great an attraction when he's on the bench as when he's on the field—something that Babe Ruth could not achieve." Critics fondly sketched Diz's dugout ragings, the insults flung at umpires and opponents alike. Once again, it appeared, the Master was embronzed and infallible. Even Dean's expressed desire to bypass the All-Star Game—"I need my rest," he chimed—produced little written wrath. Only the insistence of Cardinal officials, who demanded that he play, led Diz to Washington on July 7, confiding at the airport, "I'm just a Boy Scout, here to do my good All-Star deed."

As applause swirled about him, his career at heights rivalling the harvest weeks of 1934, Dizzy Dean met debacle and defeat. Pitching at Griffith Stadium, within one strike of holding the American League scoreless for the third inning in a row, Diz yielded a single to Joe DiMaggio. Lou Gehrig followed with a titanic home run high over the right field fence. Miffed at Gehrig's audacity, Dean dismissed catcher Gabby Hartnett's signal—"He wanted a curve," Diz rued later—and grooved a fast ball to Earl Averill, the next batter. Averill responded with a line drive that struck a glancing blow off Dean's left toe, forcing him from the game and ultimately aborting his career.

"Your big toe is fractured," a doctor told Diz.

"No, it ain't," Dean said. "It's broke."

The Cardinals were in fourth place, trailing the Giants and Pirates, five games behind the league-leading Cubs. Saying, "My big toe's so sore I can't even put a shoe on," Diz rallied to the cause nonetheless. Wearing a spiked shoe with the toe plate cut out, Dean took his next pitching turn with a splint on the toe. "This was ten days after I broke it," Diz said, "and I was asked to report to the club at Boston, which I did. Frisch asked if I could pitch when I showed up. I did. I gave him a pretty good game but lost. And the toe wasn't healed. I couldn't pivot for my follow-through, and I hurt my arm favoring the toe." His overhand delivery failing, Dean began to throw with a semi-sidearm motion, further straining his arm. Only four weeks before, Diz had won his twelfth game, edging Cincinnati, 1-0. "It was one of the best games I ever pitched," he said. "I was on my way to my best season." Enter Earl Averill—and disaster as well.

On August 27, pitching against Philadelphia, Dizzy faced two batters and departed, helpless against the pain which plagued his arm. "I'm worried," he said. "When I was hurt last month we were two and one half games out of first place. Before I come back the club was eleven games out. How they gonna survive?" Dean's survival was equally suspect; Diz suffered from bursitis of the right shoulder, and complete rest was prescribed.

After returning on September 8, his verdict a 4-0 loss to the Cubs, Diz was urged by Rickey to forget baseball during 1938. "Take the season off, use it as a tonic," he said. "Build up your baseball morale." Dean declined, fleeing South on October 17 to Bradenton, where a doctor adorned his shoulder with adhesive tape, hoping to hold the injured muscles intact. Within several weeks the bandages were gone, Ol' Diz taking to the fairways and streams. His arm was fine, he said; no doctor would guide his course. Dean bought a Bradenton filling station, named it after himself, then began greasing chassis and servicing cars. "Everyone who wants an autographed picture," promised Diz, ever the entrepreneur, "can have one free, and that ain't no lie. I had too much trouble this year to start falsifying my ads."

Earlier that year Dean had flaunted his gall, betting he could strike out Vince DiMaggio four straight times in Boston, later ordering rookie catcher Bruce Ogrodowski to drop DiMaggio's ninth-inning pop foul fly so he could complete the streak. "Drop it, drop it," he screamed to Ogrodowski, now startled and chagrined. "Dammit, if you want to catch me again, drop it." The ball fell untouched. Frisch, leaping to his feet, smashed his head on the concrete dugout roof. Dean retreated to the mound and calmly struck DiMaggio out, the fourth and final time. Dean's talent once made such daring within constant reach. Now, in late 1937, injury had come, ebbing his stature, and Diz must seek the caution he previously spurned. For 1938 the Cardinals bid $10,000; Diz countered with twice that sum. "Diz's offer to accept a reduction from the $25,000 he made last year is intriguing," Dan Daniel wrote. "It marks his first retrogression since he came into baseball, his first admission that Jay Hanna Dean isn't what he used to be. And that, *mes amis,* is somewhat more than startling." On February 23, his salary leverage slashed, Ol' Diz signed for $17,500, delighted to earn even that restricted sum. The Cardinals, he knew, were anxious to unload him; one month earlier J. Edgar Hoover disclosed that Dean escaped kidnapping only because the plotters felt St. Louis would not offer $50,000 for his release. "They couldn't get anything but my filling station in Bradenton. I haven't got anything that would make me worth kidnapping," Dean said. Which was precisely the Cardinals' fear.

In April, Dean and his teammates ventured north, their destination the annual pre-season city series between the Cardinals and Browns.

This year, at least. few in St. Louis seemed to care; neither team was headed anywhere but down. Rumors intensified that Ol' Diz would promptly be dealt away. "Yes, the Cubs are interested in Dizzy Dean," said Clarence Rowland, a Chicago scout, "and Mr. Rickey seems wanting to sell him."

"Clarence, you don't want Dean," Rickey told him. "His arm is dead."

"Well, maybe we do."

"I'll give you permission to talk to Dean and Frisch," Rickey replied, "and if you still want him, you can have him, but I want to go on record as having told you his arm is gone."

Within twenty-four hours Rowland returned. Dean was soon a Cub, dealt for outfielder Tuck Stainback, pitchers Clyde Shoun, Curt Davis and $185,000. His new teammates were delighted, his old incensed. "I'm tickled to death we got him," roared Charlie Grimm. Pepper Martin was more resigned. "There goes our pennant and World Series money," to which Terry Moore echoed, "Yeah, we would have been a cinch to win." Unlike the Cardinals, Ol' Diz publicly welcomed the change. "I hate to leave the fellows," Dean said, "but I'm glad to leave St. Louis for the Cubs." Privately his manner was less buoyant and relieved.

"I was in the Cardinal office the day Diz was traded," said Bob Broeg. "The Cardinals had just completed the exhibition game, and they called a press conference. In comes Diz to say good-bye to Miss Murphy, long-time secretary to Breadon. And he was really shook—there were tears in his eyes. When he got to Chicago, he regained his aplomb and says, 'I'm glad to get rid of those cheap bastards in St. Louis.' But he was really hurt, and no amount of blabber by him could deny the fact."

America was stunned, Chicago rivals distinctly nonplussed. "I'm puzzled by the deal," Bill Terry said. "I would have bid more for Dean. The Cardinals were had." Not unexpectedly, Rickey's estimate diverged. "Even when he's good, one pitcher does not make a club. All I will say is that the Dean of today is not the Dean of old." Cub partisans, paying little heed, stormed the Wrigley Field gates. Owner P. K. Wrigley, exulting with them, said, "Dean is in perfect physical shape," a phrase he would rapidly disdain, and claimed Diz might mean the pennant, a pledge Wrigley later recalled with relish.

Dizzy Dean had won one hundred and thirty-three games; he would win only seventeen more. Diz traveled to Chicago and demanded a raise, then swept to Cincinnati and his Cub road debut. There, surrounded by a shield of writers and photographers, Dean focused on the city he once called home. "I don't know what St. Louis is going to do," Diz said. "I've been worrying for the Cardinals the last six years. Now they'll have to worry for themselves." The Cardinals soon had reason for concern, losing seven of their first eight games. Meanwhile, pitching at Crosley Field, Dean downed Cincinnati for his first victory as a Cub, yielding eight hits in a 10-4 romp. "What a club those Cubs are,"

Dizzy Dean warms up on the sidelines at Crosley Field, Cincinnati, as he prepares for his first game as a Chicago Cub in April, 1938.

he marveled that night. "They're the greatest bunch I've ever seen. They pulled fielding plays out there behind me today that the Cardinals couldn't have handled in a hundred years."

Four days later, braving winds and dampened skies, 34,520 jammed Wrigley Field to see Ol' Diz confront the Cardinals. "Remember, Diz was sold as damaged goods," Broeg said. "Everybody knew he had a sore arm. But Diz slow-balled the Cardinals to death—oh, how they wanted to beat him—and he still had the great motion, control and rhythm. No fastball, just great slow stuff. It was one of the great victories in the history of baseball." Dean allowed only four scattered hits, blanking the Redbirds, 4-0. Afterward, as thousands crowded around the runway to cheer his shutout work, Ol' Diz sought out the attentive press. "Just twenty-eight more to go," he said. "Boy, that's the big one, the one I had to have. It's upward, it's upward from here on out."

Yet Dizzy's resurgence was more uproarious than real. In an April 29 game he tired, pulled a muscle and left. On May 3 Diz pitched six innings, then faltered again. Several days hence the inevitable climax occurred; Dean was sidelined for more than four weeks, the cause a slight tear in the fibers of the right deltoid muscles, the shoulder cap used in raising the arm. Severely inflamed, the arm was weak. "Rest should have corrected the weakness," John F. Davis, Cub physician, said, "but Dean probably brought on the present condition by putting too much of a strain on his arm before it was ready." Ol' Diz must rest; Cub fortunes will falter in his absence.

Never before had prolonged injury faced him. As Dizzy sulked, speculation mounted. Was he forever disabled? Would the Cubs discard him? Had unending labor of summers past finally laid him low? To Chicago officials, Dean's fall was especially ill-timed. Recent renovation of Wrigley Field had cost one million dollars, a debt Ol' Diz's gate appeal would have largely offset. "We don't think of Diz in terms of his arm alone," Wrigley concurred, adding, "Diz loves baseball whether he's pitching or not. He'll be valuable to us in any role." To Cardinal patrons, once uplifted by Ol' Diz and cheered by his presence, Dean's injury brought little cause to bewail. Even Diz's legacy was casually brushed aside; a former Cardinal, requesting a St. Louis baseball uniform, received the Great One's old suit. "We haven't any use for it anymore," the Cardinal letter said, and none for Ol' Diz, either.

On May 18, pleading for a chance to pitch, Dean saw both Grimm and Davis reject his appeal. One month later, still inactive, Diz learned that the deltoid muscle had healed. No matter; harsh pain persisted, and soon even pleas were passé. Seeking a cure, Diz said he was "tired and disgusted with big specialists and scientific solutions," and vowed to try "old goose-grease and turpentine. Just like my folks used to rub on my chest." By July 9, frustrated for weeks, Diz threatened to sue the Cardinals for $250,000, saying Frisch had made him pitch too quickly after his 1937 injury, thereby harming the Master's arm. "Dizzy will pitch in the near future," Wrigley subsequently promised. "I'm going to put him to work. He has lots of courage and he's anxious to get going."

Dean's agony ceased, albeit momentarily, on July 17. Pitching well, relying on courage and control, Dean downed Boston, 3-1, as 35,623 cheered at Wrigley Field. The next week, following Grimm's dismissal and Gabby Hartnett's emergence as Cub manager, 42,373 in the North-side Chicago ballpark watched Diz best New York, 3-1, his third complete game and fifth victory of the year. Physical hurt was more formidable than even the best of opposing teams, however, and in August Dean was shelved anew, his shoulder abused and sore. With Ol' Diz absent, the Cubs faltered badly, then rallied in September as Pittsburgh's first place advantage—once impregnable—began un-accountably to fade. "You can bet we ain't gonna give up that World Series dough without plenty of fight," Diz said. "If we don't make a fight from now on to the wire then I'm dizzier than they say I am."

The Pirates, undaunted, began to print World Series tickets, but by September 27 their edge had dwindled to one and a half games. Stripped of momentum, Pittsburgh arrived in Chicago for a three-game series, the pennant very much unsealed. "Diz had pitched only sporadically," Broeg recalled, "but now Hartnett brought him out of mothballs." Reporters from around the nation flocked to Wrigley Field. So did Judge Landis and both league presidents. So, too, did another overflow throng, 42,238, which roared as Ol' Diz kept the Pirates scoreless for eight innings, yielding only seven hits. When he finally wearied, relieved by Bill Lee with two out in the ninth inning, the crowd stood and cheered en masse, each crescendo louder than the one before. The game ended shortly, a victory for Chicago, 2-1. "Diz was the superb pitcher yester-day," Warren Brown wrote. "He pitched with his head, and he pitched with his heart and the triumph was justly his." Hartnett was more prosaic. "He's got the greatest heart of any pitcher that ever toed the rubber."

Seeking a novel effect, Dizzy cloaked his reaction in religious garb. "It was the Lord," he said of his victory over Pittsburgh. "He had his arms around me all the time, yes sir, like to choke me, He held me so tight. Whenever I started to go wild, he just patted me on the head and the next guy popped up. It's a grand feeling." That spirit, Dean insisted, had its origin in his youth. "My uncle was the Reverend Bland R. Dean. He rose each week to preach, and I sure did like to hear him talk. I like the part about how God played fair with those who played fair with him," Diz continued. "I was always solemn like after listening to Uncle Bland—he could make things sound so real. I think I took up the collection for him after a sermon in a tent, but maybe I'm not sure. It was either me or Paul. Maybe me and Paul together. Anyway, he never objected to us or anybody else playing ball on Sunday. Some-times he'd go himself after his preaching was done. He wasn't no Rickey," who himself was bemoaning a Cardinal and attendance collapse.

The Cubs trailed the Pirates, now thoroughly dazed, by one-half game. The next day, September 28, while darkness haunted Wrigley Field, a 5-5 game about to be declared a tie, Gabby Hartnett smashed a home run in the bottom of the ninth inning. "The homer," one account read, "topped off as thrilling an afternoon as any sports carnival could produce." Hartnett labeled his blow "the biggest thrill of my life," and the Chicago Historical Society requested the bat for permanent display. One day later Chicago extended its lead to one and a half games, routing Pittsburgh, 10-1, and virtually deciding the pennant's fate. The official climax came when Charley Root beat St. Louis, 10-3, his victory ousting the Pirates at last. Thousands of Chicagoans jammed the Illinois Central Depot to welcome the conquerer Cubs back home; Ol' Diz and Pat, entrapped in a swirling mob, were bundled in a fire department vehicle and whisked safely away.

The World Series followed, one-sided but taut. The New York Yankees, seeking a third consecutive crown, opened with Red Ruffing, who downed the Cubs, 3-1, in the classic's initial game. Short on pitchers, striving to avoid two straight setbacks at Wrigley Field, Hartnett countered the next day with Dizzy Dean. Unexplainably, in one inning after another, Dean held the Yankees at bay. "Lord knows how he held the Yankees off," George Kirksey wrote. "He didn't have anything but a change of pace. First he would throw a slow ball. Then he would throw a slower ball. Then he would throw one so lazy, so soft, so absolutely devoid of stuff, that a handwriting expert sitting in the stands would have read Ford Frick's character from his signature on the ball." The overpowering Dean, the strikeout artist of old, held sway no longer; in his place was an artist who relied upon perfection of craft. Through seven innings New York scored twice, both runs coming when Cub third baseman Stan Hack and shortstop Billy Jurges, each chasing a routine ground ball, collided in the second inning. Yet Dean soon silenced Yankee bats, ultimately leading, 3-2. "First it was astounding, then incredible, then just plain annoying," said Joe Williams, "to see Dean take one Yankee hitter after another and make a first-class ape out of him."

With two outs in the eighth inning, Myril Hoag reached base. Disaster ensued. Dean threw three balls, two strikes, then served a pitch which Frank Crosetti sent to the left-field bleachers. The Yankees led, 4-3. Dizzy Dean's final fling with high theater was done. As Crosetti toured the bases, Jay Hanna cursed his lot. "You'd never have done that to me," he screamed, "if I'd had my fastball." To which the Yankee shortstop replied, "I know, Diz. I know."

The crowd at Wrigley Field turned silent, struck mute by Crosetti's blast. "An awful stillness was felt in the press box, too," Lloyd Lewis wrote. "It was as if the American press, for whom Dean has done much more than it could have done for him, had suddenly stopped out of respect for him. It was a great salute to what each writer feared deep down inside might well be the passing of a great man."

For Ol' Diz, the ninth inning was equally bleak. Joe DiMaggio unloaded a two-run homer, afflicting Dean further and concluding the Master's demise. Diz left amid a cacophony of sound, strode up a runway and fled from view. "I didn't have nothin'," he said. "I had no license to beat anybody. But they could have cut my arm off in the clubhouse if I'd won that one."

While the Yankees gathered in the clubhouse, there to serenade writers with "The Sidewalks of New York," Diz sought refuge in the afterglow of autumns past. "He gave it his best," said Pat. "It was wonderful he went as far as he did." The Cubs lost the third game, 5-2, then completed their Series ouster with a setback in the final contest, 8-3. Heroic in defeat, Dean returned to Dallas, where he lured hosannas from Gabby Hartnett, who promised, "I'm keeping Dean in 1939, because I believe the big fellow can come back." And Associated Press, which ranked Diz third in "Comeback of the Year" voting. And the Winnebago (Wisconsin) Indians, who inducted Dean into their tribe and named him Chief Nekoosa, or Swift Running Water. Dean's image was fully restored, his bank account intact. Neither fame nor wealth, though, could aid his arm, or revive the victories which had formerly been so profuse.

"My arm is OK again," he said, discarding reality, as 1939 dawned. "I know because I took a peek at those X-Rays yesterday before they were dry and Ol' Diz has been X-rayed so often he's an expert." Dean rested his shoulder and lowered his sights. Once Diz had vowed to starve before signing for $10,000; in early March, he reversed his stance and relinquished hope. The season began and Ol' Diz ached. On April 28 he was floored by a line drive which deflected off his head. Four days later, his head uninjured, his right arm hurt, Dizzy admitted the severity of his woes. "My arm," he sorrowed, "is sore as the deuce."

Amid Dean's growing despair, his penchant for the bizarre survived. During early June the Cubs traveled to New York, Diz emerging one morning with a cut on his once-fabled arm. He was instant news once more. Dean told one writer that a lion had attacked him in a taxicab. He told another that a cigar case shattered in the hotel lobby, the flying glass slicing his arm. To yet another, Diz confided that an ill-placed night lamp, one unseen and in his way, had done him accidental harm. Dean adored his newly-regained notice, but Gabby Hartnett had endured enough, ordering Diz home, a move that delighted several jealous teammates and provoked the Great One's wrath. "All it is is a little scratch," he professed. "I don't belong by myself. I belong with the team. What are they trying to do, make a goat out of me? I wonder what's behind it all, anyway." Amused no longer, Dean's lust for notoriety turned to rancor instead. "I never thought," he said, fuming, "that a little scratch would move Hitler and the WPA off page one."

The fading months of 1939 went badly. By October, Wrigley would only say, "Dean can stay with us if he's sound," a goal Diz found elusive and increasingly removed.

"I've talked a lot in my day, but quote me right on this, will you?" Ol' Diz implored in early 1940. "My arm's bad and this is my last chance in baseball. If I don't make it this time, I'm through forever." Dean's prognosis was hardly harsh. He stumbled through spring training, a pallid shadow of his former self, then was fined $100 on April 9 for curfew violations. Diz balked and threatened to retire. But with Dean on the skids, Hartnett called the shots, and Dizzy soon succumbed.

In April, Dean pitched at Sportsman's Park, where nearly empty stands greeted his St. Louis return debut. One month later, still stumbling, Diz was banished to the bullpen. Eventually, hoping that extended minor league duty would help rediscover his form, Dean asked the Cubs to demote him. Any National League club could have claimed Diz for $7,500, but none chose to chance the sum. Ten years earlier Dean had pitched at Tulsa; now he sought there to salvage his career. On June 3, hours after he fell from a moving car when the door suddenly opened, Dizzy Dean was waived to the Texas League. "Thus a mourning wreath," Williams wrote, "is placed on one of the most memorable right arms that ever came into baseball—and one of the most colorful characters." Unusually subdued, the Deans left Chicago, Pat pledging they would return. By late August, in fact, they had; Dean's record at Tulsa was 8-8, moving Wrigley to grant him one final reprieve. The magic was gone, however, and so, too, Dizzy's right arm.

Diz conceded on May 14, 1941, asking Wrigley to release him. The Cub owner refused. "Your petition is denied," he said. "Come downtown tomorrow and we'll sign a contract as a coach." Even in Dean's new capacity, turmoil strayed the Great One's way; on June 7, six months before the Japanese assaulted Pearl Harbor, Diz verbally scored umpire Reardon, drawing a five-day suspension and fifty dollar fine. Dean owned no desire to ever manage a major league team; when coaching also paled, he turned to an even more intriguing and lucrative locale—baseball's broadcast booth. Tomorrow he would leave the Cubs, Diz told reporters on July 3. His contract with Falstaff Brewery, which called for $10,000 per year, meant that Dean would broadcast St. Louis Cardinal games through 1943.

"I think I'm going to like radio," Diz bellowed, fleeing Chicago for the riches which lay ahead. Radio, which had not seen Dean's likes before, would become rather fond of him as well.

III

During the 1930s, baseball belonged to a select group of figures, not the least of whom were Joe McCarthy and Jay Hanna Dean. Baseball was really the only game that mattered then, long before the influx of other sports which endangered its national supremacy. Starting in 1931, and for the next fifteen years, McCarthy's New York Yankee teams won eight pennants and seven World Series, a record only Casey Stengel would eclipse. McCarthy's was an age of fabled

Joe McCarthy managed the New York Yankees during the 1930s.

managers, from Frisch to McGraw to Connie Mack, and McCarthy's fame was the most pronounced.

Philadelphian by birth, Victorian by nature, Joseph Vincent McCarthy was a stern, almost imperious autocrat. Jimmy Dykes once tagged him a ''push-button'' manager, a label which provoked instant rage. Others called him the greatest manager to ever grace the diamond game. Whatever names were uttered, or qualities ascribed, America knew him as Marse Joe.

Marse Joe was a throwback to an earlier, more ordered era. His bent was conservative; McCarthy cherished corporate pride, and admonished his players to show calm and dignity, lest they jeopardize the Yankee image. He dealt with his players on a no-nonsense basis founded on authority and respect. Some called it fear, or paranoia, or the resultant stirrings of a complex and troubled man. Few doubted that McCarthy was hard, or that he commanded the grudging notice of his underlings. ''He was the greatest manager I ever had,'' marveled Ted Williams, who sought to mirror Joe's austere bearing and exact approach.

When McCarthy's temper flared, some sensed that not only jobs or careers were at stake, but also arms, legs, jaws and possibly life itself. Those tactics worked expertly in New York. There McCarthy was blessed with men the caliber of Ruth, Dickey, Lopat, DiMaggio, Ruffing, Lefty Gomez, and Lou Gehrig who, to McCarthy, was less player than son. While New York strode triumphant, fielding baseball's greatest succession of teams, by 1933 the Cardinals had begun their dominance of the National League as well. Within the next fourteen years they won five pennants and three World Series, outflanking every club but the Yanks.

"We had some marvelous teams back then, but so did St. Louis. How good the Cardinals were I couldn't exactly say," said McCarthy, notoriously reluctant to compare teams he had seen, worried that players not selected might feel excluded or otherwise maligned. "I don't like to rate fellows. Never have.

"People have been after me for years to list an all-Yankee team or an all-opponents team. Well, they'll never get me to do it. I'll tell you that. But I will say this about Dizzy Dean. He had a whale of a lot of courage. He had good nerve; he knew he could pitch and he flaunted what he had. Some people say there's a big difference between gall and guts, and they claim all Diz had was gall. I say he had 'em both. He was as gutsy as they come."

In 1945, McCarthy moved to western New York, where he and his wife bought a home in East Amherst, a Buffalo suburb. Five years later he returned, a man in exile, fired by the Red Sox and resigned never to manage again. Two decades later, he was nearing ninety, a gentleman farmer with sixty-two acres surrounding his home. He still followed baseball, even in a city which had consistently bungled its chances for a major league team. His wife died in 1971. Since then he had been largely ignored by a baseball establishment long noted for shunting aside its legends once their value was past. Even so, he now seemed placid and unruffled. A creek glided gently before his house. At final peace with himself, McCarthy's focus shifted to the 1930s, a decade in which Marse Joe had thrived.

"All the talk that came from the National League was about Dean then," McCarthy said. "Of course, he was the big show there for almost the whole decade. We had our stars in the American League, but Dean was the big news in the other circuit. It's funny. People remember him from the days in St. Louis, but I was with him for two events that had even more importance.

"You remember the All-Star Game in 1937, when Earl Averill hit a line drive that broke Diz's toe? Diz tried to come back too soon afterward and hurt his career. Well," McCarthy said, "folks don't recall that Dean was one out away from getting out of the inning. He tried to slip a fast one past Lou Gehrig"—a quick, fleeting smile—"and Lou hit it a mile. Creamed it. Diz was so mad that he grooved one to Averill and . . . that was that.

"The next event happened the next year, when Dean was with the Cubs. He'd been traded from St. Louis earlier in the season. And he didn't have it anymore; a lot of his stuff was gone. He'd lost the old blazer, as he called it. But," and here McCarthy began to laugh, "that old son of a gun, he had us beat until the eighth inning. He didn't have a thing, and he still almost beat us. Diz had a heart, I'll tell you that."

Spirits may muse about how well Dean and McCarthy would have

Yankee first baseman, Lou Gehrig, chats with New York manager Joe McCarthy after Gehrig returned from the Mayo Clinic. Tests showed Gehrig was seriously ill. (AP Wirephoto)

fared; how could two such disparate figures merge? Perhaps easily; often abrasive toward lesser men, McCarthy was far more tolerant of leading players. A minor league retread as a player, McCarthy told Ted Williams, "If I could hit like you can, no one would have to give me a salary to stay in baseball. I'd pay so that I could play this game."

With the Yankees, McCarthy always ordered players to wear a suit and tie on road trips. When he was named Red Sox manager in 1948, though, knowing Ted Williams' reputation as a man who refused to wear any type of tie, McCarthy strode into the team's spring training dining room adorned in a wild sportshirt. "Anyone," he loudly announced, "who can't get along with a .400 hitter is crazy." Undoubtedly McCarthy would have altered his style to suit Dean, too. For all his fame as a martinet, Marse Joe was flexible in his treatment of players who could seal or undo his pennant hopes.

Perhaps it was Lou Gehrig's refusal to accept this status, a favored station his heroics had earned, which so endeared him to McCarthy. The two shared many tenets—dignity and decorum, a defensive mistrust of the outside world, a pragmatic, coldly efficient view of life, and an abiding love of baseball for what it had brought them. They also shared a common loyalty to family and close friends, and a realization that their public profiles lacked the flamboyance which drew plaudits toward Williams, Ruth, and Dean.

"Ruth got the headlines, so did Diz," Marse Joe said, "but it was Lou who came through for you in the clutch above all others. He was wonderful to have managed (1931-39), wonderful to have known. When we needed a lift, you'd look to him, and Lou seldom failed you."

Lou brought coherence amid the turbulence of life, a continuity which McCarthy urgently required, lest his fixed view of life be disrupted forever. McCarthy needed ordered bearings. Life was fraught with danger, even success was not absolved of peril. Gehrig's solidity provided a calming effect; his presence reassured Marse Joe that existence lacked neither structure nor sense.

McCarthy recounted an evening with Casey Stengel as they traveled via railroad in the 1940s to New York. Looking out at the wavering farmhouse lights, ones which rushed through the darkened landscape, McCarthy had paused and said, "You know, Case, that's the life for me. Nothing to worry about except get up and do the milking. Sometimes I think I'm in the greatest business in the world. Then you lose four straight and want to change places with the farmer."

Thirty years and a million memories later, Joe McCarthy had finally realized that once distant goal. His manner was, as always, gruff and reserved. Yet there was a tranquility to his speech, and a sincerity which was genuine and real. Eight months later Joseph McCarthy was dead. Repose, that elusive ally, had found Marse Joe at last.

Chapter Six

Sweet Summer, Chastened Fall

I

During the 1930s and the next decade beyond, with television an incipient vision, radio thrust baseball into the nation's living rooms, creating millions of new-found fans. For decades newspapers had been the sole gospel of big-league gossip. Now a new medium took hold, and baseball broadcasters were off and speaking. With no picture to assist them, announcers became the sole link between the happening and their public. If the broadcaster was memorable, then so was the event. At once intimate and homespun, radio lent itself to magic and melodrama. Americans knew and cherished their favorite announcer's style—the charm and eloquence of Walter Lanier (Red) Barber, the calm and fluency of Bob Elson, the vibrancy and vocal sweep which Mel Allen portrayed. Radio alone did not lift baseball from its medieval station to a more enlightened level, but it assuredly led the way.

On August 5, 1921, the media movement erupted. Over KDKA, the nation's first radio station, Harold Arlin aired radio's first baseball game. Crudely, hesitantly, the romance between baseball and radio started. By 1924, with Chicago the pioneer, regular play-by-play coverage began; P.K. Wrigley found seven outlets which would broadcast Cub games, both home and away. Road games were made possible by Western Union, whose ballpark operators relayed pitch-by-pitch signals to announcers located in the station's studio, data received and transferred to their audience. Thus re-created contests were born, broadcast by men miles away from the games they described. Some

117

stations, WHO in Des Moines, for one, specialized in re-creations. Their broadcaster was a promising, resonant comer named Dutch Reagan. Thirty-five years later, his first name Ronald, he became the Governor of California.

Even in its formative stages, radio endowed each season's climax—the World Series—with a stunning and unprecedented appeal. Aired over two, often three networks, usually uplifted by Graham McNamee, the country's most prominent announcer, the Series lured a national cult which quickly developed and never ebbed. The broadcasts, it soon became apparent, could do much to advance baseball's national prestige. Still, many baseball owners initially resisted the tide, disdaining both radio and the promise it held. Some viewed the past as sacrosanct and unmarred; radio was new, its future impact fearsome and unknown. Some felt radio would over-expose their sport and dilute its allure, claims which proved absurd and false. Others, their disquiet verging on hysteria, warned that radio would keep fans at home and away from the ballparks they owned. "Nobody was neutral about this new medium of instant communication," said Red Barber, no neutral himself. "Some powerful men in both baseball and football were deathly afraid . . . They said, 'Who will pay for something they can get for free?' "

In 1932, with Depression poverty curbing box-office receipts, baseball owners strove to ban radio from all major league parks. Though the movement failed, New York's three franchises agreed to boycott the medium. Two years later, with attendance still plunging, they signed a five-year pact that kept their games off radio through 1938. Enter Larry MacPhail, doer, seer and president of the Brooklyn Dodgers. One year of the ban remained when MacPhail arrived. Within months he notified the Yankees and Giants that Brooklyn would take to the air in 1939—a decision which forced them to follow suit. "MacPhail wanted radio. He believed in it, in its promotional power, in its reaching of the game to women, and he especially wanted his out-of-town games to keep the fans in touch with the ball club no matter where it went," said Barber, Dodger announcer from 1939 through 1953. "He became sold on its power. He grasped immediately that radio turned a game played by two teams into a contest involving personalities who had hopes, fears, families, troubles, blue or brown eyes." With New York aboard, radio's surge crested, its impact heightened further by Jay Hanna Dean.

"Diz never announced. He just sort of talked the game," said Bill MacPhail, son to Larry, and Director of CBS Sports from 1955 through 1974. "That's the way he was on television, on radio before. You felt you were around a potbellied stove and he was speaking to you. He was funny, warm. He didn't let you listen or watch. He *made* you." So, too, did other figures during radio's halcyon years, long before television emerged to dominate and rule. Announcers could be biased, blind, prejudiced and provincial. They could not, must not, however, be placid or blasé. Baseball voices strove for flair and flamboyance; even late-season games between cellar-contending clubs took on an almost theatrical, Armageddon aura.

During the past decade play-by-play broadcasting has leaned decidedly toward mellow, impassive reporting. Not so in 1941. Announcers spurned restraint and opted for extravagance instead. Most adopted any rhetoric which would glorify themselves, their team, even the sponsors who underwrote their career. Barber spurred baseball's image at Cincinnati and Brooklyn; an entire generation of listeners echoed his trademark terms. When a fight erupted, a "rhubarb" was underway. The bases "FOB" (full of Brooklyns) meant the "ol' pea patch" was disturbed. While Barber unfurled his siren-sweet tongue, Mel Allen held forth as voice of the Yankees. A batter with a full count prompted Allen's "three and two, what'll he do?" To Mel, home runs became "Ballantine Blasts" or "White Owl Wallops"; a moment of surpassing drama demanded "How About That!" At St. Louis, Harry Caray made "Holy Cow" a Midwestern ritual, unleashed when the Cardinals stormed from behind. At Washington, Arch McDonald carried the gimmickry even further. Senator runners on the bases were "ducks on the pond." A pitch across the plate was "right down Broadway." Joe DiMaggio became the "Yankee Clipper."

Few cities were blessed with announcers more raucous than Pittsburgh; broadcasters there were *expected* to root. Whenever a Pirate home run neared, Rosey Rowswell screamed, "Open the window, Aunt Minnie, here she comes," then had his assistant, Bob Prince, shatter a glass in the booth behind. To partisans at home, the broken glass was Aunt Minnie's window. "That's too bad," Rosey mourned. "Aunt Minnie never made it." Prince, who became head man during the 1950's, developed a style even more bizarre; home runs were greeted with cries of "Kiss It Good-bye" and "How Sweet It Is," the latter a phrase borrowed by Jackie Gleason and made nationally known. When Prince wanted a double play, the Pirates needing the bases cleaned, Pittsburgh locals heard "Give me the Hoover, give me the Hoover." A runner trying for two bases became "a bug loose on the rug," a debated call "close as fuzz on a tick's ear." The era was rowdy, the fervor undimmed. "This indifferent age of broadcasting," Caray grumbled twenty years later. " 'Ball one. Strike one. Ball two.' People fall asleep, and it probably hurts the game more than anything else." Few snored in 1941, the date that Ol' Diz debuted; fans shifted between fury and allegiance, but not many became bored by Sominex-like announcers.

Only thirty, yet condemned by some as a figure from decades past, Dizzy Dean beguiled St. Louis on the air. Charming and exuberant, Ol' Diz broadcast in a manner which differed from any heard before or since. Runners "slud," Dean's personal past tense form of the verb slide. Batters "swang." Pitchers "throwed" the ball with great "spart." ("Spart," Diz confided in late 1941, "is pretty much like gumption or fight. Like the Spart of St. Louis, that plane Lindbergh flowed to Europe.") No one had a more distinct vernacular than Ol'

Diz; few had a more homespun style, or made his malapropisms more memorable. A batter looked "mighty hitterish," Dean would claim, adding, "He's standing confidentially at the plate."

"You learn 'em English and I'll learn 'em baseball," Diz once promised a grammar teacher, a doctrine which never changed. Cardinal patrons heard *karm* ("He karmed a double off the wall"). *Marn* ("Podner, he's really marn in a mess") and *airs* ("Three runs, five hits, no airs"). St. Louis and its environs were greeted, some said attacked, by a chorus of even more enigmatic words. *Rawzum* ("The hitter put some rawzum on his bat"). *Thang* ("The only thang wrong with him is his arm"). *Tetch* ("Ol' Diz'll tetch him what's what"). Unashamedly, Dean mirrored the backwoods lingo learned in Lucas and a hundred towns its size. About a sordid colleague, Dean proclaimed, "He's just a *main* guy." When a game approached curfew time, Diz disclosed, "We've got less than an *are* left." Like slud, tell, too, acquired a past tense. "I *toad* Frisch never to yank me." Ozark verse swept onward, ridiculed by the elect, beloved by the masses, most of whom were too embroiled in laughter to be offended or appalled.

Saying, "I hope I'm as good a sports announcer as I was a pitcher," Dean faced the microphone in April, 1941. He had never before done play-by-play. "Now I know," he confided, "how a prisoner feels walking to his death." Concern was fleeting; within weeks one survey showed that eighty-two per cent of St. Louis' radio audience, an astounding total, regularly turned to Ol' Diz and his daily assaults. Dean was delighted, Falstaff Brewery shocked; few had envisioned idolatry of this degree. To fans at home, Diz urged, "Don't fail to miss tomorrow's game." To Cardinals in the dugout, he conversed by signals from the booth. To batters at the plate, he lent counsel and support. "Well, here's Enos Slaughter, my ol' pal," he bellowed. "Come on, now. Knock the ball down that guy's throat." Purists gasped but ratings rose. When critics decried his syntax, Dean snorted, "Sin tax? Are those jokers down in Washington putting a tax on that, too?" To those who disparaged his colloquial manner, Diz was ready with his response. "When I tell people that the score is nothin-nothin and nobody's winning, why, folks know exactly what the score is. I just talk common sense."

Each game was a new venture, starring and orchestrated by Dizzy Dean. "I never keep a scorecard or the batting averuges," he said. "I hate statics (statistics). What I got to know I keep in my haid." The ad-lib became pervasive; what new atrocities, fans wondered, would Ol' Diz make known? This batter had an "unorsodock stance." Give that shortstop "a sist." A one-handed catch was "a la carte." A play made adroitly was "nonchalloted," a pop fly a "can of corn." Swinging at a bad pitch comprised a "fishing trip." A strikeout victim strode "disgustilly back to the bainch." When Cleveland loaded the bases, "that loads the Injuns full of bases." An expert critic was a "what's whatter." A manager "argyin' with an umparr (umpire) is like

Dizzy Dean broadcasts one of his early radio programs adorned by his white stetson hat that later became his trademark.

argyin' with a stump. Maybe you city folks don't know what a stump is. Wal, it's somethin' a tree has been cut down off of.'' Amid the novel phrases, butchered names remained. Mort Cooper became ''Cupper,'' Stan Musial ''Moo-zell.'' A Washington catcher, Tony Giuliani, was rechristened ''Julie-Annie.'' With Ed Hanyzewski, a Chicago pitcher not noted for his skills, Dizzy shifted oral tactics. ''I liked to have broken my jaw tryin' to pronounce that one,'' he said. ''But I said his name by just holdin' my nose and sneezing.''

Dean's liberties with language aroused often impassioned unrest. The St. Louis Board of Education, bemoaning his diction, urged in 1942 that Diz be removed from the air, a demand Falstaff turned aside and Dean dismissed. ''A lot of folks that ain't saying ain't,'' he said, ''ain't eating.'' As the quarrel continued, emotions rose. ''I am one of your fans,'' the mother of a young girl, aged ten, wrote in a letter to Dean. ''I like the Cardinals and, of course, I like baseball. I just want to plead with you on one point—the point of your English. Please refrain from saying, 'ain't, throwed and swang.' Honestly, Mr. Dean, it's amusing to me, but my little daughter, Mary, is now talking like that and when I try to correct her she sasses me back and says, 'Well, that's the way Dizzy says it.' So please have a heart.''

''I ain't done nothin' about my language yet,'' Dean's response began, ''but I want to say one thing. It don't make no difference how you say it, just so you say it in a way that makes sense. Did you ever meet anybody in your life that didn't know what ain't means?'' Common sense, Diz said, would dictate her answer.

While Ol' Diz rambled, the Cardinals thrived. Spurred by the pitching of Cooper and John Beazley, lifted by the daily talent of Musial and Country Slaughter, steadied by the infield excellence of Marty Marion, St. Louis held off Brooklyn in September, 1942. With the pennant won, Diz extended a public pledge. ''Folks, we win at last,'' he said over the air, ''and we want all you baseball fans to come up here and have some drinks and food on our sponsor,'' an impromptu promise which Falstaff must honor, for scores of fans believed.

In October the Cardinals won the World Series, four games to one, and Ol' Diz was named the announcer with baseball's worst diction. Momentarily, at least, it seemed that both might be quickly silenced; a movement started to ban the sport during the rest of World War II. All major league players, critics cried, should forsake the diamond game and defend their country instead. Dean's sentiments differed. ''The people want baseball. They need it,'' Diz said, confiding that a perforated ear had forced the army to deny his pleas for military tour. In June, 1943, although Diz said he might rejoin the playing ranks— ''I've had offers from the Red Sox, A's and Browns''—the Master soon chose the wealth and security which radio supplied. ''Cardinal fans rejoice,'' one account began. ''It may be the more you hear a broadcaster the more you can go for him.'' Our favorite broadcaster is Dizzy Dean. His appeal is the human, natural Will Rogers manner in which he draws the great unseen millions to his knees and keeps them there, beaming and blubbering, that marks him as a man apart. He tosses 'em in the old barrel of brotherhood and churns 'em around good,'' tortured grammar which would have done even Ol' Diz proud.

Aided by two St. Louis pennants, Voice of the first-place Cardinals and Browns, Dean strode triumphant across 1944. Named by *The Sporting News* as the year's best broadcaster, Ol' Diz became ''even more a terrific radio favorite in St. Louis in 1944,'' the paper said, ''an accomplishment all the more remarkable because his broadcasts were carried over only stations with limited power''—WEW, St. Louis, for afternoon games, and WTMV, East St. Louis, for evening encounters. In future years KMOX, a St. Louis station of fifty thousand watts, would beam Cardinal games into as many as forty-five states; now, however, the hinterlands were cheated, unable to hear the boasts of its native and most vocal son. ''Sure wish those folks could hear,'' he said. ''That's important to Ol' Diz.'' So was unflagging candor.

During World War II radio personnel were forbidden to mention how the weather was, lest the Japanese and Germans use the data to further their cause. Dean skirted the issue and drove the facts home. ''I can't tell you folks why this here game is stopped,'' he confided as rain pelted Sportsman's Park, ''but I'll tell you what. If you just stick your head outside the nearest window, you'll know what I mean.'' During another game, Diz loudly belched. ''Oh, excuse me, folks,'' he said, turning to partner Johnny O'Hara. ''You know, John, it's very impolite to belch, especially over the mike, unless you excuse yourself. I done belched and I done excused myself, so let's go. Everything is hunky-dory,'' except, that is, for the scores of protests which indignant listeners filed. Even that outcry paled when Dizzy used the airwaves to publicly support a candidate in the 1944 Presidential election. Letters and telephone calls flooded Falstaff and Dean's two stations; thereafter, many baseball broadcasts carried a tagline disclaiming any Dean views as its own.

The ongoing ruckus hardly ruffled Ol' Diz; verbal mayhem was his daily creed. ''The peanut venders is going through the stands trying to sell their peanuts,'' he said one lackluster afternoon. ''They are not doing so good because there is more of them than there is of customers.'' When the game grew dull, Diz grew restless, roaming far afield, ignoring play-by-play to spin some favored tales. ''Me and Paul was always set down first at the spelling bees,'' he announced abruptly during a one-sided encounter. ''The best spellers on our bench was Lydie and May George . . . They'd be last up there spelling and then they'd butt heads to see who won . . . What was I talking about on them Red Sox? . . . Oh yeah, if Williams will cut more of them fouls into singles he will be batting a million.'' Falstaff cringed but interest soared; only the most effete, it seemed, found offense with Dizzy's barnyard bearing.

Rarely was Dean's rapport more evident than in 1946. Appalled at his rhetoric, convinced that Diz would undermine their in-class endeavors, the English Teachers Association of Missouri complained to the Federal Communications Committee. Dizzy Dean, they said, was a cultural hazard, a buffoon bordering on illiteracy. Reaction was immediate and unyielding. Dean's home station, now WIL, was bombarded by hundreds of letters endorsing Ol' Diz. So was the association. So, too, the *St. Louis Globe-Democrat,* which defended Dean's broadcasts in an editorial attacking the teachers for ''smugness.'' Many pens advised the English teachers to mind their own business, staying clear of sports; others insisted Diz's impact on their children was more favorable than the teachers involved. The outcome clear, Diz turned gracious amid success. ''I see where some of the teachers in the Association is saying I'm butchering up the English language a bit,'' he said. ''All I got to say is that when me and my brother Paul were picking cotton in Arkansas, we didn't have no chance to go to school much. All I say is that I'm very happy that kids are getting that chance today.'' Vindication his, Diz saw the Cardinals win the National League pennant, downing Brooklyn in the playoffs, then described St. Louis' roaring World Series victory over Boston, the seventh game marked by Enos Slaughter's epic dash from first base to home. Afterward he returned to Dallas, where Dean awaited 1947 and the broadcasts of both St. Louis teams he would surely air again.

Sam Breadon, however, had grown greedy and wise. In prior years only Cardinals' and Browns' home contests had been broadcast live; now, sensing the influence radio could provide, Breadon opted for a schedule comprised of all one hundred and fifty-four games. Every inning of every Cardinal game could at last be heard, not only in St. Louis but in the hinterlands as well; a regional network, created shortly after that, eventually included one hundred and twenty-four stations in fourteen Midwestern, Southern and Southwest states. Exclusive local radio rights were given to two St. Louis stations—WEW in the afternoon, WTMV at night. Seeking his announcers, distrusting Dean's proclivity for the unknown, Breadon chose Harry Caray and Gabby Street, leaving Ol' Diz and O'Hara to the hapless Browns. "Radio surveys for 1946 showed Dean had the largest baseball following in St. Louis," said Browns' general manager Bill DeWitt. "We're happy to offer Dizzy the opportunity to continue his contacts with his large local following." Diz expressed enchantment with the divided booth approach. "I'm happy to be out of the Cardinal chain, the office part, anyway, but I'll still root for the Cardinals, because they're a great bunch," said Dean, concluding with a promise not to "toss up any soft ones" in their defense.

"All who cherish the inalienable rights of free speech and abhor censorship, as well as students of Elizabethan English," wrote Jack Clarke in the *Chicago Sun,* "view with dismay Sam Breadon's decision to let Ol' Diz go. Blessed with the gift of tongues, Dean proved to be an extraordinarily popular announcer. When Dean did not have at his disposal a word suitable for the occasion, he simply invented one," a device which proved less worrisome to Bill DeWitt than Diz's disapproval of the 1947 cellar-dwelling Browns. Months before the regular season ended, the Browns doomed to finish eighth in an eight-team league, Dean became an irritant to DeWitt and other Brown officials, who dared not release him because of his massive appeal. The reason? Dizzy's assaults against his employers grew more pervasive as 1947 advanced. "Gosh, folks," he said as the Browns stumbled onward. "I ain't pitched baseball since 1941, but I feel sure I could go out there and do better than a lot of these throwers who are drawing big salaries as major league pitchers." Daring the Browns to activate him, Diz issued his challenge daily. "I'll pitch for nothin'," he said. With his club headed nowhere, hoping that Dean's active comeback might help ticket sales, DeWitt finally succumbed. Dean signed a contract for $1, declared "it's the best contract I ever got, 'cause it's the first one I haven't sent back for more money," then began pounding himself into shape. On September 28, after the previous day's crowd had totaled three hundred and fifteen, Dean took the mound at Sportsman's Park. While the game meant nothing, the Browns' third-largest crowd of the year (15,916) came to see the Great One—still unable to throw hard—dazzle the White Sox with craft and control. Thirty-seven, graying and rotund, he allowed no runs in four innings, yielding only three hits and collecting one himself. Dean's departure was self-inflicted; lining a single to

The stands were crowded when Dizzy Dean returned to the mound in 1947 to pitch against the Chicago White Sox for the St. Louis Browns in a regular-season game.

left field, he strove for two bases and pulled a muscle in his leg. Her husband limping as he rose, seated in a box next to the St. Louis dugout, Pat Dean leaned over and yelled to manager Muddy Ruel, "Get him out of there before he kills himself!"

Dean left readily, his playing career done, and escaped once more to Dallas. There, in a November 23 debut which became all too memorable, Jay Hanna turned to football for the first and last time. "They knocked me plumb out of the box," Dean said after his broadcast ceased. "Football's too tough on me. The only play I called right was the kickoff." Haunting the airwaves of station WLIF, Diz called the officials "umpires." Referees were "those guys wearing striped pajamas." The head linesman was "a guy who must be low on ammunition or a poor shot, because I ain't seen him hit nobody." For Dizzy Dean, football and fiasco merged; in 1948 he reverted solely to baseball, where his immodest manner was best displayed. "I've always said it pays to be a character, especially on radio," he said. "Since I was young people has tried to tell me that modesty is the best policy, and that a feller of genuine ability don't have to show hisself off. Don't ever believe it! I've seen plenty of people that gots lots on the ball but no fans in the bleachers. They don't get the pretty gal or the heavy dough. They don't get elected president or nothin'. And do you know what their trouble is?" Diz paused for dramatic effect. "They just don't have enough confidence in theirself." Dean was seldom troubled by that flaw, nor by subtlety, either. As the 1940s closed, and the Browns continued their unending sleepwalk, Dean noticed a crowd swirling around a Sportsman's Park entrance ramp. "Ah don't know what's going on down there, folks," Dean said over the air, "but there's some kind of commotion about a big, fat lady."

An advertising agency companion, seated next to Dean, gasped in semi-shock. Tugging at Dizzy's sleeve, he panted, "That's the Queen of the Netherlands."

Murmuring surprise, Diz relayed the information, then inquired, "Where is the Netherlands, anyway?"

"It's Holland, Diz," the man whispered. "It's Holland."

"The fat lady is the Queen of Holland, folks," Diz informed the audience. "I don't know why the heck they didn't say that in the first place." Career diplomats were hardly enthralled.

Neither was Happy Chandler, the new Commissioner of Baseball, who questioned Dean about charges that he laid wages on a baseball game. "Maybe I have made some bets with some of my millionaire oil friends in Texas," Diz explained, "but only on golf and horse races, never for myself on ballgames. Lord knows I ain't a-woofin'."

Neither were St. Louis pitchers, ridiculed by Ol' Diz for walking sixteen Philadelphia batters on June 21, 1948. "If I'd pitched nine straight balls when I broke into this game," he exclaimed, "I'd a wrote Ma and Pa and told 'em to put in another acre of cotton because I was coming back home."

Dizzy Dean (right) interviews New York Yankee manager Casey Stengel in 1951, Dean's second year as Yankee TV broadcaster.

Neither was the Denver English Study Group, which once more decried Dizzy's verbal wont. Arriving at Denver's Union Station, present to dedicate a new minor league park, Dean was greeted by placards labeled, "Keep Dizzy Dean off the air. He's a menace to the English Language."

And neither, ultimately, was Ol' Diz. For years he had lambasted the Browns, etching their feeble exploits in comic terms. "I slud along with them as long as I could," Diz said several years later, "but I eventual made up my mind to quit. I was tired of being asked to talk up 'the great Browns,' and being called a liar by the standings of the clubs. One day I said the Browns were nothing but a lot of Humpty Dumpties. And that was the end of the Dizzy Dean broadcasting career in St. Louis." In March of 1950, finally tiring of the Browns' hapless state, Dean agreed to a $20,000 position with the Texas League's Dallas club; his bellows, one thought, would presently pervade the Southwest. But

Dan Topping, co-owner of the New York Yankees, an avid golfer whom Dean would later invariably best, desired a new broadcaster of his own. Dallas freed Dean and Diz called Topping. Within hours he was radio's no more, leaving for New York and television, the stripling which would bring him fortune and acclaim. "I'm through talking about things," Diz said, "that folks ain't seeing." Arriving in Manhattan, Dean found that along with "commentating" during a game, his duties would include a pre- and post-game program. "This here interviewing ain't in my contract," Diz complained. "This ain't no job you give me. It's a sentence. I feel like a mortar." Dean soon relented (his $25,000 salary saw to that) and chose Yankee manager Casey Stengel as his first television guest.

"Mr. Stingle," he drawled, "I'm a stranger around these parts, and I'd appreciate it if you would sort of give me a hand in this interview."

"Sure, son," answered Casey, whose 1950 Yankees would win their second of five World Series in a row. "I can see where you'd feel like a stranger in Yankee Stadium after all your years in the National League."

"You ain't just a-woofin', Mr. Stingle."

"Well, boy, you ought to begin this interview by asking me how my ballclub is shaping up. And I ought to answer you by saying we got pretty good infielding and pretty good outfielding and pretty good reserves and we got pretty good pitching and pretty good hitting. And then, son," his monologue persisting, "you ought to ask where I figure we'll finish up in the race. And I ought to answer you that—"

Encamped in New York, entrapped by foreign environs, Ol' Diz was besieged by media counsel. Alter your style, the advisers said. Corn pone might thrive in St. Louis, but New York was more polished and blasé. "You know what some of these advertising guys are trying to do?" marveled Pat. "They're trying to get Diz to speak English." Why, she asked, tamper with success? At Yankee Stadium, as in Sportsman's Park, Diz 'just talked' his games, echoing the eloquence of Lucas and Bond.

No diction lessons, he said, could change his native mold. "Nobody's going to differentiate me," Diz vowed. "Don't get me wrong. I believe in education, but I don't miss it. As long as I kin do arithmetic I'm all right."

If New Yorkers failed to comprehend Ol' Diz, why, that would merely even the score. "I never could make out what they was saying, either," Diz said. Once, years before at Ebbets Field, shrill cries had lured him from the dugout. "I looked up in the stands and there was two fellers, hollerin' and beltin' each other all around. I leaned up in the dugout and listened real good. They was hollerin' for about five minutes, but I swear I couldn't make out a single word they said."

Accents notwithstanding, Ol' Diz gained critical applause. To Vincent X. Flaherty, "Dean is the hottest thing in television. I'm not taking anything away from Milton Berle or any of the others, but ol' Jerome Hanna Dizzy Dean is the kingpin of TV." To Ed Sullivan, "the story of Dizzy Dean would be a natural for Hollywood—a composite of Will Rogers, Mountain hero Sgt. York and Frank Merriwell. Baseball, the American game, has no more truly American saga than his." To sportswriter Hugh Bradley, Diz already had "wrestlers writhing jealously and is casting the maidenly mayhemers of the Roller Derby to spill new buckets of blood in order to compete with Dizzy." To Frank Conniff, Diz was "the next big rage of television. He'll be the video's delight in a matter of weeks."

Even in New York, where artificiality prospers, Dean's prose continued Byzantine and real. With Clarence Wotowicz, a rookie Yankee outfielder, Diz verged on mock despair. "You gotta let him go," he told Stengel. "I'll never be able to say that."

"He's gone, Dean ol' boy," Casey retorted. "When I heard you were going to do our games, I knew I couldn't keep him. Now look our lineup over carefully and anybody you can't pronounce, I'll trade."

Syntax-mauling remained Dizzy's verbal mode. "They got to be my own words," he said, "because nobody else would have 'em." Chico Carrasquel was "that hitter with the three K's in his name." Because the next hitter was a pathetic soul, Johnny Mize was "purply passed." Tommy Henrich became "Henricks" or "Henry," Phil Rizzuto "Rizoota" or "Rizooti." Yogi Berra was renamed "Berry, Barry" or "Barrow." Roy Campanella was christened "Campanellie," Brooklyn pitcher Willie Ramsdell "Ramsdale." A fine hitter "laid the ol' timber on that one," a pitcher "polished the old apple." Once Diz was called upon to narrate the opera *Carmen*. The toreador became "tudor," Carmen "common." When commentator H. V. Kaltenborn denounced Dean's prose, Ol' Diz was moved to reply, "Wal, Mister Kaltinbomb, I heard you once and I couldn't find a word you used in the dickshunary."

While Dean's rhetoric worsened, his candor, if possible, grew. Diz had rarely been sheepish about stating his convictions; now, his ego buoyed by New York's reception, his financial security assured, he discarded all caution and further indulged himself. Of umpire William McKinley, who made a decision Diz disclaimed, Dean said, "Why, they shot the wrong McKinley." To beer sponsors who prepared commercials for him to read, Diz replied, "If them guys want me to sell their stuff, they'll just leave me alone. I'll sell that stuff just as fast as a monkey can skip up a tree," which, of course, he immediately did. Of baseball rules, Diz shrugged, "I don't know any, and don't care to. I have to do this job my own way. Sure, sometimes I get too frank. But it ain't venemous. It's just Dizzy Dean." To viewers who scored Dean's lack of pretense, he answered, "I say, 'Bauer hit the dirt.' Guys write in and ask why I don't say, 'Bauer slid.' Well, when you hit the dirt, you really hit the dirt. Ain't nothin' polite about that." Batting averages "throw me off the beam." Managers have "the easiest job in baseball. There's one guy who should pay to get into the park." Critics who claimed Diz deliberately mangled his broadcasts were "way off base. It's just the best I know. Don't forget," he said, "I'm still getting educated. I like to read to my wife, Patsy. I mispronounce some word and she calls me on it every time."

Ozark inflections were more alien than accepted in New York. Few, even so, would dispute Dizzy's stature, or deny that he had become insufferably rich. In 1951 alone Dean's salary touched six figures, a hefty, almost staggering sum by that era's standard. From Yankee games he collected $40,000, the rest from land and business ventures, and chances often beckoned for more abundance still. Once a radio executive, having heard Dean's recital of *Carmen,* urged Diz to become an off-season disc jockey, playing and commenting on classical music. Dizzy rejected the offer with the same frankness used to declare himself "amongst" the greatest pitchers ever. "You want me to play this sympathetic (symphonic) music and commertate about these Rooshian and French and Kraut composers?" he mused. "Me pronounce them composers' names? Why, I can't even pronounce everybody's name in the Cleveland Indians' infield."

There was always much of the rustic in Dizzy Dean, but precious little bumpkin. Those who tagged Ol' Diz as rural and crude, or snidely dismissed him as a hayseed, overlooked the complexity which baffled even associates and friends; on the air, with New York his stage, Dean's many dimensions became palpable and beloved.

Times were when the flip, aw-shucks comic surfaced. Nineteen-fifty saw Diz and concert singer Jessica Dragonette perform a duet of the "Wabash Cannonball." When the music stopped, Dean asked blithely, "Is it true you girls are real tempermental?"

The courtly, demure good ol' boy was present, too. In the early 1950s Dean appeared on "What's My Line," then one of the nation's most oft-discussed programs. Seeking his identity, Arlene Francis, blindfolded, said, "The guest could be Dizzy Dean," to which fellow panelist Dorothy Kilgallen replied, "Oh, no, this man is too intelligent." Later she apologized. His feelings unruffled, Diz did a semibow and said, "That's perfectly all right, ma'am. You never meant no harm."

Another role was the voice of indignancy. During one game four balks were called on an opposing pitcher. Situated in the broadcast booth, Diz stridently objected. The umpires, he said, were mocking the sport. "You know what I'd do if I was out there," he advised his viewers. "I'd take offen my glove and I'd give it to the umparr and I'd give him the ball and I'd tell him, 'Say, Mr. Umparr, you know so much about how a fellow ought to pitch, well sir, you pitch and let me umparr.' "

When the need demanded, Diz could become author of the virtuoso ad-lib. "That Ted Williams," he said, "he reminds me of a long-legged pelican," a phrase which prompted one local wag to say, "Diz just says whatever comes into his head—even if it's nothing."

Towering, though, above all Dean's roles was the folk seer, the teller of stories and scenes; awkward pauses in a game were few and seldom noted. Diz regaled viewers with a medley of hillbilly tunes, with anecdotes of Frankie Frisch and the Mudcat Band, with a detailed sketch of the fried chicken Pat would set on the table when Ol' Diz strode home—and with the portraits only Jay Hanna could verbally construct.

"That there Yogi Berra," he exclaimed, "is the heartiest-eating ballplayer I have knowed since Babe Ruth. Yogi needs a half-dozen hot dogs and three or four bags of popcorn just to keep going during a game. Then he's ready for the biggest plate of spaghetti in town after the game. I'd rather take a span of mules to feed than Yogi."

One vignette involved a dog named Suds. Sighting a flock of pigeons above Yankee Stadium, Dean's rapt notice rose. "Swing up the camera, Mr. Cameraman, and let everybody see the birds," he shouted. The camera swung and Ol' Diz sighed. "Wish my old Texas meat dog, Suds, was here. Best bird-hunting dog I ever owned. The skillet never gets rusty when Suds is around."

Yarns arose about fishing. "Man, wait 'til I get home to them streams." Or traveling. "I think I'll take a trip to Novus Scofus." Or the St. Louis Browns. "The Browns is sluggish, but they ain't really as bad as they've showed in New York," he said. "It must be something about ol' Gotham or this stadium that makes them Browns lose their pose," which converted, naturally, to poise.

Dean retained his poise, all right, but the Yankees soon lost Ol' Diz. Tired of urban congestion ("That New York," he snapped, "it's just too big for a country boy"), knowing his image was resented by several front-office figures ("Can you imagine a less dignified clown?" one laughed), aware that the Yankees wanted Joe DiMaggio as a post-game television host, Dean returned to St. Louis in October, 1951. He would broadcast Browns' games, Falstaff announced, with Bud Blattner over the brewery's twenty-station network. Diz also teamed with Al Helfer on Mutual Broadcast System's "Game of the Day" series, radio broadcasts aired over the network's affiliate stations. "If the Browns are hot, I'll do a lot of their games," Dean said. "If not, I'll be with Mutual," a pledge which told America where Dean would spend most of 1952. Entrapped in a futile fight for survival, the Browns finished seventh. Two years later they became the Baltimore Orioles.

Diz was far more favored than the Browns, and few events were kinder than Twentieth-Century Fox's 1951 decision to make a movie of his life. "Jees," Diz chortled over the movie rights, "they're going to give me fifty thousand smackers just fer *livin'*." Priorities varied. Instinctively, Pat Dean ordered the company to stagger Dizzy's payments over the next five years, easing their tax burden. Paul Dean, wary and unsure, balked at Fox's $15,000 offer. "Finally, I said I'd give him $5,000 of my own rights if he'd sign the dang contract," his brother later recalled, "or we might never have got the movie made." Diz was more intrigued by whom would play the leading man. Told that Dan Dailey had been cast as Ol' Diz, only to suffer a nervous disorder, Dean roared, "That figures. After this Danny feller found out he was going to have to take my part he went nuts." When Dailey

Dizzy Dean rehearses "Wabash Cannonball" as he prepares to make his first recording for Colonial Records, Chapel Hill, North Carolina, in 1954.

recovered, he shared top billing with Joanne Dru (Patricia Dean). Richard Crenna, later of "Real McCoys" television fame, played brother Paul. "The Pride of St. Louis," a ninety-three minute film, debuted at New York's Rivoli Theatre in 1952. Reviews were widely mixed. Ken Smith labeled the movie "one of the worst I've ever seen." Tagging the script "howlingly humorous," Bosley Crowther said, "It is not Dizzy Dean, the Cardinal pitcher, who is the hero of this film. It is Dizzy Dean, the character, the whiz from the Ozark hills." Calling Dan Dailey's role "a masterpiece," Alton Cook claimed Dean's career had "become an engaging and amiable comedy." Perhaps another account most closely defined the film. "It isn't a bad picture, except that one of baseball's most vivid personalities has been hammered into the formula—boyhood, rookie, star, love," the story read. "It isn't fair to Ol' Diz. There's never been another like him."

The premier over, Dean's focus shifted to politics, Ol' Diz endorsing Dwight Eisenhower's presidential campaign. "I made $125,000 last year," he disclosed. "That was during the government of Harry Truman. And I guarantee you I had more take home pay when I was in the Cardinal gang, who never were knowed as fellows who give nothin' for nothin'." His focus shifted to Falstaff, who ordered publication of a new booklet, *Dizzy Dean's Baseball Dictionary*. And to Bill Veeck, pioneering owner of the Browns, who proclaimed May 25, 1952, as Dizzy Dean Day at Sportsman's Park. With more than twenty-three thousand fans attending, Diz was given a goat, chickens and two prize Hereford cows.

Sigma Delta Chi, the professional journalism fraternity, granted Dean a Doctor of Slanguage Degree as well. Adorned in academic robes, the Master accepted, saying, "I got as far in school as the Second Reader, only I didn't learn it all."

The following year, favored once more, Diz was inducted into the Hall of Fame, where he again lent support to a favored theme. "It's pretty nice for an ol' Arkansas cotton picker to be up here with these city boys," said Dean, who told the throng in Cooperstown, "The Good Lord was good to me. He gave me a strong body, a good right arm and a weak mind," failing to mention a new home in Dallas, oil investments and three hundred-acre farm, all of which were his alone.

Dean completed the season, then saw the St. Louis Browns dissolve. While the club fled to Baltimore, Ol' Diz returned home. There he spoke of his love for music—"First time I ever heard them guitar notes in 'Great Speckled Birds,' they brang the hair up on my neck"—and signed a contract for his initial record. Since 1941, when he performed it publicly for the first time, Dizzy Dean and "Wabash Cannonball" had been inexorably linked. "I sanged it during a dull game," Diz said. "I like to a blew them all out of the tub." Now, in late 1954, Colonial Records of Chapel Hill, North Carolina, issued "Wabash Cannonball" with "You Don't Have to Be from the Country" on the reverse side, both warbled by the Great One's baritone voice. One disc jockey played the record seven times in a row; the demand in small towns and cities staggered even Colonial officials. Ultimately, with Dean's thrust and blessing, the "Wabash Cannonball" almost surpassed "Take Me out to the Ballgame" as baseball's most cherished ballad. That, however, required the mystique of national television, a medium which enshrined forever Dean's image as a folk hero, which canonized the legend and made extravagant his appeal.

II

Downtown Stamford, Connecticut's Roger Smith Hotel towered above adjacent blocks. Inside was a bar, uncrowded and dark. Now sixty-three, the man at a corner table rose and gave greeting.

"How you doing?" he said. "Always good to see you."

"That goes double for me, Mel," I said.

For twenty-five years Melvin Israel Allen commanded the most fanatical following of any announcer in the nation. Over a Northeastern network of more than fifty stations, some of which reached to the Rockies, his exuberant praise of New York Yankee feats brought genuine excitement to small burgs and cities, to provinces located hundreds of miles from the ballpark in the Bronx. Partisans hung on every word. Critics claimed he talked too much, a complaint which masked their true intent. The woods were full of Yankee-haters, and Mel Allen drew the haters' wrath. Few questioned his talent, or denied the impact he made.

Across America the republic's baseball cult divided into two schools —those who proclaimed that Allen was nearly as exciting as being at the ballpark and those who prayed that an attack of laryngitis would silence him forever. Vocal, dramatic, a reporter of unequaled skills, Allen lent music to his voice, a voice which spoke for hours and boasted a sustaining quality few could rival and none surpassed. He began in 1939, an Alabamian in New York. In 1964 he was fired, a stunning dismissal which drew the public's rage. In between 1939 and 1964 he did radio and television for the Yankees. He announced more World Series games than any man in baseball annals. He televised the All-Star Game, the Rose Bowl, the East-West football classic, and heavyweight fights. He became the sports voice of Movietone Newsreels. He was the most famous sportscaster in the world. He worked with Red Barber, with Curt Gowdy, with Russ Hodges and Jim Woods—and with Jay Hanna Dean, another Southern boy come north.

"I found Diz a lot of fun," Mel began. "He was always so chock-full of stories. I'd love to hear them. He had, as you know, this great sense of humor. And he had fun in all phases of his life—work, recreation. He used to love to golf; matter of fact, Diz came to the Yankees because Dan Topping was a great friend of his. And they were friends largely because Dan liked to golf with Diz."

Diz joined Mel in 1950. "He did some radio, but mostly TV. What I remember about Diz was this—he was a personality more than a broadcaster. He could get serious with you once in a while, but once he announced solo, when he did play-by-play, it was show-biz time. Missing a pitch or two didn't faze him. And he was smart, intelligent— and how he loved to sing that song. What was it? The artillery. . . ?"

"Wabash Cannonball!" I said.

"That's right," he said, smiling, "that's what I meant. Diz had a method and a style all his own. And he knew what he was doing. Some of the things he did—a guy slud into third—they were professional. Once he said slid correctly, by mistake, and he corrected himself. He wanted to goof up. But even more of his muffs were natural. The guy just didn't have much education. But he had an excitement about him. He was a great name. And boy, was he an extrovert."

Mel Allen was rather expressive, too. For a quarter of a century he broadcast baseball with expansive detail, lending to his profession enormous charm and color. Baseball buffs suffered with his puns ("There was no power shortage on that one," Allen roared as Mickey Mantle, moments after the lights had been restored at an evening game, slammed a booming home run). They echoed his cheers, rejoiced in his prose, repeated his trademark phrase. "How about that!" arose in 1949;

Mel Allen (center) was easily America's most famous and highly paid sports-caster in 1959.

for a decade and more afterward, Allen and his fans delighted in using the cherished chant. When Mantle homered, when Ford rallied in the clutch, when Yogi Berra demolished a rival team's hopes—"How about that!" was sure to follow. Long before the 1970s, when announcers began reaping more notice than the sports events themselves, Mel Allen had become a household name.

Few remembered Mel Allen for his reportorial skills. They revered, instead, the voice, deep and vibrant, the voice which lured and never tired, which made an audience listen—even Yankee-haters. They loved the pet terms ("Ballantine Blast . . . White Owl Wallop") that Allen invented and brought national fame; or the exuberance which seemed to mark every inning of every game; or the emotions he aroused among even the most inactive of fans. Announcers today, I said, seem unable to stir the same response.

"That's the other side of the coin," he replied, staring at the sunlight. "There are the big mouths, the ones who dominate an event. And then there are the others, actually quite a few, who tend toward dry, matter-of-fact announcing.

"A lot of guys today, they don't say much. And it gets to be a real bore, which all goes back to the fact that too many people in TV think you don't have to talk. The picture, they say, will tell the story. You don't have to say a thing."

"But that was never your style," I protested. "You loved to talk."

"Yes, some people said so," said Allen, laughing. "But seriously, there are a lot of things going on, things the camera can't show. A base runner maybe takes a shorter lead off first. Or the left fielder moves to his right two steps. Or the third baseman moves in and to his bag. You see, baseball's a hard game to televise—the camera can't show the whole field. So it's your job, it's your duty," he continued, slapping his knees, "to tell details, to offset what the viewer can't see at home."

Mel Allen paused. "I run into people all the time," he said. "Most of them say, 'Jimminy Cricket, the games now seem so slow. There must be something going on, but the announcers just sit back and don't say a thing.' People tell me they used to enjoy our games when the rain stopped play. Then we'd swap stories and we'd really roam. I could never have been aloof, reserved. Man, I got into a ballgame. I got involved." So, too, did those who listened.

Despite his national stature, the network exposure he gained, Allen was most vividly linked with New York. From 1947 through 1964, eighteen years in which they were idolized and defiled, the Yankees won 1,748 games, fifteen pennants and ten World Series, success equaled neither before nor since. One's sentiments toward Allen rested mostly upon one's allegiance. Yankee partisans, arrogant in perpetual victory, marveled at Allen's penchant for drama, his capacity for verbal grace. Yankee-haters, equally as legion, grew vehement in defeat. One embittered soul sent telegrams to *any* club which beat New York, even though its sole victory might be the finale of a five-game series. Another sent a wire which reached Allen during the second inning of a 1958 World Series game. "Allen, you Yankee-lover," it read, "shut up." The message was sent two hours *before* the game began.

"I never tried to be controversial," Allen said, "but you naturally were so because of the team you were with. You couldn't escape. People said I rooted. Hell, no. If these guys had heard some other announcers—Bob Prince, a good friend of mine, in Pittsburgh, or Harry Caray and Jack Brickhouse in the Midwest—they'd never have said I was biased. Those announcers *literally* root. I never tried that; New York was too cosmopolitan. It had transients from other parts of the country who rooted for other teams. I couldn't have been biased. This town wouldn't have allowed it."

"Yes," I agreed, "but critics said you were partisan".

"No, they didn't," he said, nearly shouting. "They said I was prejudiced. You see, there's a difference. Prejudice, you see only one side; partisan, you see both sides and give full credit, but you obviously favor one side. I was loyal to the Yankees. I worked for them. And I was partisan, not biased. I had respect for the opposition.

"Oh, I got more excited for the home club, caused partially by the fact that you had more home fans in the ballpark. They shoved you up—their waves of noise made you more vocal. When they shouted, you would, too. But I never really cheered. You fit your broadcasting style to fit your area, and in New York you couldn't be a shill."

"Even so," I said "people threw barbs your way."

"Everybody loves a winner," he said quietly and with pride, "yet they love to knock a winner, too. And what there is about human nature that makes folks do that, I don't know. They never knock a man who doesn't show his head."

Allen's urbanity suited Manhattan well. But Ol' Diz had also survived there, indeed flourished, and few would label his bearing unduly suave.

"Oh, Diz did OK," Mel conceded, "but he wasn't accepted with overpowering force. Diz was too folksy, too rural. Maybe he was before his time. I know that in 1950 country and western music would never have gone over in this area. Now it does. Another factor was that Dean broadcast daily here. Singing a song constantly, mispronouncing names all the time—people got tired of them. And it's strange that a guy like Diz, as popular as he was, wasn't a gigantic hit. It just goes to show you how tough the business is."

"Dean was hailed critically, your ratings were high," I said, "and when Diz left New York for St. Louis, he did so on his own."

While Allen gloried in the role of public figure, at ease on television, at home in crowds, rare were those who knew him.

"Yeah, that's right," Allen said. "Don't get me wrong—he did a good job. And I think if I'd had the chance to work with him directly over radio, Diz would have developed into an excellent announcer. He could call a play, don't misunderstand, it was just the way he called it. You couldn't fault his excitement, the feeling he put into a game. If only he'd been a little more sophisticated." Silence followed. Then quiet laughter. Then the inevitable praise, delivered with warmth, meant to allay any criticism implied. "I'll say this for Diz. He was a helluva guy and people loved him. Maybe not his style, but as a person, yes."

Now, as a decade or two earlier, the character of Mel Allen tended to be baffling and elusive. There was a complexity to his manner, and an element of sadness, too, which lured sympathy from even his most ardent foes. Unmarried, childless, Allen sought in public the solace his private fortunes denied. His career was his life, the wife and children he never had.

Another spirit remained which could not be easily denied. The Allen of 1957 was a sponsor's delight, a man who helped sales by crying, "Go grab yourself a Ballantine," then unveiled his omnipresent White Owl cigar. The Allen of twenty years later strove valiantly to sell himself; the delivery was halting and deliberate, his phrases less assured, the poise less evident than during the harvest years.

Where was Allen's aura, the enchanting talents of old? During the late 1960s, he and his younger brother, Larry, purchased a Canada Dry Bottling Company in Stamford, where I first met him in 1972.

Driving to dinner, Allen turned wistful and depressed, his manner quite unlike the person who once uplifted innumerable springs and summers.

After dinner we returned to the Canada Dry plant, where Allen deliberately backed his sedan into one of the company trucks. "I've told those drivers a thousand times not to park in my parking space," Mel said as he started his car in reverse. "They've hit me enough times, so I figure I owe 'em one." Two years later, when I next saw him, the agony and disquiet had faded, or at least become submerged. Mel seemed relaxed and convivial, gracious and aware. Then, as now, Allen remained a complex and solitary prism. Who would ever penetrate this gifted and perplexing man?

The Yankees fired Allen in early October, 1964, an error of staggering effect; New Yorkers, who prided themselves on immunity to surprise, found themselves, for once, truly shocked. Several months later NBC stripped Mel of the Rose Bowl and other football events, giving them to Curt Gowdy, his former assistant in New York. Utterly unforseen, the disclosures prompted a torrent of unbridled reports. "Rumors ran wild," Mel said, rumors he was powerless to check.

Meanwhile, thousands of letters, many of them bitter and impassioned, flooded Yankee offices on the victim's behalf. Stunned by the outpouring and intensity of Allen support, the Yankees refused comment on Mel's dismissal. NBC followed suit. So, to his ultimate chagrin, did the principal himself. "The Yankees never held a press conference to announce my leaving," Mel complained. "They just let it leak out. So there were all sort of lies spread around. And when people are left to believe anything, they're going to believe the worst."

Even today, Allen insisted, he was unsure why the Yankees fired him. "I walked in to sign what I thought would be a new contract. Suddenly Topping said, 'I got some bad news for you.'

"And I said, 'What's that, Dan?'

"He said, 'Well, Mel, we're going to make some changes. We're not going to renew your contract.' "

Allen's voice grew soft, the tortured memories again aroused. "They never gave me any reason," Mel repeated. "All Dan said was, 'It wasn't anything you did, and it wasn't CBS,' " which had recently purchased the club.

"So I said, 'Well, that leaves only one party' "—Ballantine Beer, known to millions as *the* Yankee sponsors, located in Newark, N.J. but seeking to expand. "They'd made a real bad mistake," Allen said. "Most breweries had built smaller affiliates around the country, cutting shipping costs. Ballantine hadn't. Instead they enlarged their home brewery and produced all the stuff there. The transportation costs were bad, just awful, and they started struggling just to stay alive. They knew they had to cut the budget, and heads started to roll. And my head was among them."

What had prompted Mel Allen's stunning fall? The answer lay in the turbulent career to which he clung, the unending hours he scheduled. They at last became the unconquered foe.

"Mel could never sit down and enjoy himself," said an announcer who worked during Allen's era, who knew him better than most. "After a game all of us would go to Toots Shors in New York. And Mel would get on the telephone and call up an agency guy in, say, Cleveland, to see if he could do a lousy show on radio at midnight. Or he'd fly to Chicago for a commercial. You couldn't get through to Mel. He had this obsession, this burning desire to do all the events, *all* the big ones, to become the best-paid announcer for sports in America. And I said to him, 'You've achieved your goal. You're single. What the hell are you doing? Why don't you slow down?'

"But he couldn't. He just rushed and ran. And eventually it cost him. He started to ramble; you couldn't shut him up. He had everybody befuddled. And what happened was that, trying to keep himself going for all these things, Mel took a pill in the morning to get up, a pill at night to sleep, a pill to control his weight. His metabolism got so fouled up he didn't know what he was taking, or when. He drove himself ragged. It was one of the saddest things I've ever seen."

The Yankees hired Joe Garagiola in December, 1964. "As my replacement, I wished him nothing but the best," Allen said. Early in 1965 Curt Gowdy was signed as both baseball and football voice for NBC. Mel Allen was out. "Here, also, it was financial," he said. "NBC was going in with the American Football League in 1965. And Curt had got in on the ground floor with the football people—he had excellent contacts. So when the network grabbed the AFL, Gowdy was the natural choice. Then they put him on baseball as well. Saved 'em some money. They only had to pay one guy, not two."

Mel Allen's fortunes, cresting in early 1964, had shattered within a year. Alone and incredulous, still stunned by the flood tide of change, he broadcast Milwaukee games in 1965, then was bypassed when the Braves headed South the following season. In 1966 he commuted to Cleveland, televising games on a limited scale. He did weekend sports for the NBC affiliate in New York. Nowhere, however, were there rave reviews.

"Hell," Allen said as he straddled the chair. "I could have gone with four, five clubs. There were always, in fact, possibilities right here." During 1966, George Weiss, former Yankee general manager then president of the Mets, rendered a tentative bid. "He was a real good friend. He wanted me bad." But Rheingold Beer served as the chief Met sponsor; Allen's reign with Ballantine, once the envy of his peers, returned to curse his lot. "They were real nice about it," he recalled. "All they said was, 'Mel, every time you say Rheingold, people are still going to think Ballantine.' That association becomes negative. You get stereotyped."

There had been times, he said, when other clubs desired his presence. "Johnny McHale of Montreal wanted me to come and broadcast his games," Allen claimed. "And Charles Finley—ol' Charlie O.—wanted

Mel Allen (right) waves to the crowd at Yankee Stadium on "Mel Allen Day,"
1950. Former Postmaster General James Farley presides at the ceremony.

me to go with him to Oakland in 1968, when the A's moved West. We had a long talk, real long. But we'd just bought the Canada Dry franchise in Stamford and I didn't want to walk away. So I told Charley, 'I'll broadcast your games if I can live here during the off-season.' But he wanted me all year, you know, to do publicity stuff, to promote the team, and I just couldn't. "Anyhow," he said, "who the hell wants to leave New York? After you've been at the top, everything else is downhill."

Mel Allen and his beloved Bronx Bombers both collapsed. By 1965, crippled by injury and age, the Yankees' dynasty ended. Boredom enwrapped the broadcast booth, mediocrity the field. One year later the team finished tenth in the ten-team league. During the late 1960s, reeling from defeat, club officials disclosed a five-year program; another pennant was its aim. The Yankees entered 1976, when the famine finally ended, in the ninth year of their five-year plan.

"You know," Allen remarked, "letters poured in after I left. And over ten years later it hasn't stopped yet. People are still writing in to the Yankees, wondering where Mel is. And that's unusual. I mean, cripe, you take movie stars—three years of inactivity, and they're forgotten." Not Mel Allen. Who could forget him?

"Sure I'd love to rejoin them," Allen said, "but, hell, I'm doing a lot now." He listed his current trades. He was employed as Director of Public Relations for Canada Dry. He would host a syndicated program for major league baseball. He was involved with a radio series, "Mel Allen Remembers," for Mobil Oil. A year before he had appeared on "The Way It Was," a highly-acclaimed television show. Yet these were relatively minor parts; the limelight eluded him.

"You know," said Allen, "if a network or baseball job came along, I'd grab it in a minute. Because this other work is not really my bag. Sports announcing is, always has been, and I have to hope my chance will come again."

III

Wrapped in jargon of two decades later, the CBS "Game of the Week" became a happening, caused partly by its novelty, partly by baseball's immense prestige, partly by the fluency which Bud Blattner and Pee Wee Reese revealed. Yet looming above them all, casting a specter across the 1950's and 60's vision of televised sports, was the enormous, usually inflated figure of Dizzy Dean. "He created the audience before we ever said a word," recalled Blattner, who preceded Reese as television sidekick to Ol' Diz. "It was going to be Dizzy Dean on the CBS 'Game of the Week' with me, or like, with podner."

From 1955 to 1965 Dean and "podner" comprised sport's most celebrated announcing duo. During the first two seasons a Saturday game was broadcast each week over CBS affiliate stations; in 1957 a Sunday game was added. Almost twenty years later ABC claimed "Monday Night Football" altered the evening routine and viewing penchant of millions of Americans, that the broadcasts lured clusters of converted fans around television sets in living rooms and bars. Accepted even as gospel, a dubious assumption indeed, its effect paled beside the ovations which greeted "Game of the Week" and Jay Hanna Dean. "Monday Night Football" polished, stylized, improved upon series which had come before; ABC's gamble was that sports broadcasts in prime time were not destined to fail. CBS's stakes were just as high and far more uncertain. No weekly series had ever been broadcast nationally; Dean and his cohorts charted totally virgin ground. Had the endeavor flopped, its impact might have radically altered the future fortunes of televised sports. Instead, the opposite occurred, and a bonanza of staggering dimensions unfurled.

From the "Game of the Week," sponsors reaped profits, Reese and Blattner national notice, Dean celebrity status and CBS an audience which staggered industry brass. "The reaction was stunning. Just stunning," said Bill MacPhail, director of CBS Sports during Dizzy's reign. "We'd get reports from towns like Cedar Rapids, Iowa, or Little Rock, and they'd simply close down in the afternoon when Dean was on." By 1957 NBC, all too aware of Ol' Diz's success, began a weekly Saturday series of its own. Two years later it entered the Sunday field. The contest became no contest; CBS lured ratings which often doubled its principal rival. Dean and Blattner, then Ol' Diz and Reese, bordered on the invincible, and the tides, soon irrevocably behind them, were never turned aside. "Dean's popularity, and thus his broadcasts, were enormously powerful in the small towns," said MacPhail, graying at sixty-two. "In the hinterlands it was incredible. Watching Dizzy Dean was a religion. An absolute religion."

Dean's revival hour blanketed most of the nation. Like NBC, CBS was not allowed to beam its weekly encounters into American and National League cities. Major league moguls, fearful that national broadcasts might harm their own regional networks, made sure the rivalry never arose; both league's cities were always blacked out. While Denver and Buffalo chortled at the tales that Ol' Diz spun, New York remained without his weekend laughs. Dallas and Miami rollicked with Dean's comic presence, but Cleveland and Chicago were given pablum as network fare instead. "We used to have split programming. The major league cities got golf or tennis or stuff like that," said MacPhail. "Today you couldn't do it. You couldn't leave out New York and Detroit and the other big towns. But back then—the 50s and 60s— network sports weren't that powerful yet. We could be more daring. We could give Dean's series his chance."

Week after raucous week Ol' Diz was at America's disposal. Until 1958, when New York's National League teams moved west, Los Angeles and San Francisco gave witness to the humor which Dean weekly spawned. The Far West, the Southwest, the Rockies and Midwest Plains—all served to underscore Dizzy's mounting allure. So, too, the South, Dean's own by custom and tradition, compelled by his message and stirred by his style. "All this land was untapped territory. It wasn't until the mid-sixties that these places began to get major league teams. Before that, they were ours. We went in every week.'' Only in the teeming Northeast, where many major league franchises lay, did ''Game of the Week'' sporadically appear. Even here, the mosaic was mixed. Though Manhattan and its environs saw Dean not, New York's other urban centers—Rochester, Syracuse, Albany and Buffalo—alternately derided his antics and delighted in their effect. Entering New England, the split continued; Boston was without access, Hartford and Montpelier with. Despite the affiliate split, one constant remained; wherever shown, ''Game of the Week'' demolished opposing programs that had the ill-fortune to appear. One could visit Scranton, Pa., for instance, if one were so inclined, and find network ratings which neared any the bedrock South could compile. ''I didn't care for him personally,'' MacPhail continued, ''but on the air you had to like him. During *any* broadcast you had to laugh nine, ten times.'' At the least, memory claimed.

Dean's esteem, and the approval which met his comic thrusts, rose yearly amid taut, competitive times. During the late 1950s more than a thousand radio stations, all involved with individual clubs, saturated the country with play-by-play. The Mutual Broadcast Company, airing its ''Game of the Day'' each afternoon from a major league park, sent daily radio accounts to another five hundred affiliates. By 1960, with ABC now hosting a Saturday series, three television networks also shared in baseball's media wars. One hundred and twenty-three games were broadcast nationally, compared with forty-one fifteen years later, five per weekend against two in 1977. Radio, which had served to widen baseball's mystique, was eclipsed by a visual addiction that turned overwhelming in scope. While Barber and Allen lifted baseball's appeal in Brooklyn and New York, Vin Scully molded interest at Ebbets Field and the Los Angeles Coliseum. The Giants' Russ Hodges spanned the continent, announcing from the Polo Grounds, then Candlestick Park, while Waite Hoyt tested well-crafted yarns amid the boundless memories of Crosley Field. There were other figures, too, voices like Ernie Harwell with the Giants and Orioles, Gowdy with the Yankees and Red Sox, Jack Buck at ABC and Lindsey Nelson with NBC, Bob Elson at Comiskey Park and Bob Wolff in Washington. Radio and television gave baseball an unprecedented lure; not until the mid-1960s, when baseball reduced its network schedule, its national voices becoming unforgivably reserved, did the diamond game's place in Americana finally falter and recede.

During the ten years after 1955, however, few thought of decline or fall. Television was still new, a precocious infant inviting novelty and daring. Baseball was ushered into America's homes, into the social center of its life. If the broadcasts were vibrant, viewers thought, why then, so must the game. Style eclipsed substance; announcers became part-informer, part-observer, part-Broadway performer . . . ie. Dizzy Dean.

Ol' Diz sensed instinctively what scores of polished, solemn announcers a decade later failed totally to grasp. "Baseball's fundamental weakness on TV is the long wait between pitches," columnist Jack Craig once wrote. "And for most kids, the slow pace is intolerable . . . If a sport turns off youngsters at the TV level, it seriously reduces efforts to lure them later on." Baseball does not inherently televise well. The 'long wait between pitches' lingers, the 'slow pace' remains. The television screen negates the sweep of ballfield and diamond; the major battle between hitter and pitcher can transcend into televised boredom. Football telecasts much more adroitly—both teams are wholly viewed on the TV screen, the action visibly developing, its movement easily followed. Not so with the summer game. Unlike football, baseball cannot "sell itself" on television; its announcers must undertake that task. This Allen and Barber understood; they went on to enliven as well as report their work. They were forceful and persuasive, and in large part responsible for cloaking baseball in semi-deity garb. "It's not play-by-play that matters," said Bob Prince, "it's what's said between the pitches that counts." Hampered by silent souls, announcers who sparsely report the unfolding drama, baseball can become a crashing bore. By the early 1970s, baseball's network image boasted as much exuberance as a morning stroll through the Abbey of the Genesee. Small wonder several doctors advised heart patients to adopt NBC's Saturday "Game of the Week"; if that failed to calm them, what would? Enlivened, however, by announcers who lend a native eloquence, who *use* the game's languid tempo to intersperse narrative and comic prose, baseball can be riotously entertaining, unsurpassed among its athletic peers. Prince and Harry Caray would flourish in any sport; only here, however, could their flair and flavor wholly thrive. Above the field, as upon it, the solitary artist excels.

Few excelled more than Jay Hanna Dean. "Our success wasn't that we were smarter than NBC, or that our production was more skilled. It was Dean," said MacPhail, dismissed by CBS in 1974, now Vice President of Robert Wold Broadcast Company in New York. "He was just very homey. It was warm, very warm, and very homespun, and very much accepted."

Few reaped more riches than Diz. "It was a funny format, the "Game of the Week." Falstaff owned the broadcasts—we didn't. We aired the show, but the rights were their's. They made a mint, we got the ratings. We were very proud of the Dean-Falstaff thing. And we were quite upset when it ended."

Few lent more humor, either. "This," said MacPhail, reverting to a cigarette and adjusting his tie, "is where Dean's pioneering took effect. He was the first announcer *ever* to inject comedy into a game. And I think an overriding concern today is that too many guys take themselves too seriously on televised sports. Of course, there was always a question of when he was acting and when he was not—I think some of Diz's funnies on the air were put on, some of his pronunciations.

But we never discouraged it, because it added to his color. And you don't mess with success.

"He was two different people," MacPhail said, his manner minus warmth. "He was much warmer, in fact, on the air. I'm not saying at times he wasn't funny in person, even though it might disgust you how he was constantly played up to—Gene Kirby, his producer, in particular, was like a caddie to him, barking at his slightest whim— but on his broadcasts, it was impossible not to sit there and roar. You got to like him. Colorful, funny, obviously knowledgeable.

"I wouldn't say he was just a big hillbilly," he said, "because he could be very cunning. I know he played golf with some big people— the head of Goodyear and J. Walter Thompson— and I'd hear stories about his integrity. It seems Diz would play very poorly with them, then the next day, after they'd made a bet for $2,000, he'd come back and shoot an eighty-two. Set them up and win. So there were some bad vibes." He paused, looking much like his father. "No, he was just not my type of person. Very hard to handle—he'd do what he wanted to. I also recognized, of course, that there was never any thought of getting rid of him and replacing Ol' Diz. None at all. *Ever.*"

Americans saw only the public Dean and thought they knew the private. Intuitively, without backstage counsel, Ol' Diz realized the essence of his appeal. "The thing I've got to guard against," Dean confided as 1955 dawned, "is improvement. If I start talking better," citing a danger which never approached, "they'll throw me out." Beneath the facade lay an abundance of parts, roles which varied in intent and degree. Diz could be the pitcher's ally, pleading for a legalized spitball. "A pitcher these days really needs a shotgun out there, but I guess that's against the law. The ball they're playing with is not just lively, it's hysterical." Or a friend to players fading and almost done. "I ain't hesertant to knock," he said, "but not a guy who's slipping. Times like that, a feller needs a lift." He could praise the grace of baseball, "It's made me what I was," then assault the sport as commercial and cold. "It's strictly a business. You see the same thing at the park every day, and that's why people stay home and watch TV. I'm talking against my livelihood now, but that's the truth."

Truth, Diz knew, was an attribute he could afford to uphold; financially, he hardly needed CBS' presence, though his ego assuredly did. Irritated by Dean's autonomy, MacPhail required him, nonetheless; to dump the Master would enrage hundreds of satellite stations. Wealth and security meant unbridled freedom, no one permitted to censor or review. Diplomacy was not completely shunned (Dean once refused to do a Falstaff beer commercial—because the day was Mother's Day), but Ol' Diz became noted more for candor, much of it outrageous. What, fans asked, would Ol' Diz say next? No one seemed to know, least of all Bill MacPhail. "We had no control over what he'd do each week. I'd sit there in front of the television and cringe."

Dean turned rebel while his series thrived. Over CBS, he publicly praised "The Dinah Shore Show," one of NBC's most valued ventures. "It's the best variety show on TV," Diz boasted, moving MacPhail to shudder and wince. "These things just weren't done, plugging a rival network," MacPhail remembered. "But we couldn't tell Dizzy not to do it, because if you did, he'd get more determined that he would." An ardent airplane foe, Dean chastised them on the air. "Here CBS is selling time to American and United Airlines," said MacPhail, "and Dean says, 'Podner, I hate to fly, but if you have to, Eastern is much the best.' And I'd die. Just die.'"

Seeking to avoid the game's tailend teams, CBS purchased games from the reigning powers. "We didn't want to televise losing clubs, so we showed lots of Yankee games, some Cardinals, etc.," said MacPhail. "But we didn't have rights to all the teams. It would have been economically unfeasible." Thus occurred one of Dean's more memorable barbs. "I don't know how our folks come off callin' this the 'Game of the Week,' " Diz told CBS viewers during a one-sided encounter. "There's a much better game—Dodgers and Giants—*over on NBC.*"

Dizzy's honesty touched other topics, too. Long before the phrase acquired in-vogue acceptance, Jay Hanna Dean described baseball 'like it was,' usually couched in biting terms. Kid-gloves treatment was out, blunt reportage in. Why "purty up" a game, he asked. A mediocre pitcher had "nothin' on the ball 'cept a cover," a hapless hitter "couldn't hit home plate with a hoe." Umpires were a choice subject for attack. Once Diz beguiled viewers with an incident from several decades past. "I kept disputing the umpire's call one afternoon," he said, "and that evening I run into the umpire at a chop house. 'That was quite a game out there today, wasn't it?' I asked him. 'What a shame get to see it.' " Few mortals were sacred. "That batter shakin' his head down there—he don't know what's going on," Diz said while a dispute engulfed the field. "I don't know what he don't know, but I know he don't know. Look at the umpires," he roared. "They don't know, either. If I knowed what they don't know, folks, I'd sure tell you. And I ain't just a-kiddin'.''

Dean's language, erratic at best, turned ungodly as "Game of the Week" progressed. Diz achieved what no team in baseball could even attempt—make a shambles of the New York Yankees. Television viewers, accustomed to Yankee clubs which made an annual mockery of the pennant race, saw Ol' Diz shuffle the players en masse. Tony Kuebaak replaced Tony Kubek; Bobby Risharsen, Richardson. Mickey Mantle became Mannle; Moose Skowron, Scarn; Enos Slaughter, the former Cardinal warrior, was converted into Enose Slooter. New York's battery changed from Jim Coates and Elston Howard to Jim Coots and Estone Howard, with Ryn Duurn (formerly Ryne Duren) in relief. Across the dugout sauntered Casey Stingle (Stengel), shouting advice to reserve Marv Thornberry (Throneberry), counsel the future New York Met utterly failed to heed.

Dean's thrusts were not reserved for Yankees only; open season was cast upon any players whose names ran two syllables or more. Once he and Kirby, subbing for Reese, aired a game from Cincinnati. "They had all kinds of guys with long names," Diz said. "Ted Kluszewski was on third. Somebody like Odrowski on second, maybe Timowitz on first. Boy, was I sweatin', hopin' nobody'd get a hit and I wouldn't have to call all them names." Rebuking Dean's desire, the Reds' batter lashed a line drive toward left-center field, worth two bases and certain to score three runs. "There's a long drive," Dean screamed, sensing danger as the fractured runners streaked toward home. "Yep, it's a long drive—and here's Gene Kirby to tell you all about it." Which, of course, Gene did, friend and caddie still.

Earthy, uninhibited, his gospel impelled by the times, Ol' Diz became companion for five hundred afternoons. "In many of the cities, even more so the small towns, that he appeared," marveled MacPhail, "it was all that was discussed. If you asked folks what their top ten programs were all week, he'd be right up there." For inhabitants of the Dakota plains, of Virginia's swaying hills, of the sweeping farmlands of upstate New York, Dean was more than "right up there"; he became a part of life. Each weekend the ritual occurred. Saturday broke teeming and hot; why was the sun always present? Sandlot games came first, their impact heightened as one's age declined. Each player aped a major league figure; some chose Roberto Clemente, others Mantle, or Mays. Late-morning television followed. For hours we sat transfixed, enamored by the deeds of Sky King and Dennis the Menace and Woody Woodpecker and a dozen idols more. Roy Rogers and Dale Evans were giants among the heroes we craved. Lunch came next, quickly ordered and hurriedly consumed. Then more television—Cliff Arquette as Charlie Weaver, Dennis James and his Saturday newsreel, cartoons combed from forgotten files. At 1:45 "Baseball Leadoff" appeared, hosted by Gerry Coleman or Pee Wee Reese or Ol' Diz himself. Two o'clock meant the "Game of the Week." Viewers loved Dean's plots and stories, the telegrams read to "good ol' folks" back home, the "Wabash Cannonball" sung weekly, the comedy which rounded out scenes. Sunday's scenario, too, followed strictly patterned parts; the morning paper, church, a wild exodus as the benediction ended, the short trek home. The game began and you were "podner" once more. Dean made you laugh. He made you listen. He made life gentle. He let you love.

Even dull games seemed intriguing, the exact opposite of NBC's decade-after weekend effect. Each broadcast became vintage ad-lib. Once Diz consumed a watermelon while describing the action below. Another afternoon, while Reese aired play-by-play, the camera shifted to a closeup of Dean slumped backward, snoring as he slept. When Reese boasted of a catfish, twelve to fifteen inches long, that he had recently caught, Diz was waiting with his response. "Pee Wee, we've got 'em down in Mississippi like that, too," Dean roared, "but that's

Dizzy Dean gives the camera a wry look in 1964. (AP Wirephoto)

between the eyes!'' Familial affection thrived, and laughter, too. Always laughter. During one game Pee Wee turned to Dean, asking, ''Diz, you watched this pitcher out there for about four innings and he's been throwing that ball and I mean doing a great job. What would you say he's throwing out there?'' Nonplussed, Diz surveyed the playing field. ''Well, Pee Wee,'' he replied, ''I *have* been watching him four innings and after watching him four innings I believe that's a baseball.'' Often Dean turned impulsive; ''Announcers are too dull,'' he sighed, and weekly he tried to remedy that defect. Once, with cold winds sweeping Wrigley Field, chilling him before the game was half done, Ol' Diz grasped the mike and said, ''I've had enough of this. I'm going,'' then departed the park, leaving Reese to finish the broadcast alone. There were other exits, too, many caused by Dean's craving for ballyard food. Armed with hot dogs in one hand, peanuts in another, Diz made a fetish of stadium cuisine. Pictures abounded of Dean ambling downward from the broadcast booth, straining the rope ladder as he descended, his interest focused on the concession stand ahead.

Not even the most riveting of games deterred him. ''Pee Wee, I'm going out for a hamburger,'' he said, the score tied, 1-1. Below the eighth inning progressed. ''You want one?''

''Yeah, I'll take one.''

''Pickles, lettuce or mustard?''

''See if they have some onions,'' Reese replied, the nation watching half amusedly, half in disbelief.

''It was a circus,'' said MacPhail, ''informal, harmless, lovable and live.'' Diz appealed to the rural, and to the suburbs and small cities, too. Yet perhaps only in the culture of the small town and devout America, among the bastions of sincere allegiance, only here was Jay Hanna's impact wholly felt. These were Dean's people, by faith and background, the sturdy image of America's old-stock heart. Vibrant, triumphant, the symbol of the bucolic made good, he uplifted their values and gave credence to their trust. ''People identified with him,'' my father often said. ''They felt like somehow he knew them.'' Dean became plain folks, almost family, defender of the mores his flock endorsed. Less than well-bred himself, Diz appealed to the sober masses who enriched America and gave her meaning—the high school teacher, the general druggist, the retired mailman, the men who owned their farms. Middle brow, middle age, largely middle class, they adored Dizzy Dean in a quiet way too deep for applause. These were the Eisenhower years, the good and tranquil years, and Dean's manner fit them well. Main Street ruled America, and Main Street loved Ol' Diz. Even during the early 1960s, when turmoil and filth began to gnaw, crime and cynicism starting their incessant rise, Dean's mystique flourished and endured. Madness came from the nation's leaders, Diz said; the ''podners'' for whom he spoke kept the treasured faith.

So, too, did ''Game of the Week,'' buoyed by the plaudits which flooded its way. ''I loved the games, I enjoyed folks, the wonderful mail we received,'' Diz said in the early 1970s. ''I don't mean to say it boastfully, but I had a lot of friends in this country. And the fans loved our broadcasts. I still hear it ever' day.'' Not always, ostensibly, had emotions been so serene. In 1957, at age forty-six, Dean threatened to leave the series, discarding baseball and his $62,500 salary. ''If I'm ever going to enjoy life, it's now,'' said Dean. ''The time to live is between forty-five and sixty.'' But retirement paled and Ol' Diz returned. Two years later Bud Blattner resigned, victim of Dean's impatience and his own ideals. ''There was a lot of friction between them,'' said MacPhail, ''and in effect, Dizzy forced him out. A case here of Dizzy not being a kind of person I admire.'' Blattner's departure was never fully explained; only when out of baseball, his announcing career over, did Bud make public the dilemma Diz induced. In 1960, with Blattner gone, Reese sputtered badly in the season's early weeks. Nervous, far from glib, he had done no previous play-by-play. ''Pee Wee got off to a bad start,'' MacPhail recalled. ''He just didn't fit in the groove. But he came on fast; before long, he was plainly super.''

Blattner's ogre turned tutor for Pee Wee Reese, and the pair teamed superbly, one from the mid-South, one from the deep South. Even the absurdity of 1964, when the Congress of Racial Equality denounced Ol' Diz, scoring his habit of praising the "good people down in Mississippi," failed to alter their unchanging eclat. "I say nice things about people in Kansas and California, too," Diz protested, not grasping the intolerance which CORE displayed. "I don't hate *anyone*."

How square, critics chorused. How insufferably pious. How embarrassing and uncouth. Without malice or harmful intent, Dean found himself under assault by the double standard many of the self-styled "better people" would ultimately enshrine. Question a minority group's cause and a score of columnists condemn your worth. Obscene and bigoted, the elitists say. To their tormented minds, somehow praise of Southern whites becomes equally obscene. After all, they claim, the South is prejudiced, its "good people" racist boors. Who says? Their best friends tell them so. Georgetown cocktail gossip accepts the fable as fact. Syndicated organs echo the erroneous bunk. Each mistruth reinforces another; of such are the seeds of bias and hypocrisy sown. Reverse discrimination thrived. To fair-minded Americans, however, Americans who brushed CORE's babble aside, Dean lent a continuity to the transient quality of life, a normalcy amid the changing times which we urgently required, lest change overwhelm us all.

Perhaps, one mused, "Game of the Week" would last forever. "The novelty never wore off," said MacPhail, "but other factors emerged as too important to ignore." One became pro football, its mystique molded by television, its image as a contemporary sport shaped to fit the electronic times. Through national television, pro football had created an enormous impact on the mass buying public; each team shared equally in network receipts, Green Bay no less than the New York Giants. Each baseball team had its own separate television package, an ideal format for teams in the lucrative markets but fatal for most of the others. "The rich clubs were getting richer, the poor were getting killed. Baseball owners had seen what football had done," MacPhail continued. "Now they wanted to do the same—get their national network together—with all the clubs involved."

Dean's "Game of the Week" had bypassed all major league cities; baseball's new series, announced on December 15, 1964, would be seen in every city, major or not. One selected game would be shown every Saturday, the rights distributed equally among all twenty teams. "All three networks were invited to bid for the series," said MacPhail. "We declined our chance.

"We hadn't paid much for the rights to Dean's series," he said. "We were getting away with murder, in fact. And the reason was that the broadcasts didn't go into the big towns—New York, Chicago and the rest. We got great ratings elsewhere for peanuts. Now, in late '64, baseball wanted millions for its package." Televised baseball was national in scope. ABC purchased the "Game of the Week," yielding

$300,000 to each major league club, but ratings floundered and the network lost face. At CBS, where the Yankees had one year left on their network contract, Dean and Reese embarked upon the 1965 "Yankee Baseball Game of the Week." They broadcast all twenty-one Yankee home weekend encounters. They hosted a sports series on Sunday afternoon. They hoped, too, (vainly, as it happened) that baseball would soon divide its television rights among two networks, one of which they then might join. When the Yankee series ended, the CBS contract ceased. On October 19, 1965, John Fetzer, Detroit Tiger owner and chairman of the major league radio-television committee, announced that baseball and NBC had signed an exclusive three-year contract. Only one network would broadcast the summer game through 1968, Fetzer disclosed, a policy which damaged the sport and devastated its appeal, which—when extended through 1975—proved almost disastrous in its overall effect.

A major sponsor of NBC's new weekly series, Falstaff pushed and prodded the name of Dizzy Dean. Hire him, officials hinted, or their money might defect elsewhere. Intent on a more urbane veneer, NBC opted for Curt Gowdy, voice of the Boston Red Sox, solid, colorless, a reporter of unquestioned skills; clarity, not drama, was his television forté. Gowdy preferred Ted Williams as his network partner. Rebuffed, he chose Pee Wee Reese. Ol' Diz was out, his "Game of the Week," already crippled, now extinct. "I called the sports department at NBC for almost a week," Dean said, incensed, in March, 1966. "Once they said the guy I wanted was asleep. Another time they said another man was working. A third time the secretary told the man that I was calling and the man said he was out. I broadcast these games for eleven years and now no one'll even talk to me." Distraught and shaken, Diz bemoaned the game he loved. "Baseball's getting in an awful fix. Fans can only see twenty-eight games a year on one network. Used to be you could see fifty-five or sixty. There used to be four games a week, now there's one. Just what's happening. *What is happening?*" No one could tell him, for no one knew.

"We simple people really miss Dizzy Dean," an Alabamian, writing to *The Sporting News,* grieved nearly a decade later. By then, aided by Gowdy and Tony Kubek, sterility and network baseball had become more married than Bogart and Bacall. "He added life to the game. Maybe not perfect English all the time, but lots of clean, wholesome fun. Baseball has always been just for ordinary folks like myself. Please give us plain Americans Ol' Diz back." He had been the most gloriously talented announcer in baseball's tide of times. Now he was gone forever, his voice silenced, his work undone. Few, in early 1966, could measure the good and bad, the sincerity and hypocrisy, of Jay Hanna (Dizzy) Dean. One could be certain only that America had loved his message— its naivete, its homespun craft, its seeming warmth and goodness. Perhaps, one hoped, such a nation was great because it, too, was good. Perhaps there was some of Ol' Diz in us all.

IV

For twenty-six years Robert (Buddy) Blattner had broadcast major league baseball. Now he was unemployed and Christmas lay eight days away. Two months earlier he had been fired by the Kansas City Royals, a club for whom he had announced since its 1969 inception. "I've broadcast for almost as long as I can remember," Blattner said, adding without sorrow, "Lately, I've been sitting by the telephone, just waiting. Time slips away, you know," and the telephone remained mute.

Tall, white-haired and stylish, Buddy Blattner was one of the early pioneers in a movement which ultimately swept radio and television—the tidal wave of athletes turned announcers. At sixteen the world's doubles table tennis champion, Blattner played five seasons with the Cardinals, the Phillies and the Giants of New York. He performed with agility and he played with grace, drawing notice as an infielder who offset banjo hitting with fluidity and range. In 1949, when Blattner retired, he exchanged the field for the broadcast booth. Articulate and soft-spoken, he became one of the few players in any sport to make the transition with unquestioned success. For three years he served as the voice of the St. Louis Browns, for nine as broadcaster for the St. Louis basketball Hawks. In 1960-61 he telecast Cardinal games, then left the next year for California and the American League Angels. Seven years later Blattner returned to the Midwest, site of his home and heritage. Another seven years had passed since then, and so, too, perhaps his career.

"I knew a couple months ago the Royals' situation wasn't going to work out," he said. "They had some turnover in Kansas City, and I knew my time was short. Since then there have been some jobs come up, ones I've missed. There was a spot here when Jack Buck left the Cardinals (he returned shortly afterward), but I applied too late. And there was the Pittsburgh job open, after Bob Prince was fired. I could have gone there, but they wanted me year-round. I would have had to make the banquet tour during the off-season, and it meant starting a new life. I would have had to be away from my family, my grandchildren. It's not worth it."

Native urgings meant much to Blattner. St. Louis was his home, a fact evoking memories money could not eclipse. "I can go a couple places broadcasting and make a lot of dough," he claimed, "but I am thinking very seriously of just moving into private industry. That way I could stay here, where all my friends and family are. That's what's important. You see, certain people have to be before a microphone—their egos just drive them there. I like to think I'm not like that. I've always broadcast because it was a way of making a living. I enjoy it, but I don't need it." Gratitude and humility marked Blattner's veneer, and there was in all he said, even in his appraisal of his current woes, a total absence of embittered grief, of the rancor and venom which might have been expected to color his remarks.

An infielder for the St. Louis Cardinals, Buddy Blattner trains for the upcoming season of 1942.

"There are things you can't buy with money," he said. "I don't have a dime, but I've lived like a millionaire." Those sentiments, and his emergence as a solid, mature announcer, earned him high marks in St. Louis, California, and Kansas City, where ratings were healthy and his broadcasts won widespread applause. They also helped to thrust Blattner upon the most memorable part of his career—an association with Dizzy Dean on the CBS "Game of the Week"—and the most electric five years of his life.

"I was doing Browns' games and working for Falstaff in St. Louis at the time," Blattner said. "And Falstaff got this property and put it all together. It was quite an undertaking—no weekly series like this had ever been tried before. But they sold the idea to CBS, and then came to me, in large part, I suppose, because I worked for them. Well, by the time I was approached Diz had done a couple games in the 1955 season with other men around the country, but I started in right after I was hired. And I suppose Diz thought he could trust me. After all, I'd known him so long. He didn't want anyone to be prying into his popularity or thinking that someone would pull the rug out from under him."

Blattner never hurt Diz, but the series did Bud Blattner no harm, either.

"I must honestly say 'Game of the Week' made me. I vaulted into a higher money bracket. I received renown around the country. I was able to hold Little League clinics around the country for Falstaff, things like that I wanted to do. And what made it so beautiful was that those were the days when my kids were growing up, and I was home for four solid days a week. I thoroughly enjoyed those years—they were vintage, they were great.

"We didn't know what to expect when the series began," he said. "I think Falstaff was surprised by our success. They started with some fear and trepidation. But only for a year. By then they knew they had a gold mine. We worked withan agency in New York—Dancer, Fitzgerald and Sample—and they put four or five men full-time on the account. They really promoted the games, and always in conjunction with the brewery, because Falstaff was the only sponsor—they owned 'Game of the Week' lock, stock and barrel. And I knew Falstaff cherished it. They made a lot of money, and they paid well, as breweries are prone to do."

At first, Blattner said, no friction hampered sidekick and star. Or the network and its affiliate stations. Or the two announcers and the players they described. "It was so gratifying," he said. "All the way down the line—CBS, the viewers at home, us as well. And there was never anything negative. We were honest, not cynical. We had no axes to grind."

"Nineteen fifty-five, the first season, just took off like gangbusters. It was like feeding the multitudes. Like the Sermon on the Mount. As you recall, people were getting baseball in the hinterlands, major league style, for the first time in their living rooms. These fans, scattered through the country, had never seen a major league game. They'd heard them, but not viewed on television except for the World Series, and suddenly they're getting a game every week. It was great for several reasons. We were getting national exposure doing something we liked to do. We thought we were doing it well. And we knew the people out there were accepting what we did. I mean, our mail was incredible.

"Surprisingly, our biggest fans were those in the movie industry. I remember Clark Gable coming to us with a story. Clark would play golf on Saturday and he'd start at something like six in the morning. Why? Because our games came into Los Angeles on CBS real early. So he'd play nine holes, then go into the saloon and grab a sandwich and beer and watch the game. Then he went out and played the last nine holes. We got bundles of mail from the entire entertainment industry—musicians, actors, actresses are often great sports fans. And many at that time, most in fact, were all baseball because it was really the only game in town."

Baseball was now hardly the only game in town, largely because it televised nationally on Saturday, leaving the Sabbath open for local broadcasts by the twenty-six major league teams. Blattner and Dean did well both days, but the viewing audience was greater on Sunday.

"Saturday is your weak day, Sunday better," he said. "In fact, baseball today is missing the boat by not shifting the 'Game of the Week' to Sunday. You see, because Saturday is your first day of the weekend, during the summer you're going to play golf. You've been in the office all week and now you're going to cut the lawn. Or take the kids swimming or horseback riding. You're going to do something, and when it's so gorgeous outside on Saturday, you're not going to stay inside and watch baseball."

Even now television ratings for Saturday are poor, but Blattner and Dean prospered, Saturday or not. "With us it was a novelty, too. This was such an event for people who had never seen major league baseball before. Now they began to know the teams in the major leagues and the great players who maybe wouldn't make the one event people had seen—the Series. So people arranged their golf games and their outings around 'Game of the Week' on Saturday. Maybe they set aside Sunday to go boating. Then we went Sunday, too, and maybe they didn't go boating at all."

"The ratings stayed tremendously high in every market we were in. And beer sales, in every market they were in, Falstaff led, like two to one. This marked the vintage years for Falstaff as well as the 'Game of the Week,' and that event, I believe, made them."

NBC was their rival. "Their threat never bothered us," he said. "And they brought the big guns in—Leo Durocher, Fred Haney, Lindsey Nelson. I just figured 'Let's don't change a thing. Just do what we're doing.' And we did, and we just overpowered them. But again, by that time we'd been with the people in America two or three years. We'd become a part of their weekend schedule."

One could claim, without fear of virulent dispute, that Dizzy Dean and "Game of the Week" were totally intertwined. To mention one was to mean the other. "Each helped make the other," Blattner said. "The 'Game of the Week' was a tremendous vehicle for Dean, who in the mid-50s was almost at his zenith of popularity. He was doing television specials out of Hollywood—Dinah Shore and so on. He was a national celebrity, one of the best known, most beloved people in the nation. Not just in sports, in the entire nation. The 'Game of the Week' series gave him a forum. Plus, he had been, and would remain, a Hall of Fame pitcher, recognized as such.

"He related because he was Dizzy. He's going to say anything because he's Dizzy, and he *was* Dizzy. He didn't do baseball games like anybody else. He didn't want to. I was always there, of course, to get viewers back on the track, so he could do anything he wanted.

"As I say, he had certain expressions which people took to. He had stories, little anecdotes that he would tell about the Gas House Gang, about different pitchers. And he could use me as a crutch. You know, here I was, a little old .250 hitter, and I was made to order for him. 'Podner,' he'd say, 'you'd be duck soup for me.'

"Diz loved to agitate, although Diz didn't like to be agitated. That was one quirk of his personality—I'll mention others later—that people really didn't know. For the public Diz had a ready smile. Privately, his temper was a little short. And he didn't argue per se. He'd walk away, like 'get me out of here, podner, get me out of here.' Diz liked the adulation of the crowd, and then after that, he wanted to get out. In other words, get your ovation and scram."

Diz's style on the air was unique, but how did he know that it would be accepted, much less prized?

"Don't forget that Dizzy had done some broadcasts in St. Louis earlier," Blattner said, "where everybody loved him. So he had some prior work. But I don't think that Dean ever walked with me for the first time to do 'Game of the Week' and said, 'You lucky people, you, around the country. You lucky slobs, I'm going to attack you,' or 'I can say anything I want to say.'

"Diz didn't know if he was going to be good, bad or indifferent. He cared whether he was, but he still had the indifference that could be enjoyed only by one who knew he could make a living in some other way. He didn't need the money from 'Game of the Week'; I think he made enough money playing golf to last him the rest of his life. And I suspect he thought he would succeed on the air; there was a certain command that he possessed. Some said almost arrogance. But he never really assaulted viewers. Oh, he did say things, you know, that once in a while would bother people. The only time he'd really get upset during a game is when he'd told a person how to bet on a game and then his advice turned sour.

"People were forever calling Diz—they'd call from Texas and everywhere—asking, 'Who's going to win?'

"And he'd say, 'Well, I think the White Sox are going to win.' So if the White Sox pitcher was doing badly, Diz would get mad. You know, he'd just rip him. 'Can't see how a fella can pitch like that,' Diz would fume," and here Blattner's voice became hurried and animated. " 'Come on, throw the ball. Get the ball over the plate,' or 'podner, throw the ball. Nibble, nibble.'

"For the listener, it was kind of different," Blattner continued. "He enjoyed it. But Diz always had to have someone who could come back,

Dean (left) and Buddy Blattner were a broadcasting team for CBS Television's "Game of the Week" from 1955 through 1959.

put the game in perspective and get the right score. This is where I came in. And the amazing thing was how little Diz knew about baseball. As far as being a manager to construct the game, when to bunt, when to hit and run, how you put the lineup together so, for instance, the second batter could push the ball around—no, Diz didn't know. And he didn't want to discuss the inner workings of baseball. 'Score some runs,' he'd say. Man, Diz was just down to the basics."

"Game of the Week" viewers assumed that Dean sought the lime-light, Blattner the shadows, and thought them both content there. They accepted the public image of Dean as lovable, rambunctious and eccentric, of his sidekick as unpretentious, Rotarian and well-informed. Diz was a household word, Blattner the neighbor next door. Those conceptions were not entirely valid, one realized, but they were less erroneous than true. The pair cut wildly disparate figures, a fact that helped to cause their on-camera success.

"We *were* different," Blattner said. "We complemented each other. Because actually, Diz would be in a bad humor—and we couldn't understand how he could be tired, because he only worked two days a week and didn't work very hard then. He was more worried about catching his plane back to Dallas than he was about finishing the last two innings.

"But anyway, he'd be grumpy, and I could say something which would allow him a line to get on me and he would brighten up just like a new penny. Then he'd have fun. This was his crutch. He had to feel important, wanted and to know that he was a big cheese. And he was always bolstered by his wife, who was a good businesswoman and would tell him how good he was and what a following he had."

But Blattner's role never caused regret. "You see, if the roles had been reversed, if I'd had the name and image and following that Diz had, I would have expected someone working with me to perform the same function. I never felt like an interloper. I knew I made a definite contribution. We made a good team because I really didn't care what Diz said.

"If the people wanted his humor, fine. But we also knew, from our mail, that people wanted some relief, too. He gave everything but the ballgame, which they liked, but then I'd come back on and reconstruct what happened during his two innings. I'd give the averages which he hadn't. So they got both sides of the spectrum. And it worked well. We played off one another, 'cause I knew Diz like the back of my hand. I knew when he'd react. I knew when he wouldn't.

"Why some things fell flat when Dean worked with Pee Wee Reese in the sixties," he said hesitantly. "Pee Wee was an outstanding hitter. So there was no need to play my .250 against Diz's thirty games. See, with Reese and Dean, Pee Wee didn't want him to talk about, 'That's how they got you out, podner,' because maybe they didn't get Pee Wee out. Or Reese would say, 'I hit guys like you, Diz, like I owned them.' And Diz didn't like it. Those things didn't play well.

"I actually received," he continued, smiling wistfully, "a degree of a sympathetic following. Diz knew he couldn't bury me, and he didn't try. I would say things that I knew would get a charge from him, phrases that I knew he'd pick up. Because he was just waiting for a crumb he could really run with. All the public saw was Diz making cracks at my expense. But these things were important to him—he had to get a laugh. Maybe it was at your detriment, but you were primarily being a straight man for his part of the performance. He needed those laughs."

The man described by Blattner differed widely from the jaunty, self-assured qualities usually identified with Dizzy Dean. He made him sound wary, almost insecure.

"Well, there was some of that," he said, "and a lot of it came from not having an education. He was very aware of what he missed. But more of it came from selfishness. Having always been the big man, he was determined to remain so. And he respected me, because he never told me a lot of the stories he had told others, 'cause he knew I'd never buy them. He knew I knew him too well.

"To the public, though, people who didn't know him, he told stories that he knew you wanted to hear. He pleased you and built himself up. And it wasn't a bad way, really, because everybody was happy. Oh, off the air he might tell me, 'Those clowns on the field, those humpty-dumpties,' but on mike the only guys he'd really get on were the pitchers.

"The general public didn't really know Diz," he said. "Dean was a character. He enjoyed being a character and he was smart enough never to get out of character. That was the most important thing he did in his life. When you're tabbed with the name of Dizzy, you're not expected to have a Phi Beta Kappa key dangling from your watch-fob.

"Diz was, in the expression of many athletes, 'dumb like a fox.' He knew what would work and he was on a perfect vehicle, the 'Game of the Week,' which was twice a week. He made sure, with rare exceptions, that he didn't prepare, because people didn't want him to be a prepared broadcaster. They expected him, they wanted him, to demolish the game.

"And the techniques that worked for him, he continued to use. He also was in a different locale for most games, so he could get away with using the same expressions week after week. Diz was not, by nature and education, a linguist. Names were a little bit difficult. But he had a good memory. People don't realize that. He remembered particular things that he'd said to a particular writer ten years earlier. He might have told fifty other writers a different story, but he remembered which story went with which guy."

Diz improvised eloquently, Blattner conceded, but the Master also strove to reinforce what the public already believed; one remembrance, Bud insisted, was especially intense. Asked to broadcast a mid-1950s contest over Mutual Radio's "Game of the Day," Dean called Blattner and convinced him to fly to Detroit. "That's where the game was,"

Blattner noted, ''and the press box was about nine thousand feet in the air. It looked like the Singer Midgets were performing. Anyway, to sketch the story, I told Diz to do the first two innings. You had to get his part in there quickly because at any time he might get up and leave. So he did the first inning and, I tell you, he actually did a standard play-by-play and put things together pretty well. The actual structure was good, so unlike all the chaos Diz specialized in on ''Game of the Week.''

''Well, Diz leaned over to me after the first inning and said, 'That's enough of that. Now I'm going to start making money.' And he just butchered up the next inning above and beyond recall. He started talking about his friends down in Texas and about quail and duck hunting. Everything but the game. And he brought in a few products that weren't to be sponsored—like Grandma's Biscuits or something. I guess he'd just gotten in five hundred pounds of meal or biscuit mix from Grandma's and he wanted to thank her.

''When I said he didn't prepare, that's not quite right,'' Blattner said of Dean's calculated style. ''He would actually pre-plan his mistakes, which shows an intelligence again. 'I'm going to butcher this up today, it'll be in the second inning,' he'd say. He would program when he was going to mention so and so, and how he would tie it in. Viewers roared—they'd never heard anything quite like it. But he was good, and he knew what he was doing.

''Diz could have done standard play-by-play, but he didn't want to. And he had a homey voice, it wasn't bad, and it was the tone of the South and Midwest. And,'' he said, ''it worked. Diz was in six figures all the time. He picked up so much money, or as much as he wanted to, with all the TV specials.

''Every two weeks or so, there'd be someone in from New York or Los Angeles coming to Diz with a script for a television series. Hermione Gingold, for one. Diz would get all excited about that for a while and then he'd drop the idea. He didn't want to work that much. He'd relegate himself to three specials a year, but he could have done as many as he wanted. He was unique, let no one argue to the contrary.''

Television has long been marred by ego-mongerers who are false and shallow and constantly ''on.'' The man in the chair to my left, however, seemed real and genuine, the breach between his on and off-presence remarkably slight. Dean gravitated toward both extremes.

''The Dean on air wasn't his real personality. He was possibly more warm on the air than he was as a person. You see, Diz created many illusions that he didn't try to eliminate. One was that he was a big drinker, which wasn't true. Diz worked for Falstaff, and you got the impression, just from his innuendos during the course of the afternoon, that he's had fourteen beers during the game. Well, I never saw Diz take a drop prior to or during a game in all my years with him. Now, Diz didn't slur, and he never got silly or obscene. But he got so big, and he was always mentioning booze, that you thought, 'Boy, this guy's a big drinker. He can really handle it.'

"Another illusion was that he was a mammoth eater. You know, he talked about food all the time. He wanted to get all the plugs in—he went from biscuits to corn meal to steaks to a certain kind of pork chops that he'd had somewhere. And when you looked at him, you swore he really did gulp down all those things. But the truth was that he'd just become too inactive. The only thing Diz did was golf, and even there, he rode the cart. And he never had to walk fifty feet, 'cause he hit the ball up the middle. And he was one of the greatest putters I've ever seen.

"People thought of Diz as everybody's friend, as a guy surrounded by family and pals," Blattner said, "but one of the biggest things that hurt Diz was the fact they didn't have children. It's a shame because I believe—some will disagree with me—that he would have been a good father. The problem was that when all this notoriety and adulation came his way, fortune as well as fame, he had very few to share it with. And he became basically selfish. He could handle success publicly, but he became very private. And primarily through his wife, they guarded everything they had, and they had no one to center their attentions on except themselves.

"Another misconception was that Dean had a close circle of friends. *No.* People all knew Diz and he always had a smile and he'd take off the sombrero and say, 'Hi, podner.' He didn't know anybody's name, of course, but people thought, 'Oh, my goodness, he knew me,' cause he said podner. So in this regard Diz was very private. He was more prone to indulge himself, outgoing only when it was a matter that he should turn it on to please his fans.

"Diz's image was, and he loved this, the guy that just dropped off the back of the truck, bare-footed, and wandered into town, saying, 'Fellas, what's it all about?' But he was just about two steps ahead of you all the way."

What Blattner meant, one assumed, was that Dean's image was largely facade. "Some of it was a put-on," he agreed, "but some of it was quite sincere. America knew Dean was a great showman. Dizzy knew what the people wanted from Diz and Dizzy Dean gave it to them.

"He knew of his great popularity and became a bit lazy with it. All of us started doing more work because we were doing his." Blattner paused. The smile faded. "There was this conflict between the on and off-air Dean I've mentioned. There was also an amazing complexity to the man. He could be quite bright, quite knowing, and yet the other side of the coin, he could be so naive about things, it would stun you. At once he was sophisticated, almost worldly. He had the capacity to be the backroom brawler, to own a bookie's shop. And yet he was so innocent—he knew nothing about home life and family. I suppose this comes from the places that he'd seen, all the big cities he'd been exposed to, and yet there was still the rural naivete to him.

"As a 'country bumpkin,' you'd think Diz's socks wouldn't match and his shoes would be unshined. But Diz was classy. He was a meticulous dresser—not fancy, and he wasn't vain, and his image was of the big hat—but Dean dressed very well. And to look neat, as Diz did, when he was huge was quite a trick.

"There were conflicts within him, too. I can't say that he was basically kind. He wasn't, and he wasn't overly considerate, either. Yet there were times when someone touched him, and he could be almost tender—whether it was show or not, I don't know. But he'd spend some time with a little kid, then say, 'Let's get out of here.' Diz was not a reader, yet he'd prop up on his bed in the hotel room when we were on the road and start reading a paper. Just at the time, incidentally, when you'd think Diz would be out on the town. These were some of the paradoxes.

"Dizzy Dean," Blattner stated, "was instantly capable of the lure. This was his public image—the people's choice. When we walked down Broadway or Lexington Avenue in New York, there'd be a mob around him. And he'd say, 'Hi, folks,' then grab a cab and beat it. He wanted out. He wanted that sanctuary—to be away from people. On the 'Game of the Week', we'd get in a town on Friday and Diz would get a suite and he wouldn't leave. We'd even have dinner up there.

"Diz had morals. He had values. I don't doubt that for a minute. And he knew that he couldn't cross a line in public and make a fool of himself, or the public would disapprove. There he showed a great deal of discretion. But there were conflicts. And America still thought of him, nonetheless, as a wild man, a harmless, lovable wild man, drinking and eating up a storm."

Dean and Blattner presided over some of baseball's most splendid seasons. The game was intimate, more of a family affair. Ballparks were cramped and unpretentious, crowds raucous and exuberant. There were fewer teams to follow (sixteen), two leagues instead of two divisions, less talk of talent dilution and inferior personnel. Only four hundred players wore the major league tag, and many were the Americans who knew them all. Mantle and Mays and Musial strode across the American summer. Williams and Berra lent a luster to their game. Even lesser lights, men like Arnold Earley and Marv Grissom and the immortal Wayne Terwilliger, left an impression which far surpassed their skills. For baseball, for Bud Blattner, some would argue, for America, the 1950s comprised among the best of years.

By 1959, with the Dodgers and Giants on the West Coast, no section of the country was without rooting interest or partisan concern. The "Game of the Week" reveled in profits and unbroken cheers. Baseball basked in two furious pennant races—the Yankees upset by the Chicago White Sox, Milwaukee tying Los Angeles for the National League crown. Rumors multiplied that expansion would soon occur, or that something called the Continental League might surface within a year. On Saturday, September 26, 1959, the Braves downed Philadelphia, 3-2, and moved into a tie for first place with Los Angeles, which bowed to the Cubs, 12-2, at Chicago on the "Game of the Week." The next day, the season's finale, Milwaukee won, the Dodgers won, and Buddy

Blattner's career with CBS and Dizzy Dean came to a stunning and irreparable close.

Saturday, the 26th, had concluded that year's "Game of the Week." "It marked our fiftieth broadcast of the year," Blattner said, "and we weren't scheduled to do Sunday because of a football conflict. So we were officially done for the year. However, Falstaff had said if the race ended in a tie, they'd do the playoffs." Blattner returned to St. Louis, Diz stayed in Chicago, each awaiting Sunday's outcomes.

"It was about four o'clock in the afternoon," he said. "I was out in the driveway washing the car. I got a phone call saying both the Braves and L.A. had won and the National League playoffs were on." Moments later Blattner called Dean. He suggested they meet in Chicago, then drive ninety miles to Milwaukee, where the playoff series would start the following day.

"While I was flying to Chicago," he said, "unbeknownst to me, Diz and Gene Kirby, our producer, had gone to a place to eat." So began the events that led to Blattner's leaving. The crisis took birth in St. Louis, where Falstaff, having vowed to broadcast the playoff games, found itself unable to solely underwrite their cost. Casting about for financial aid, the brewery came upon L&M cigarettes, which consented to co-sponsor the network's endeavor. Falstaff was relieved, L&M delighted. Only Dizzy Dean and his imminent fiasco remained.

For years, with increasing frequency and relish, Ol' Diz had made much of his aversion to cigarettes. "Man, I never felt so good since I threw that last cigarette out," he said amid most weekend games, claims hardly endearing him to L&M; Dean's zealotry, always resented, was presently recalled. When Falstaff decided to team with L&M, it yielded the right to choose the playoff announcers—and the cigarette company, understandably, wanted no part of Diz. Dean was off the playoff broadcasts, Blattner on. "Diz," a Falstaff spokesman told him, "we just can't hack this whole thing alone and L&M won't accept you. Bud'll do the game, and we'll get George Kell to help him out."

None of which Blattner knew. "I was at the Knickerbocker Hotel in Chicago," he said, "but Diz wasn't there. And I couldn't figure out why. So I sit, in the hotel lobby, waiting like a little boy. Well, it gets to about eight o'clock in the evening. And finally here comes Diz flying across the lobby, knocking old ladies down with their packages, and right by me he goes to the phones. And there he starts screaming to these agency people in New York. I've never seen him so mad. I mean, he was just out of his mind. And all I find out is that L&M is going to be one of the sponsors, which was fine with me.

"It was a little while later when I heard Diz say, 'Well, I'll tell you one thing. They're not going to get away with it.' This was the first inkling I had that maybe cigarettes wouldn't want him. And the agency just told him to return to Dallas and forget the game. Well, now he's really burned; his pride's been hurt. So he comes back," Blattner said in a way that was halting and slow, "with a statement that anybody who appeared in the playoffs would be off the 'Game of the Week' forever.

"It was obviously aimed at me. And I told him, 'For God's sake, Diz, why don't you just forget it? You don't want to do the game anyway. We'll have to do this game in Milwaukee, then fly to the Coast.' Pat was there and it was just a very bad scene. They were tremendously upset and there's not a God-damned thing I could do.

"My point to Diz was, 'If you want to go with me, fine. Gene, the same with you. But I'm going to grab the rented car and get to Milwaukee. I have a job to do.' Gene thought if we discussed it more, maybe Diz would drop the whole thing and go back to Dallas. But all I said was 'Diz, there's not a thing I can do. If you want, I'll call up and plead for you, but these people, I guess, are very adamant about your not doing the game.' So Kirby went with me and Diz said he was going to stay up all night calling agency people. I couldn't imagine him doing that, but in the end, he did."

Blattner's smile grasped the middle road between compassion and disdain. "We got in Milwaukee at two in the morning," he said. "I got up five hours later to try and find someone who could pull the whole show together. I find George Kell—he did American League games— and he hadn't been contacted until four in the morning. Can you believe it?

"George had never done a National League game in his life. He didn't have a pencil, paper, scorecard, anything. I told him not to worry about it, that we'd get through. So we got to the ballpark about ten. I'm heading toward the broadcast booth, and I was halfway up the ramp, and Gene Kirby is coming down. And he said to me, 'Podner, can't believe it.'

"I don't know what made me say this, but I said, 'Well, Gene, am I off the game?'

"And Kirby said, 'Podner, yeah.' What Dean had done was say that if I was on the playoffs, he'd never come back for 'Game of the Week.' "

Dean, then, had forced him out.

"And Falstaff misjudged me badly," he said. "They thought I'd be happy to return to St. Louis and get paid for the playoffs I hadn't broadcast. After all, they thought, what did I care? Well, I came down the ramp and called New York and dictated my resignation as of right there. I had a couple years left with Falstaff and CBS, but after several thousand dollars in lawyer fees and three months I finally escaped the contract, too."

His sentiments were surprising. Here, perhaps, was a man who still respected character and values, who regarded neither as outmoded nor passé. Why didn't he accept the money and remain with Dean? Why leave the series he loved?

"It was strictly a matter of pride," he said, his manner resorting less to pomp than matter of fact. "I never could have looked in the mirror again had I said, 'Well, I'll take the dough and flee and then come back in the booth with Diz next year.' And I left, quite bluntly,

Buddy Blattner (right), Dean's former CBS broadcast partner, announces a game for the Kansas City Royals.

Another athlete turned announcer, Buddy Blattner broadcast major league baseball for twenty-six years.

the best job in the country, but it all evened out as the years went by.

"I think he (Dean) was very sorry about it, even though he really was behind my ouster. Again, he acted in that selfish vein of his. Falstaff said to me, 'Stay on, you know Diz didn't mean what he said.' And I said, 'Quite likely he didn't,' but in no way was I about to be dictated to. I never blamed Falstaff—they never tried to hurt me or take me off the playoffs. But Diz was self-centered, and this really got to him, that he could be kicked off and I would go on.

"I never held any great hatred for Diz," he insisted. "He did something that was a big hurt to me, and that's partly why you're the first person I've ever told this publicly to. I didn't want to air my grievances out loud. But I reacted in 1959 in a way as a man I knew I had to.

"And Diz, whenever we met in later years, he always made out like nothing had ever happened. And Diz could do this so beautifully. You know, bad things that he'd done, he'd forget tomorrow. Our paths didn't cross that much, of course, even though he did one game with me in Kansas City and another in Chicago. Both during the 60s. I never felt that Diz wanted me to get fired, but it happened anyway. You see, I couldn't back down; even if I'd gone on the playoffs, and Diz had in the end relented, there would have been an uneasiness all the time. So once Dean dropped the hammer, I had to leave."

Blattner's Dean rarely knew contrition; one suspected that apologies were blatantly unknown. "Oh, he never apologized," Blattner said. "His only reaction was utter amazement, as though I'd lost my mind. And the country was surprised. That's why I kept my story to myself, because I didn't think it was a story for public consumption. That is," he said, "until now."

V

He had become, as Red Barber called him, "a captain among men," leader of the Brooklyn Dodgers for a decade and a half. A Southerner, his childhood home forty miles from Louisville, he helped to mold baseball's racial calm, his aid a solace for Jackie Robinson's grief. Involved with baseball's first wholly national series, NBC's "Game of the Week," he won the laughter of many, the applause of more. Settled and assured at fifty-eight, however, he flung aside those memories and named a rival choice instead.

"My six years with Diz," he said, choosing slowly his words, "1960 through '65, they were the best years of my life."

Kentucky-born and bred, Harold Henry (Pee Wee) Reese moved haltingly from high school to Brooklyn. "I weighed only a hundred and ten pounds my senior year," he said. "Who wants a runt like that?" Skeptical about his future prospects, Reese spent two years with the Kentucky Phone Company, gaining thirty pounds and playing baseball on the side. The Presbyterian Church League was the early forum, shortstop his locale. In 1937, to Pee Wee's surprise, he was signed by

PeeWee Reese in his prime as shortstop for the Brooklyn Dodgers.

the Louisville Colonels, purchased by the Boston Red Sox the following year. "Boston paid $195,000 for the club," one wag suggested. "All but five of the dough went for that kid at shortstop." Reese flowered in 1938. He led the American Association in stolen bases, thirty-five. He led in triples, eighteen. He batted .279 and fielded with poise. "I was happy at Louisville," Reese recalled. "I was near my parents, near my girlfriend, near my home."

Security collapsed as the 1940s dawned; twenty years after selling Babe Ruth to the New York Yankees, the Red Sox peddled Reese to Brooklyn for $150,000. Joe Cronin, manager of the Red Sox, was also their shortstop; perhaps he feared Pee Wee's competitive skills. "I was miserable when I went to Brooklyn. I didn't want to go. But it was probably, next to Diz, the best thing that ever happened to me." Even at Brooklyn, misfortune early arose. During Reese's first year, he broke his hand and was beaned. In 1941 he made forty-one errors, high for any shortstop in the league, and saw his batting average plummet to .228. Next season Pee Wee's hitting spurted, his fielding improved. He stayed the Brooklyn shortstop for twelve more years. He helped with his bat and glove, and more with his spirit than both. Brooklyn fans, noted for their harsh, biting edge, reveled in Reese's growth, his quiet humor, his droll, almost courtly ways. More than thirty thousand of the faithful flocked to Ebbets Field for Pee Wee Reese night, striking matches as the field lights dimmed, there to show their love. When the Dodgers left Brooklyn in 1957, an exit that stripped the borough of identity and civic pride, its denizens mourned No. 1 more than most, Pee Wee the captain still.

Reflexes fading, his legs soiled by wear, Reese, now captain of the Los Angeles Dodgers, passed forty in 1958. Walter Alston, ever unsung, remained owner Walter O'Malley's manager. "I kept The Dodgers, too, were aging, marred by injury and decline. "They knew they weren't going to contend. I guess they wanted me for my name." Memories of Reese base hits crested a continent and ballpark away. Meanwhile, marooned in California, Pee Wee hit .224 and the Dodgers collapsed. Third the year before, Los Angeles placed seventh, two games removed from last. Only the Phillies lay beneath. Reese retired and became a coach. He had emerged, insiders said in 1959, as Alston's obvious successor. "Mr. O'Malley kept saying, 'Pee Wee, one day you're going to manage this club,' and I said, 'Mr. O'Malley, there ain't no way.' "

With Maury Wills at shortstop, Los Angeles won the World Series in 1959. "I was making $20,000 coaching," Pee Wee said. "That was unheard of; the only reason I got so much was because of my career before. But where are you going as a coach? I would have floundered around in baseball, I'm sure." Autumn brought Reese's blessing and Blattner's curse. "Buddy had a lot of trouble with Diz. I don't know the story, all I know is that he resigned." And Reese replaced him.

"We considered several people," Bill MacPhail had said, "but Pee Wee always led the list. We wanted him very much," his name, his manner, his soft-spoken Kentucky charm. Seeking consent, Gene Kirby flew to Louisville from New York. Agency personnel followed. So, also did phone calls from Patricia Dean, urging Pee Wee to join Ol' Diz. Reese balked; he had never done an inning of play-by-play. "I didn't think I was that much of an extrovert," he said. "I didn't want to bomb." Again Pat persisted. Reese's wife backed the cause. Perplexed and torn, Pee Wee consulted Buzzie Bavasi, Dodger general manager, a man, unlike O'Malley, whom Reese respected and liked. "Why in the hell don't you try it?" Bavasi asked. "More than likely, you'll screw it up, but even if you do, you can always come back and have a job with us." Amused by Bavasi's counsel, Reese endorsed it, too. He would team with Ol' Diz, Pee Wee disclosed. A neophyte to television, he would chance face and reputation on a medium he barely knew.

"You bet I was frightened," he said. "I mean, this was all new to me. All that winter, before the 1960 season came, I'd have a projector and baseball tape set up in the basement. Kirby came here and worked with me. I worked on the video. Then I'd talk, talk, talk." "It comes spring training," Reese continued, "and we get a little tape recorder and used that. Then at night, Gene and I'd go back to the hotel and we'd listen to what I'd done. Usually what I'd done wrong. And Diz," he broke off, laughing, "he'd come in some afternoons and say, 'Podner, having a little trouble? Let me show you how to do this stuff.' And he'd sit down and sing 'Wabash Cannonball.' 'That's all there is to it,' he'd say. But mostly it was work—how to project, how to watch the game, when to watch the monitor, when not to.

"I kept thinking, what happens if I can't say anything? What happens if the guy says, 'Ten seconds 'til air time' and I freeze? We did all that work in the winter and then we went to New York before the season started and watched a game Mel Allen had done—I watched how he set the tempo—and with all this, the first game I did, I *still* had problems. But I'll say this," he said, "working with Diz, it was the best thing that ever happened to me."

Baseball has spawned several marvelous broadcast crews. The Yankees' trio of Allen, Barber and Jim (The Possum) Woods excelled from 1954 through 1956. Brooklyn laid claim to Barber, Scully and Connie Desmond several years before. Two decades later, while Woods and Ned Martin sparkled as announcers for the Boston Red Sox, ABC lent to America the equally gifted duo of Keith Jackson and Bob Uecker. By late summer, 1960, however, Ol' Diz and Pee Wee surely ranked among the best. "I guess I came on pretty well," Pee Wee conceded, "but Ol' Diz really helped. Just being Diz relaxed me. He knew when I was out on a limb, when I was uneasy.

"Diz was super. He'd come in and kid me when I was unsure. 'Podner,' he'd say, 'let me take over here,' or 'Podner, let me say something,' or 'You got this all fouled up.' And we laughed about it, I guess, as only two former ballplayers could. You know, if there was a professional announcer up there and I made a mistake, it was terrible. Like when I worked with Curt Gowdy."

"But Diz never took it as a plague upon the craft. We'd just sit there and laugh, and so would our viewers.

"Well, a majority of 'em did, anyway," Reese said, humility yielding to working pride. "To this day people talk to me about it. Yesterday a guy looked at me—I was at a filling station—and he said, 'You're not Pee Wee Reese, are you?' I said yes. And the first thing he said was, 'Baseball hasn't been the same since you and Diz left.' That's how it was—you either raved about us or said, 'Jees, I can't stand these guys.' There was no middle ground."

"I liked working with both Diz and Gowdy," Reese said, "but it was so different. With Diz, we just kind of went on the air, pushed a button and said, 'Here we go.' With NBC, it was a Cecil B. DeMille production. All these guys passing around statistics and the rest—Diz used to call them statics. It was just so much more *fun* the way we did it before."

Reese had called these his most memorable years. Now, he clapped his palms as though to press his convictions home. "I can remember one Friday night we were in Cleveland. And I got a call from Diz late at night—I was in the hotel room. 'Podner,' he said, 'guess who's in town?'

"I said to him, 'Diz, I have no idea. What in the devil you want?' We were kidding, of course.

"Diz said, 'We got Roy Acuff,' and I said, 'So what?'

"Well, Dean, he loved Roy Acuff. 'Let's go down,' he said, which meant, of course, we're going down. Because if Diz wanted it, I'd say OK, Diz, let's go. So I got out of bed and we went to hear Roy Acuff. And I *enjoyed* it." Sincerity, one sensed, had always been Reese's strength. "Met Roy Acuff for the first time. A heluva guy. And real country. But I loved these things—seeing Diz have a few drinks, have a few laughs."

With the memory of Diz's image a frown appeared. "Oh, I know what people said. But I swear to God," he said, raising his hand, "hope I drop dead, I never saw that man take one drink before a game."

"Never," Reese repeated. "Oh, he'd get a sandwich a lot of times during a game, especially if it was dull, and he'd make a big to do. They'd get a shot of Diz eating the stuff. Or we'd come into Philadelphia and they'd play up Diz stumbling down the rungs which hung from the booth. Diz would really put it on. He loved to play the ham." Diz with sandwich, Diz with beer, Diz atop the old rope ladder. Memories became real again as Pee Wee spoke.

"We were at the New York airport," he recalled, "and I was walking ahead of Diz. He had the hat, the big boots on. All the porters, everybody saying, 'Hi, Mr. Dean.' 'Hi, Diz. How ya doing?' 'Hi, podner.' And Diz shouts to me, 'Pee Wee.'

" 'Yeah, what do you want?' " Reese said.

" 'How come you played in this town for eighteen years and nobody knows Pee Wee. Everybody knows Ol' Diz.' So I shot back to him, 'If I had that cowboy hat and boots on, everybody'd know me, too.' And he just laughed. I don't think he ever got mad at me."

With Reese, like Blattner, Dean towered, unchallenged by colleague or friend. "Well, he kinda ran everything," Pee Wee conceded. "The agency, CBS. Whatever Diz says, Diz does. As they often said, the network created a monster and they weren't too sure what to do with it. It was amazing, really—Dean could tell a giant corporation what he wanted, and what he wanted, he got. Course," he said, his voice quiet but charged, "I knew who was the boss. If Diz wanted me to come eat with him in the hotel room, I did. If he didn't, I didn't. There were the Kirbys and Pee Wee Reeses and all the people at CBS. And then there was Diz. We had no friction. Never." But Blattner split violently with Dizzy Dean. Why was Reese's station more secure? "If Diz didn't like you, he'd want to see you make a fool of yourself. But he wanted to be sure I didn't. He didn't want anything to happen to me. He was kind of protective, really."

"Diz didn't resent me doing play-by-play. I remember when he first walked out of the booth and said, 'Podner, see you in two or three innings,' and then he'd go grab a steak. He let me do it solo. But," Reese continued, laughing, "he didn't stay out too long. If I got in a tight spot, he wanted to be sure he was there.

"Sometimes I'd do a commercial or an inning of play. Diz'd come on the air and say, 'Podner, I'd better pick this thing up. I think you just lost some sales.' You couldn't keep from laughing at the guy. Or I'd do a live commercial and he'd say, 'Well, podner, commercial wasn't *too* bad"—Reese paused—"but I think you better get with it next time." Or we'd get through doing a game and as soon as it was over, he had to call Mama. He had to call Pat. And Diz would say to us when he'd finished talking to Pat. 'She said I was terrific, but the other guy . . .' and of course we'd roar. We went through the same thing every week. Yes, we really had a life."

Blattner grew disgruntled with Dean's unbridled reach; Reese proved far more facile. He delighted in Dizzy's company and accepted his whims, forgave the boundless ego that soared yearly to new, more elevated heights. "I wasn't overwhelmed by Diz," he insisted. "I never felt like a poor second cousin. I always felt comfortable. Why? Because I didn't have to cater to anyone. Not even to Diz. I was just myself. Just ol' quiet Pee Wee."

"At NBC," he said, his tone strangely embittered, "they used to tell me, 'Pee Wee, don't forget the sponsors, the Gillette people, the agency people. Mention 'em on the air.'

"I'd tell 'em, 'Hey, wait a minute, I've been doing games for eight years. I don't have to start kissing anyone's rear. And they'd come right back. 'Well,' they said, 'we're just telling you.' "

Pee Wee's smile surfaced. "Maybe they were right," he said. "The next year I was fired," replaced by Tony Kubek in 1969. "That's what was great about Diz. I never felt I had to be a straight man. I only did what came natural. And I knew how much people enjoyed him. I just hoped I added something in my own quiet way."

"I never did really figure the big ox out," he confessed. "He wore the hat and this and that, like he needed to be noticed. But sometimes people bugged him and he wanted to get away, though he'd never let on.

"At dinner, when autograph hounds pestered him, Diz'd never tell them to beat it. He never let anybody know that it bothered him, which is actually a tremendous thing. I mean, Sinatra, you touch his coat and he hauls off and belts you in the mouth. Not Diz. He was unflappable. Diz always took time for people. He was extremely kind."

Kind? Blattner, and several more before, had labeled Dean less warm off the air than on, less than sensitive, less than genteel toward broadcast associates. "Oh, he had his moments," Pee Wee acknowledged, "but I think a lot of it was a ruboff from Pat. He depended on her so much. Almost like a crutch."

Aside from Pat, was Dizzy's on-camera posture a charade? "No, he was the same. Always kidding. I remember saying to him in the hotel

Dizzy Dean (left) and Pee Wee Reese joined forces for six years on CBS Television.

lobby, mockingly-like, 'Dizzy Dean. High, hard fastball . . . I wish I would have had the chance to hit against that trash.' And he'd start bringing his arm up in the air, like he was going to pitch, and I'd start to duck. Just a little gesture. But Ol' Diz loved it. He really loved people, I believe.

"I remember once," he continued, "I told Diz a story. Chris told it to me and I thought it was great. Anyway, Chris was coming out of this small town and he picked up an old farmer. 'Where can I take you?' Chris asked him.

" 'I'm going about a mile down the road,' the farmer said. 'I got a little work to do.'

"It was a real hot day," Reese related, "and as the farmer got in the car, a big Cadillac, Chris had the air conditioning on. They went down the road about half a mile. The old man turned to Chris and said, 'Son, would you stop this car?'

"Chris said, 'Why? I thought you were going down a couple of miles and cut some tobacco?'

"The old man looked at him and said, 'Yeah, but it's turned so cold that I'm going back and kill some hogs.' "

Reese laughed uproariously. "I gave Diz the story," he said, "and I told him, 'Diz, I'm going to tell this over the air.' Well, he said, 'What? You can't do that. You'll insult the intelligence of the farmer.' And he was serious about it, real concerned. Diz could be sensitive that way, more than other people realized." Left unspoken was an obvious truth: were he alive, Diz would bemoan the farmers' plight. Few cared about their intelligence, or the values they held, or the economic woes which often marred their lives. Farmers were too quaint, too homespun, too rhapsodically square. Style was all that mattered; moral substance had become a forgotten art.

Diz had style, Pee Wee said, and substance, too. "How else you gonna explain the effect he had?" Reese queried. "We didn't do that much homework. You can read all the statics you want, but if it's a dead game, all the homework in the world won't save you. And we had Diz. We didn't need statics. He was a show in himself. I'd say, 'Diz, do a little singing if the game was dull. 'Sing "Precious Memories" or something.' Or we'd get a shot of him sleeping; I signaled the monitor and nudged Diz. 'Podner,' I said, 'am I keeping you awake?' It was corny as hell, but people loved it.' " Making $20,000 yearly as coach, Reese cleared several times that amount as podner to Dizzy Dean. "I could have been paid a lot less and still loved it. People would say to me, 'Does Diz bug you? Do you mind all the corn?' And I would say to 'em, 'Hell no. It relaxed me, it made me more at ease.' No one sat there, just waiting for me to goof. We'd just sit there and laugh."

Few, least of all America's baseball public, laughed in October, 1965, when NBC officially became the summer game's sole network for the following three years. "It came out in the papers. Diz and I were at Lake Tahoe at the time. So I went to him and said, 'Hey, this could be serious. We could be in trouble.' He told me, 'Don't worry about it. We'll be all right.' " Reese flashed his whimsical smile. "And Diz had been doing this for years, so I figure he knows what's what." As usual, Reese's instincts were perceptive; he and Dean's woes were insoluble indeed. NBC sought to revamp baseball's media image, and Ol' Diz would no longer do. "Diz might have gotten a job with Curt, but he would have had to do color, not play-by-play. Diz didn't want that. And I didn't especially want Gowdy. I said, 'Look, I'd rather work with Diz on the backup game.' But that was out, too. NBC just didn't want Diz as its main guy on any broadcast. So I gave up. I went with Curt.

"You know," he said slowly, "Diz missed the 'Game of the Week.' It saddened him deeply. He still had the ego, the need to have applause. Only the applause wasn't there." Pee Wee brightened. "But he still kept the happy face, and never stopped kidding. We were up to a golf tournament in Dayton, Ohio—this was a year before he died—and I hadn't seen him in a while. And I was getting ready to tee off. Well, Diz was in back of me and he couldn't stay still. 'Podner,' he said, 'a lot of trees over on the right.' Couldn't stop needling. The next tee came up. 'What'd you get on that hole?' he'd shout after I messed up. The next tee. 'Lot of sand traps on the left.' '' A smile exploded across Pee Wee's face.

''We were just a couple of country boys that made mistakes, that said things about which people knew.'' The ''country boy's'' series was long since past; long live their ''Game of the Week.'' Did he miss the exposure, the turmoil, the national forum he owned every spring and summer week?

''Naw, not the series,'' he said, adding softly, ''not really. But I sure miss Ol' Diz.''

Chapter Seven

Dizzy Dean's America

I

The summers fled, sweet and mourning. He was older now, past sixty, the hair solid gray, the eyes blue and wistful, the bulk even larger than before. Mississippi had become his sole adopted soil, heir to Diz, wife Pat and a million memories more. Around him lingered clustered pines, the fields of clover swept by red, August evenings marked by peace and music. Home was Bond, rural and serene. Three miles away lay Wiggins, population 3,186, host to Dean's Super Shell garage. Each day strangers bid Diz greeting, the white Stetson above his head, his frame aside a cigarette machine which adorned the indoor office. Amenities passed and nostalgia flourished. "Podner," Dean said, forsaking the humor which once enchanted and entranced, "can't complain about what life brings me now." Yet his stage was dimmer, his audience reduced; bravado masked deeper, more intimate concerns. Almost plaintively, Dizzy's allies bemoaned their plight. Without Ol' Diz, "Game of the Week" had become a farce; all, they knew, could agree on that. Baseball, too, was enmeshed in doubt; its leaders stumbled onward, groping blindly for a force to guide them. And what of America, their land once divinely blessed? What had happened? Where had the dream gone wrong?

"The country's all different," said Diz, mouthing the verity which wracked his final years. "A lot of people look at you and say, 'Aw, he's old-timey.' But I'll tell you one thing. I look over the last ten years, and ten before that, and I see how we've fallen. Now time

175

progresses I know that's true. But we progress with so much trouble and grief and graft." Even here, amid tiny Stone County, unrest made ready to wrench and hurt. Four decades before, with Pat's family home set back in Wiggins woods, relatives eschewed the mere practice of locking one's doors. Neighbors were friends, trust held dear. Now, Diz said, he must secure the windows, bar the doors, use double locks to lessen his risk. "Things is happening today," Diz sorrowed, "I just don't understand." Turmoil warped the times; nothing, it seemed, remained resolute and firm. Constants were uprooted, old landmarks eroded or gone; no one, Ol' Diz included, escaped the anguish, the slow torment of change.

By the early 1970s, Dean and network baseball were long since divorced. Gone, as well, was the train Dean had helped to memorialize and enshrine. "I loved the railroads," Diz said. "You got to talk to people. You got to know 'em so well," but empathy must yield to the ledger board. Plagued by mounting losses, burdened by empty seats that graced each passenger flight, the Norfolk & Western Railroad asked the Interstate Commerce Commission to discontinue the Wabash Cannonball, the train Dean cherished, whose song he sang. "He just liked the number," Roy Acuff said. "It seemed to please and thrill him." The railroad had covered a mosaic of routes, all of which touched the sprawling Midwest. Few American treasures rivaled the nation's railroads—their imperial power and influence, their capacity for awe and wonder, the folklore and romance a sweeping heritage spawned. Few rivaled the thousands of virgin miles that graced each side, the mystique of land innocent and unknown. Trains once joined the country, their tracks a common chord. Now the Wabash Cannonball perished, its grace a victim of violent, more vulgar times. "I don't know any worse news," said Diz, informed of the train's demise. America had changed, and so, too, its modes of travel. Railroads were dying, their use and magic dimmed. Only the memories flickered. Memories, one knew, were all Diz had.

Changed, too, was the tapestry Dean's own innocence wove. "He could be so naive," Blattner had said, "it was incredible." Dizzy's unflagging trust, so often engaging, returned in early 1970 to curse his harmless intent. Closeted in Las Vegas, clad in pajamas, Dean was roused by federal agents who showed a warrant and searched his room. He was suspected, they said, of aiding gambling interests, of placing large bets for business allies. Though Pat angrily denied the charge— "This is ridiculous, it's way out in left field," she said. "I don't know what it's all about"—Diz was named co-conspirator in a federal indictment; ten others, some friends to Dean, were charged with abusing federal gambling statutes. "Mr. Dean has been very cooperative. We need witnesses like him," a federal attorney later said. "He's furnished information about people in a widespread gambling syndicate." Media accounts detailed Dizzy's dilemma; stupidity, not malice, had caused his decline. "I won't say I haven't done some foolish things in my life, but I'll tell you one thing. I have nothing to do with big-time gambling

—never did and never will,'' said Diz at a Phoenix press conference. ''I want to tell you exactly how I became engaged in this thing. It was through a friend who asked me to make wagers for him, and I did. I was told there was no harm in it. Later on I was told it was the wrong thing to do, and I stopped it.'' Where was Blattner's hustler, the conniving Diz of old? ''All I want to do is go back home and live normal,'' he concluded, ''like I have in the past thirty-nine years of professional life, teaching youngsters on the ballfield and helping them.'' Few wanted Dizzy's help during much of 1970; tinged by scandal, an unwitting aid to illegal concerns, the artless innocent stumbled home. Gullible and unaffected, Dean bore the indignity of deception and shame. Betrayed was the trust once so eagerly supplied. Where were folks' set of ethics, Diz wondered; since when were one's word and vow apart? ''People are so different now,'' he said, ''so deceitful, so dishonest.'' That also had changed; innocence, perhaps, was no longer enough.

Where, then, lay the solace, the panacea for Diz's current ills? Not, he knew, in television; the summers since 1965 had comprised baseball's lost media years. Unwilling to develop bold television policies, baseball's Neanderthals saw their sport fall far behind football in network exposure. In the suburbs and provinces, where few fans in person ever saw a game, baseball suffered its most precipitous decline; television remained their sole baseball link, and now Ol' Diz was gone. So, too, were Barber and Allen, household words driven from the air, silenced by the game they served. ''I tried to do a good job,'' Diz said. ''My broadcasts was what I thought the people would enjoy. There's not enough humor or color now. Most announcers are dull. That's it exactly.''

Even during the mid-1970s, while the game rebounded strongly in box-office receipts, baseball's media image still faltered, victim to the one-network format which did little to promote the game and less to enhance its national appeal. ''I don't see why only NBC broadcasts games,'' Diz would state indignantly. ''If they ever go back to where more than one network does a game, I'd be tickled to death to go back.'' While baseball stumbled, pro football boomed, dividing its financial spoils among all three networks. With one network, baseball received almost no notice on CBS or ABC nightly newscasts. Or on ABC sports specials. Or the CBS Sports Spectacular. Cursed by its single-network reliance, baseball must bear further the presence of bumbling color men who haunted their sport; NBC's Tony Kubek, for instance, was described by one wag as ''sounding as if he were presiding at a funeral.'' Televised sidekicks should be provocative and entertaining: Don Meredith or Bob Uecker. Kubek was neither. For years critics abused Kubek's cohort, Curt Gowdy, NBC's play-by-play announcer. They assaulted his voice, his seeming obsession with the past, his penchant for glibness and the flip approach. Yet Gowdy was weaned on baseball; he covered it longer than any other sport. Writers said Curt was dull, and assuredly Gowdy was. He would have seemed

more lively, though, had NBC dropped Kubek and chosen Dizzy
Dean instead. Ultimately, Gowdy was dropped as NBC's baseball
voice, replaced by Joe Garagiola. "I sure like those guys," Diz said,
"but I can't say I'm much excited by what I hear." Audience totals
dropped yearly as NBC's coverage took hold; one yearned vainly,
amid the rising boredom, for a glimpse of drama, of the comic color
which endeared Dean's effect.

Even more absurd, Diz complained, was baseball's refusal to televise
a Sunday network series. "That's when the game should broadcast
coast to coast," Blattner said. "Sunday is your big day, it's when your
ratings should rise. I think most people know that." Blattner knew.
Ol' Diz knew. So did the networks and the nation's fans. Why are
baseball owners always the last to know? Saturday afternoons lend
themselves to outdoor endeavor—Americans manicure their lawns,
or play golf, or ride the country roads. "It's the worst day of the week
for TV," Blattner said, and few could disagree. Sunday boasts far
greater viewing potential—more families remain at home, friends
and relatives arrive; the Sabbath spirit echoes leisurely communion
with others. Nineteen seventy-six saw major league officials finally
abort their one-network format, dividing national coverage among NBC
and ABC, the latter one of baseball's most ardent prior critics. Even
then, however, the game's media ills proved less than fully cured;
viewers saw only one more game than in seasons past. Rebuffing CBS'
offer to televise two games each weekend, baseball remained the only
major sport without weekly Sunday broadcasts, the series pro football
once exploited to trigger its meteoric rise. "Man, Sunday is the day
to take it easy," Ol' Diz often said. "Why don't them guys in baseball
wake up?" Rejecting Dean's plea, baseball executives huffed forth
their response. "We've got a good thing going," they said to outsiders.
"The devil with you." Viewers around New York City, they said, were
deluged by over one hundred and eighty Yankee and Met games combined; network exposure on Sunday would only compound the flood.
But what about fans in Denver or Buffalo, Diz retorted, or Miami
and Seattle, or the thousands of locales in between? They received
only two network games a week, a total far below what pro football
gave them when autumn neared.

"Sunday is our big day at the gate; we didn't want network TV to
cut the crowds," a leading official replied. "The owners need those
big throngs to survive." Sunday network series were also blocked by
an unspoken, yet far more important, truth; baseball's reliance on
local coverage, on its allegiance to regional television networks,
doomed the national exposure which Ol' Diz urged. "We have to
leave room for local clubs to broadcast," the official continued. "Those
area contracts are important, you know. And Sunday is their big
broadcasting day." Inexplicably, unfazed by logic, baseball shunted
national interests aside; downplayed was the lethal imbalance local
dependence caused. Amounts ranged widely for games broadcast
and television rights received. Chicagoans had access to more than

two hundred games per year, residents of San Diego none. The Boston Red Sox aired over one hundred games, a number most clubs could not approach. The rich grew richer, the poor mocked by unending neglect. Oversatured were several areas; grievously under were many more. Every Sunday, while local games enthralled New York and Boston, most locales, far less favored, many major league cities among them, were deprived of network broadcasts and the import they held. One missed Sunday baseball, and Ol' Diz, and the marvelous alliance, the spirit and mirth, which they in concert formed. "We wanted to broadcast nationally on Sunday," a high-echelon CBS executive said. "It would have been great for baseball. We would have done a hell of a job. And we kept trying to tell baseball's owners what every other sport long ago knew—national, not regional, telecasts build a sport's national appeal. But they wouldn't listen. I've seldom seen such stupidity. Incredible, absolutely incredible." Who, indeed, could tell the owners? Who could eclipse their ability to convert success into chaos, to create havoc and impair their game, to make an art form of buffoonery and blatant bungling? The 1970s gave emphasis to several glaring verities. Too often baseball was run by mental cave men, not moral and innovative souls, men who moved in ice ages, not months or even years. What even the sport's most avid partisans realized, and ultimately came to rue, was that baseball owners were rarely diverted by reason and rationale; instead they wandered aimlessly, seeking that death-wish which seemed to rule their course.

America, too, was seared by malice, a victim of its self-inflicted harm. "Why's everything fallin'?" Ol' Diz asked. "Why don't people have no respect for one another?" Faith and civility, love of country and love of God. All the trusted truths, ideals still accepted but once revered, lay under coarse and vocal siege, assaulted by the elitists Ol' Diz despised. America was wrapped in conflict, torn by riot and marred by strife. Urban violence ripped its fabric, savaged values, stained its soul. Main Street had yielded to burning streets, civil liberty to civil license. "Man," Dean said, "they tell you prayer in the classroom is illegal. Then they say riot and disorder in the classroom is OK." Drugs challenged alcohol as the nation's favorite crutch. Dizzy's decent, law-abiding, middle class Americans, citizens who cared about the flag, about patriotism, who believed in the work ethic and what it mirrored, were ridiculed by demagogic newsmen, by pseudo-intellectuals, by the street people and park preachers who insipidly equated law and order with racism and repression. Obscenity, Diz complained, had become accepted and just. Authority existed to be overthrown. Manners, he mourned, were almost passé. Why, Diz said, was decorum considered vulgar, religion gauche, morality a refuge for rustic boors? For years Dean had praised the virtues of small-town America, its sober, more decent, more respectful ways. Baseball and America merged; both were cloaked in mythic molds, divinely created, liturgically acclaimed? The 1970s brought turmoil to each; discontent swept the nation, chastened and remorse. America was God's favored province, Diz said; even the lowliest student realized that. Why, then, had we forsaken him, rebuffed his chosen course? Who, Dean wondered, could stem the madness, the barbarism which raped convention, which made Babylon enshrined? Where was the new Jerusalem, the dream to save the land? Not among the champions of Middle America, its once vocal spokesmen turned timidly mute. Nor the sanctimonious counter-culture, whose doctrine Diz detested, whose assertions he disclaimed. Nor television, either; television, Diz suggested, seemed bent on bias both disastrous and demeaned.

Fifteen, twenty years before, when God was in his heaven and television was new, Americans saw in their living rooms a reflection of their native good. Television sought to echo the nation's morals, not degrade their worth. Westerns became a predominant art form, uniquely American and media inspired. Programs thrust forth a mosaic of themes; innocence reborn, the virgin plains, ethics predominant, values revived. Cowboys, Diz rejoiced in the early 1960s, were in pervasive vogue, their merits copied and extolled. A score of folk-heroes emerged: Kit Carson, Wyatt Earp, Davey Crockett, Marshall Dillon, and the Lone Ranger—strong, silent, courageous and true. Honor must triumph, the good guys prevail. America's fiber demanded as much, and television stood ready to content those demands. Within comedy, also, the nation's innate virtue shone. These were the civil years, the wholesome years, and nightly programs reflected their spirit: "Leave It to Beaver." "Ozzie and Harriet." Sainted Ma Kettle and "The Real McCoys," Barney Fife and Tennessee Ernie Ford. The Masonic Lodge ruled America; their mores were the same: initiative, dignity, community pride. All were applauded, not scorned as outmoded and antique. A decade and more later, television's influence too often distorted and perverse, returns of past series underscored the recent fall. "Fighting on Sunday," Andy Griffith, vintage 1961, counseled son Opie. "I mean, that's disgraceful." A year before his death, Diz sorrowed, one searched vainly for such prime-time propriety now; the major networks adored the deviant and lewd. Unconcerned with its impact on the nation's youth, network television paraded a litany of permissive harm: pornography, obscenity, violence and crime. All shown nationally, sanctioned by their incessant presence on the screen. "I don't watch TV no more," Diz said in 1973, " 'cause I don't like what I see."

Square seemed evil, sardonic good. Small-town America, Ol' Diz had said, was the real America. Its locales formed the country's backbone. Politically, they comprised America's most powerful single entity. Their ethics formed the basis of accepted law and required order. Yet within the nation's largest papers, on its television screens, on the programs which shaped its emerging values and altered their worth, they were a psychic island, unable to reason or rule, to explain the spiritual collapse which endangered all they stood for and all they had built. "People gets their ideas from television," Diz said, "and gees, on television, we're practically ignored." Even during the late

1960s, with change the country's craze, a barrage of rural shows had flooded the screen—"Beverly Hillbillies," "Green Acres" and half a dozen more, all superbly supported, endorsed by the abundant ratings they lured. Within several years they were canceled, all pulled off the air, not because they were ailing or inadequately watched, but because they appealed to the 'wrong' people—rural, white, middle-income Americans. Soon not one prime-time program revolved around the fortunes of America's sixty million small-town inhabitants. "Ain't that something?" Dean marveled. "What are we—part of a different country? Sometimes I think so."

News coverage, too, Diz said, had become shamelessly debased. Security agencies, charged with protecting American interests at home and abroad, were labeled enemies of a free, informed republic. Free enterprise was attacked, the welfare state embronzed. Prudent financial policy was chastised as heartless, New York's squalid, irresponsible spending praised as compassionate and fair. Evening newscasts comprised an ongoing classic drama, its leading lights clothed in black and white. Prayer and national defense, work and order, were dismissed as archaic. Disclosure and innuendo, inevitably linked, were excused as aiding the public's right to know—or at least what the networks wanted them to know. Film distorted reality and gave us fiction instead—police were corrupt, rampaging rioters deprived, the misguided victims of societal injustice. Nightly the networks' message poured forth—the government was guilty until proven innocent, the Pentagon hired liars, its opponents practiced morality and truth. Parochial was television's perspective, pervasive its self-righteous tinge. Even locales were jaundiced; carrying tunnel vision to novel heights, network executives made New York City, home to less than five per cent of the country's populace, the setting for a plurality of prime-time shows. The national media, Diz grieved, seemed determined to warp the American fabric, to injure the majority folk culture which had molded her mystique. The country had fallen, and television remained an undeniable culprit, though Dizzy Dean was plainly absolved of blame.

For Ol' Diz and television, once joined irrevocably, had become almost wholly rent apart. Only twice during the 1970s did Diz grace baseball's network screen, both during 1973, his forum NBC's Monday "Game of the Week." "It'll sure be nice to get back, even for one time," Dean said. "Boy, am I happy. When they told me I could be on—back on network TV so I could say hello to all the fans we used to have—I was so tickled I almost shouted with joy." For a few memorable, bittersweet hours on May 21, when Ol' Diz first returned, one almost imagined that Dean had never been fired, never left the air, never been replaced by the banal flock of languid announcers who followed his presence and mocked his effect.

Even now, a decade after his network decline, Diz lent hope that life could be calmed again, that social sanity might one day be restored;

Dean's romance, the music which adorned his lyrics, arose from the fantasy he stirred. He provided what his nation still craved—laughter, warmth and pastoral poetry, the poignant longing for old-time religion and old-style ways. He made us better than we were—more gentle, more serene, more sensitive to life and love. One year later he was dead, felled by a heart attack, his three hundred pounds the lethal touch. Tears shed were less for Diz than the souls he left behind. "Podner," he had said, "Ol' Diz sure had himself some good life, yesiree." Ol' Diz, one sensed, would thrive in life-after, too. Perhaps, with Dizzy their's, the heavenly hosts were already serenaded by a rousing chorus of "Wabash Cannonball," or enveloped by the bear-hug grasp which cornered all those who neared him. "I believe you should go out and make an honest living," he often proclaimed. "When you're down, you get up again." Defeat, to Dizzy Dean, was but a momentary hardship. Death, for all its ultimacy, seemed little more than that.

Epilogue

Hattiesburg faded and the Gulf Coast neared. Biloxi lay thirty miles to the south and east, New Orleans ninety miles to the west. Route 49 yielded and a side road appeared. Past fields and lumber the highway weaved, past the timber and beef which lent the region growth, the garages marked by mud, past the pine cones and mangled sheds, the flowers splashed by hues of purple and blue. This was home country, Mississippi, sweltering yet reposed. The furies had raged a decade earlier, intolerance luring counter bigotry, violence the nation's wrath. The years since then had wrought a groping, tentative calm; unrest and quiet still grappled, each bidding for the other's soul.

Remnants, marred and aging, flanked the winding road. Perched above adjacent structures was a water tower; houses bathed beneath the sun beyond. A freight yard towered as the village drew close; near its center a box car was marooned. "Illinois Central," the deserted vessel read, "Main Line of Middle America." A feed plant and ice cream shop lined the road's leftmost curb; the Fowler Hotel, almost abandoned, adorned its right. Magnolia Drive remained the major street. The railroad terminal still stood. Train tracks split the hamlet's heart. Wiggins had changed little since Ol' Diz took leave.

Now, as twenty, fifty, a hundred years before, the South took refuge in its separate culture, the folkways had borne incessant turmoil—in literature and mores, in idiom and commerce, in the pride and poignancy

Dizzy Dean and his wife Pat look at a copy of his Hall of Fame induction plaque. Diz received the honor on July 27, 1953. (AP Wirephoto)

its embattled station caused. Diz had clasped this culture, and down-home cronies, and Wiggins guideposts as well—the post office where daily he received his mail; the furniture store where he autographed baseballs for Jimmy Davis, owner and long-time friend; the bank which he frequented with maddening occurrence. "Man, that Wiggins," Diz often said, "they got lots of good ol' boys down there." Most of Dean's old guard had since departed—Ed Taylor, financier, to Texas, Boyce Holleman, lawyer, to Gulfport, Miss., Jack McHenry, local entrepreneur, to illness which warped his strength. Few of Dean's friends lingered, left to sample the timeless ambience Wiggins continued to uphold.

Wiggins was a decent locale, its people agreed. "A God-fearing, church-going Baptist town," Jimmy Davis exclaimed. Wiggins was sober and restrained; seat of Stone County, Mississippi's smallest, it barred even the private exchange of whiskey and beer. Wiggins was also patriotic; war had deeply scarred the town. Service was respected, the flag held high, protest dismissed as obstinate and wrong. And, more than one newcomer added, Wiggins was wary, too, cautious of progress, of the slow sweep of change. "I know all small towns have faults, and Wiggins is no different," a recent transplant said. "It's closer than close-knit. But towns like this also have virtues—that's why some people stay here five, maybe six decades." Wiggins loved the native South, and America, and values, sainted landmarks, besieged but holy.

Wiggins loved Ol' Diz, too, said most, even those who questioned its complacent curb. "He'd come into town ever' morning," a resident of Pine Avenue, the business street, said. "Always had on a brilliant Hawaiian shirt, like it was flowed from the islands that day. He'd go to the post office, the bank, poke his head into stores, say hello to everybody, help 'em when he could." Death glorifies one's past; that must surely be true of Diz. Townfolk remembered his gruff, unflagging presence ("loud, not offensive"), his empathy for the common soul ("he'd be talking to a banker. Even before he was done, he'd come over and talk to me"), his penchant for charity—different from what Bud Blattner had ascribed. Mentioned were Dizzy's ventures, solely pioneered and publicly unknown—endeavors with impoverished youth, paying for vacations in New York, financing their flight from Wiggins and back; covert aid for former ballplayers, their career over and bankroll deplete; an offer to underwrite construction of Wiggins' First Baptist Church. "Diz didn't glorify these things," a Magnolia Drive inhabitant said. "He didn't go out seeking a lot of headlines. Like when he wanted to build the church. He didn't have to do it, but that's what he wanted. No strings attached. That tells you what kind of a man he was." Town officials declined Dizzy's bid; his money came from Falstaff beer. "Beer was wrong, you know. That tells you what kind of emotions run through Wiggins."

Diz? Jimmy Davis reflected. Diz was a winner. "He'd bet you five cents and fight just as hard as he would for fifty thousand dollars," said Davis, reclining in his dark cluttered office, feet upon the desk. "When he lost, he'd pay up quick. 'Fast pay makes fast friends,' Diz would roar, but he almost always won." Bulky, bespectacled, comfortable in a self-made way, Davis was early bequeathed with Ol' Diz's favor. "We had about seven or eight of us. We ate together, socialized together," befriended each other and praised Ol' Diz. "Dean was a great kidder," he said, echoing Reese's party line. "I remember once, Ed Taylor had a growth on his arm and he told Diz about it. 'Diz,' he said. 'I have to have this removed.' And Diz came back, 'Podner, I'll lay you five to one it's malignant.' " Jimmy Davis' laughter was louder than mine.

"Seriously," he said, frowning, "Diz was not a religious person in the strictest sense. But inwardly, he was very moral. His attitude toward children and his fellow man—you can't beat his behavior toward them. And after all," he paused, groping as his wife approached, "that's what it's all about." But what of Dean the hustler, the man whose behavior often wavered, inwardly or out? Had Wiggins stripped away the duality?

Pat Dean gets a helping hand from Alabama football coach Paul "Bear" Bryant during the funeral services for the late Dizzy Dean in Wiggins, Mississippi, on July 20, 1974. (AP Wirephoto)

Had the hobo triumphed for good? "Oh, Diz would win fifty dollars on blackjack," Davis whistled, "And he still loved to gamble. But he'd turn right around and buy you a fifty-dollar dinner." Here, as in Lucas, the sensitive side prevailed.

Conflicting truths tore at one's sleeve. Wiggins need not be kind to Dizzy Dean. The town reaped no profits from his past; no longer could he enrich its locals. Yet its praise seemed genuine, prompted less by deliberate intent than affection and concern. Now, as in life before, Diz was clutched to Wiggins' self-styled rustic breast. "I remember once," said a young village belle, "I was bicycling with a friend down in front of Dizzy's house. And he was sitting out on his front porch, just his underwear on. Did he run when he saw us! Embarrassed? You bet. But he was always looking to have a good image for us, for the town."

So Diz was accepted, ushered into Wiggins' 'closer than close-knit' heart. Why, though, was he so infatuated in return, so magnanimous toward a town which could not further his career, nor multiply his wealth, nor link him with influential peers? Often before, while Diz played the simple, well-meaning clown, he seemed less than harmless beneath, less than delighted with the surface role he must cradle and mold. Dean sulked at Frisch, bullied Blattner, served as benevolent despot to Kirby and Reese. Roaming Wiggins streets, however, he played the elder statesman and comic laureate, wholly at ease with both. Childless, his admirers from afar more numerous than friends, Diz had strayed from Bradenton to Dallas to Phoenix and back South, no real kinship present except for his wife. Wiggins aborted Dean's caravan, the restless soul coming home at last. Perhaps, one mused, the wanderer had yielded to constancy and peace; only here, with Diz's fall from network fame concluded, nothing now to be gained from his friendship, no self-serving favors to be wrung, only here could he sense these people with him, with him because they loved him, and sense himself complete.

He was an old-fashioned man, his values born in an earlier, more unruffled time. These people were his friends, more so than the plastic allies of the past; he enjoyed them because he trusted them, because they liked "the big ol' ox," in Reese's vivid phrase, because he shed his bravado, the image which the nation knew, and found that Wiggins reveled in what lay behind—the small-town innocent whose innocence sufficed.

"He grew to like it here," Ovin Hickman, a retired barber, said. "He found people who talked to him, who appreciated him for what he was. And always glad to talk to little people, not important people, people like me," people less little than neglected and abused. Life greeted Dizzy Dean with hardship, poverty his early, accustomed curse. Poor once himself, Diz became, in Wiggins, a tribune of the poor, the unsung, the slightly soiled, an itinerant sojourner turned squire from Bond.

I left Jimmy Davis and turned upstreet. It was altogether probable, one supposed, that neither Dean's foes nor allies ever wholly knew Ol' Diz. Neither honored what the other prized—Dizzy's capacity for charity, for spite, for fleeting malice and more lasting largesse, for the clashing emotions which altered his career. Neither grasped fully his ideals or duality, the crudity and compassion, the flights of meanness and pervasive good. Both denied the diversity of this deeply textured man. Yes, I remembered Reese saying, Ol' Diz had been insufferably complex. "Who can sort out the conflicts?" he said quietly. "Even those who knew Diz didn't know all the parts. All we know is what Diz left us. A lot of fine memories for a lot of fine folks."

"I cain't never thank him enough," Ella Mae Robertson, of Booneville, Arkansas, once had said. "That Ol' Diz, even for poor people like me, he made life fun again, he made life grand." Here in Wiggins, amid encircling Southern woods, this gentle man named Diz reaped the harvest of his years, and left what he had lived—a touch of the American Dream.

I entered Bond Cemetery. There, like Ella Mae and Pee Wee Reese and a thousand others before, I thanked Jay Hanna Dean for all he had done, and what he had meant, and what he had given us all.

Index

About the Author

One of America's fine young writers, Curt Smith is a former reporter and prize-winning author who is currently a public relations executive. Now 26, he lives with his wife in Clinton, New York.

Smith, who has written for many national publications, some of which are Associated Press, Library Journal, Gannett News Service and Baseball Bulletin, joined Hamilton College in upstate New York as a speechwriter and publicity spokesman in 1975. Since then he has won several national awards for layout, writing and graphic design. He is a member of numerous professional and civic groups, including Sigma Delta Chi, the American Association of Public Relation Directors and the Wesley Board Foundation.

A native of Caledonia, New York, Smith attended Allegheny College and Geneseo State University where he worked his way through school by holding down four jobs. In 1973 he graduated magna cum laude from Geneseo with a major in English, and minor in Speech. In 1973, too, Smith joined the Gannett Company's flagship newspaper, the Rochester *Democrat & Chronicle* as a reporter. That same year he was awarded a St. Bonaventure—*New York Times* award for "outstanding journalism" on stories about Roberto Clemente and Floyd Patterson.

Smith's first book, *America's Dizzy Dean*, has been called by veteran broadcaster Ernie Harwell "a superb portrayal of America's 'good, quiet people'—a moving plea for old-time civility and old-style morals." Of his book Smith says, "Each year produces a flood-tide of works on baseball. No year has yet produced a book on Dizzy Dean. This book is about Ol' Diz, and baseball, too—and what each has meant to the America they helped to alter and enrich."